"It's Bear Grylls-styl ..s madcap pursuit of nature's e."
THE AGE

"Exotic Booze Club is what it sounds like: a bit wild, a bit out there, a lot exotic – and the amazing thing is **all of it is true**! Stories that would make Hunter S. Thomson proud… I loved it."
EMINENT AUSTRALIAN MEDIA PERSONALITY PETER FITZSIMONS

"A country boy infects his American team with a little bit of Aussie larrikinism in a relentless quest for strange experiences and even stranger liquors… Armstrong knows how to translate weird and wonderful adventures for the rest of us to enjoy."
THE ADVOCATE

"Seat-of-the-pants expedition filmmaker Brian Armstrong has an eye for weird and wonderful alcoholic concoctions. He sources them from far corners of the world, relying on their ability to help negotiate foreign deals and dodge tropical diseases."
ASSOCIATED PRESS

"The Exotic Booze Club ticks all the boxes of a good travel memoir. It takes readers to faraway places, thrills with tales of death-defying adventure, and Armstrong's colloquial and witty prose is easy to like. Enjoy it over a drink (or two)."
THE WEST AUSTRALIAN

"Exotic Booze Club is every journalist's dream of what the profession should really be like: edgie times, memorialised by lurid but licit substances. Brian globalises a focal point of Aussie creativity – how to define nonchalance in the face of danger or adversity through the nationally preferred route to oblivion."
HON KIM BEAZLEY, AC, AUSTRALIAN AMBASSADOR TO THE UNITED STATES

"It will appeal to anyone who likes a good adventure tale, whether they are drinkers or not."
SYDNEY'S DAILY TELEGRAPH

"Armstrong's book is an excellent account of what it takes to film large-scale, on-location documentaries, and it should enhance the experience of watching such documentaries. In the meantime, I'll settle for raising a glass to the book – and to the memory of the Booze Club."
THE SYDNEY MORNING HERALD

"Keeps the reader turning every page. Verdict: Enthralling."
MELBOURNE'S HERALD SUN

Brian Armstrong is an independent Australian journalist and filmmaker and formerly a staff producer for National Geographic in Washington DC. He has produced around a hundred documentaries for National Geographic Television and other broadcasters.

National Geographic has not endorsed this book. The author is solely responsible for its contents and the views presented are his own.

First published in 2013

Copyright Brian Armstrong 2013

All rights reserved. No part of this book may be reproduced or transmitted in any form or by any means, electronic or mechanical, including photocopying, recording or by any information storage and retrieval system, without prior permission in writing from the publisher.

ISBN: 1497438705

ISBN 13: 9781497438705

www.theexoticboozeclub.com

How did two of the most sober parents on the planet have a kid like me? Cheers to Mum and Dad.

CONTENTS

	INTRODUCTION: Pre-Dinner Cocktails	ix
Chapter 1:	BEYOND THE LAVA: Russian vodka	1
Chapter 2:	CAMEL COWBOYS: Victoria Bitter	25
Chapter 3:	COBRA HUNT: Burmese Toddy	45
Chapter 4:	AMERICA'S LOST MUSTANGS: Wild Turkey Bourbon	69
Chapter 5:	INTO THE TORNADO: Don Julio Tequila	95
Chapter 6:	ATTACKS OF THE MYSTERY SHARKS: Indian Archer XXX Rum	131
Chapter 7:	KING KONG IN MY POCKET: Malagasy Vanilla-Bean Rum	149
Chapter 8:	DANGEROUS ENCOUNTERS: Chinese Godawfulgunk	165
Chapter 9:	ROLLING STONES ON THE BEACH: Brazilian Caipirinha	189
Chapter 10:	ONE LAST DRINK?	205
THE INVITATIONS		209
ACKNOWLEDGEMENTS		217

INTRODUCTION:
Pre-dinner Cocktails

The Exotic Booze Club was a real club, born in Russia and dedicated to foreign libations, exploration of the palate and storytelling. For about six years, a core group of National Geographic adventurers brought exotic alcohols from their far-off travels to my office in Washington, DC. There, from the comfort of our chairs, we'd experience tastes from around the world while sharing tales of our daring endeavors abroad.

Adventure and alcohol make a comical cocktail. If an exotic escapade doesn't seem so funny, then take another look at it through the bottom of a shot glass. That's what I gleaned from more than ten years as a fish-out-of-water Aussie, making films for the prestigious National Geographic Society.

I specialize in producing the riskiest kind of films: documentaries of expeditions. This genre is the Kama Sutra of filmmaking. To do it well, you must remain flexible and creative. You explore, but you can never be sure what you'll get. There can be a great deal of pleasure, but slip up and there may be a lot of pain as well. You must adopt different positions and approaches to get you through, and it helps to have a personal lubricant. Mine happens to be alcohol.

Responsible amounts of alcohol can lift the spirits of your crew, get you through tough times, win friends, and seal deals. I've also found that exploring and sharing alcohol in various faraway lands allows a deeper understanding of foreign customs.

The culture of drinking is steeped in history; its language is not just Australian but international, and the experience of partaking is mostly communal. The Exotic Booze Club was also all of these things. The EBC began as an underground affair, operating as it was against the very unAustralian National Geographic Society policy that prohibits the consumption of unauthorized alcohol. But for the most part, it was a gathering open to any and all brave enough, or thirsty enough,

INTRODUCTION: Pre-dinner Cocktails

to venture by my door on a Friday afternoon. We sampled more than a hundred of the strangest and sometimes vilest potions on the planet, and with each sip came a story, many a firsthand account of some faraway adventure survived by the Club's founder - me.

Over the six years of the EBC we met up about 150 times. At each meeting, my old worn-out three-seater sofa and a bunch of routinely rounded up office chairs transported drinkers from my office to faraway lands, fuelled by Czech schnapps, monk-made chartreuse and sake infused with the eviscerated remains of deadly habu snakes.

One of my favorite stories came from a petite yet feisty young producer who thought she was being cheated out of the camels she needed to carry her camera crew and equipment. She was on the Ethiopia-Eritrea border, going toe-to-toe with an Afar rebel who towered over her. (These are the warriors who are not allowed to marry until they've killed at least one other male and have proven it by displaying their victim's severed genitals to the village.) With the help of a translator, the negotiations settled in our brave producer's favor, then the warrior asked the translator in total seriousness, "She strong woman. I want to buy her. How many camels?".

Only one such EBC meeting was not held in my office. Producer Peter Getzels invited the usual suspects for a special ceremonial gathering at his house. He'd just returned from Peru with a bottle of pisco and a 1,500-year-old human skull, the latter being the by-product of a human sacrifice.

Peter, an absent-minded-professor type, had been authorized to escort the skull to the US for some forensic work. All was going smoothly until a stopover where Peter forgot to warn airport authorities of his unusual carry-on. An image of a human skull emerged on the X-ray machine and a wide-eyed operator quickly screamed for backup. Before Peter could pull out his permits, security crashed down around him. Suddenly his own head was at risk, if not literally then possibly in the embarrassing headline that flashed through his mind: Nat Geo Man Found With Head In His Hands. Peter eventually escaped, shaken but with the skull miraculously still in his possession. From then on he felt it best to store his visiting bodiless buddy at his home, where we met to swill pisco in a ritual Moche blessing.

This book is not so much an education in booze as a collection of real-life stories, and the stories behind those stories. It bursts through the sober facade of high-end documentary making and delves into the gritty world of in-the-field, seat-of-the-pants filmmaking.

Many of the producers, camera operators and other personalities in this world are wired backwards. We fly into the face of danger instead of away from it. We're often blinded by the possibility of a great shot or story and motivated by the hope that if we do well on the current assignment, we'll get to do more.

Given the nature of Nat Geo's work, some of the tales may be hard to believe. These pages are overripe with near-death experiences - crocodiles, snakes, tornados, malaria, a helicopter crash - but be assured that it's all true. If you have a taste for the exotic, enjoy a shot of humor, have a thirst for adventure or are curious how to survive a harrowing film shoot without spilling your cocktail, then read on.

Chapter 1

BEYOND THE LAVA:
Russian vodka

A great dichotomy comes with being a National Geographic film-maker: you're either thinking "I can't believe they pay me to do this" or "they just don't pay me enough to do this." The switch between those two modes can come as quickly as the swish of a crocodile's tail or as suddenly as the turn of a deadly tornado. In Russia's Far East, the switch came with a simple glance upward as we prepared to board our helicopter.

I watched as a mechanic stood atop a stepladder under the motionless blades of our 25-year-old Mi-8 chopper. Before my very eyes he reached up and began to wrap duct tape around one of the rotors. Let me make my alarm clear: *DUCT TAPE!* He wound several feet of the stuff around the blade like one might wrap a bandage around a hurt limb.

Now don't get me wrong. I've trotted out my share of duct tape and I know it has myriad uses, from repairing shoes and packing boxes to curing warts and - one would presume - sealing air ducts. But this particular use did not seem within the bounds of credulity.

I wanted to say, "Hey mate, are you nuts?" or "Where did you get your engineering degree?" or "Would you like an arc welder and some metal with that?". With the help of a translator, all I managed was a nervous, "Is everything cool?".

"No problem," came the reply. "In Afghanistan these rotors were full of bullet holes and they still kept flying. This is nothing."

What I discovered inside the aircraft made the duct tape look comparatively secure. Each side of the chopper had fold-down bench seating with no working safety belts. A dozen of us were all to sit on one side, while our gear, now fully loaded, took up the rest of the space with about as much order as a kid's closet jammed with toys - and ready to topple down at any time.

There was really only one question to answer: "were any of us going to pull out?" That just wouldn't be Geographic. Nor would it fit with the producers' mantra that the film must come first. With caution cast to the wind, we climbed in. Now there was no turning back, and perhaps just as well.

I'd flown into Moscow in the autumn of 2000, a week before I watched the duct tape-wielding mechanic tape our helicopter together. I was part of a team from Nat Geo, who were off to explore the volcanic regions of the Kamchatka Peninsula, Russia's easternmost frontier. My job was to find lava, film it, and make a documentary of the expedition. This was your grandmother's Geographic trying to fit into her new-wave preshrunk jeans: we had classic subject matter and a large multinational team of pros, but the budgets of the new millennium were too tight for our bold ambitions. We'd have to squeeze out every cent.

Upon arrival in Moscow, I joined three or four hundred human sardines immersed in a common post-flight body-odor experience. We all slowly shuffled toward two immigration officers who clearly believed that Mr. Speed and Ms. Efficiency never made it east over the rubble of the Berlin Wall. And certainly not into the secure, airconditioningless confines of international arrivals.

You can tell a lot about a city by the way its people line up. In London, for example, everything's extremely orderly and polite. It's been said that if you stand still long enough in Trafalgar Square, people will start to queue up behind you. In Italy, if you don't push in, you'll never get to the front. And in Moscow they prefer a practice best described as the "clogged funnel".

When I finally made it to the pointy end of the funnel I got "The Look." I believe it to be a uniquely Russian countenance that combines a heavy-lidded expressionless stare with a droopy-jowl grimace. The giant grouper, a tropical apex predator fish, does a fine job of this look too, but in Russia it comes with more attitude.

I countered with innocently raised eyebrows and a slightly higher pitched voice. "Is there a problem?".

Mr. Happy held up my Aussie passport. "You Australian?"
"That's right."
Happy held up my US driver's licence. "You American?"

"I live and work in America but I'm very much an Australian."

He threw me The Look again. "You wait."

He left, effectively cutting the flow of people in half, and leaving me feeling awkward and guilty in front of a giant wedge of humanity. The annoyed masses glared, now looking less like sardines and more like those predator groupers, with me as prey.

By the time I was scorned, stamped and shuffled off, my associate producer, Nancy Donnelly, had made it to the other side to deal with customs and our twenty-four bags of equipment. When you travel with film gear, certain countries require something called a carnet; essentially it's a passport for your electronics to ensure you don't sell them in your destination country and avoid stamp duty. Russia had implemented carnets just a few months before our arrival and we seemed to be their first clear-cut case of imperialistic extortionists trying to deprive Vladimir Putin of his hard-earned stamps.

Nancy had out the Russian translation of our equipment list - over 130 different items. It became clear that our customs bloke had never actually dealt with a carnet before, but he felt it necessary for us to locate every single item on the list and show him serial numbers, a process that would take hours. We'd already clocked up eighteen hours in transit and were in no mood for more.

We decided to switch tactics. Instead of racing to find every item he called from the list, we became dazed and confused. Nancy and I went to the wrong bags, pulled out the wrong gear, and had trouble finding serial numbers. But, ever helpful, we'd keep looking and discussing between ourselves which of our twenty-four bags could possibly contain Sony Sennheiser microphone SAKQ283746492.

Less than ten minutes of this and our frustrated customs guy disappeared. When he returned shortly after, he wrote out our entire list in pencil on a separate piece of paper and told us to be off. Maybe I could work with the Russians after all.

While we were dealing with our own customs issues, German adventurer and National Geographic photographer Carsten Peter had been negotiating the release of two giant silver boxes, each about half the size of a sedan, that now sat by the bus and trailer waiting to ferry us for our overnight in Moscow. Carsten was beaming that he'd gotten through the red tape unscathed and with two motorized paragliders intact. It was Carsten's intention to lug these up Kamchatka's highest volcano and fly from the top. Once airborne, he could whiz in and around the crater, snapping photos as he flew.

BEYOND THE LAVA: Russian vodka

The only time Russia has had anything remotely to do with a machine resembling a motorized paraglider was in a James Bond movie, and those scenes were set in Azerbaijan long after it split from the Soviet Union, no doubt to avoid the scrutiny of Russia's highly suspicious customs department. Carsten's accomplishment was indeed impressive - the mark of a pro.

Carsten has had about a dozen stories published in Geographic. His photos often make the cover, either in the US or in international editions. Working with him you quickly learn that two things in life make him happy: great photographs and giant bottles of Coca-Cola. He usually has an abundance of both so he's pretty much always happy. Stand between him and a good shot of a natural phenomenon and he may well sever your feet from your legs with his bare teeth, but mostly his oral fixtures are dedicated to smiling and laughing and swallowing sweet black bubbly soda. Many a girlfriend has tried to rearrange his priorities but to no avail. It would not be unusual for Carsten to drink two or three gallons of Coke in a week, yet he remains as skinny as a rake. Some magic of biomechanics allows him to transform all of that sugar into nothing other than spectacular photographs.

Judging by the current lack of blood about him, I could only assume that Carsten somehow slid through customs using only his boyish charm and contagious laugh. I wondered, as he never did, how much further that would take us. We still had a long way to go to reach the volcanic mountains on the Pacific side of the country.

Here's the thing about Russia that few really appreciate: it's humongous. If you don't believe me, get out a map and take a look. We boarded an Aeroflot jet from Moscow and flew nine time zones to get to Kamchatka that's nine time zones without leaving the country. Any further east and we'd be in the west. Kamchatka's capital, Petropavlovsk, is closer to Washington, DC than it is to Moscow. If former Alaskan governor Sarah Palin could actually keep an eye on Russia by looking out her window, as she once suggested, she d be looking at a microscopic blip on the radar of Gigantanormousland. It is the biggest country in the world and nearly twice as big as any other.

Our flight to Petropavlovsk was full, those aboard including three large dogs and a rotund flight attendant who sat in the lavatory and smoked *during* take-off. We saw less of her and more of the canines, as they were frequently exercised up and down the aisle, but our attendant did squeeze by occasionally with the two drink options on offer: water and vodka. If you were an adult, the vodka was handed to you as a given. This courtesy was my first experience of alcohol in Russia.

Carsten's support crew was also aboard. This included a French husband and wife team, Franck Tessier and Irene Margaritis, two professors from Nice who specialize in the outdoors. Franck has a great sense of humor and loves nothing more than a practical joke. In his countless joke-plotting hours, he mastered the art of impersonating the precise sound made by those shitty little mosquitoes that you can never quite see or catch but whose annoyingly persistent sound causes you to instinctively slap yourself about the head. During long, solemn hikes, Franck would sooner or later walk quietly behind some unsuspecting soul and persist with his mosquito imitation until that person was either sufficiently covered with self-inflicted red-welted slap marks, or alerted to the joke by a burst of uncontrollable laughter from witnesses further back in line.

Franck's wife, Irene, is as beautiful and temperamental as any French woman I've ever met - at least, that was her usual state. As we began our descent into Kamchatka's capital, I could see Irene lying under her seat suffering the ill effects of ten hours of free vodka. Our flight attendant waddled by and glanced down at poor Irene, but rather than assist her back into her seat she uttered something about pickles and hangovers, then proceeded to the lavatory for a quiet smoke while we landed.

Russians have a favorite saying for this part of the world: "In Kamchatka there are no roads, only directions." It seems a lot funnier before you realize that this is quite an obstacle. The peninsula stretches north south for nearly 750 miles. Out of Petropavlovsk, the paved road only covers about half of that. Where it stops is where you must use a helicopter. Which brings us back to our overloaded Mi-8 chopper.

Akin to the tractors of Kamchatka, the ageing fleet of Mi-8s is overused and tired, but with sheer grit, willpower and, apparently, duct tape, engineers somehow manage to keep them going. Seating about twenty people and a ton of equipment, they fly with two pilots and a mechanic. Having two pilots seems understandable - after all, what if one of them had a hangover in the morning? - But the need for a full-time mechanic was a little disconcerting.

Our pre-arranged chopper had come in at a disused airstrip right where our two-day drive from Petropavlovsk, and the road itself, ended. We'd sat with our mountains of gear and watched as the pilot shut down the motor and workers started unloading bucket after bucket of some orange liquid. Our Russian crew advised us not to ask too many questions about the contents, but later we learned that we'd witnessed the Russian mafia in action: the buckets were full of caviar, taken without permit, from the great salmon runs near the coast.

I would have paid more attention to this criminal act but I had become disturbed by the slightly more worrisome sight of the duct tape going around the rotor. Once airborne, we were blessed with the distraction of our spectacular surrounds and the mode soon switched back to "I don't believe they pay me to do this".

From the air, Kamchatka is a sight to behold. It is part of the Pacific Ring of Fire, a 25,000-mile horseshoe-shaped geologic hot spot. If you're a bubbling pot of magma, feeling overheated and stressed below the earth's crust, this is the place you d most likely come for relief. From New Zealand, the Ring of Fire arcs over the top of Australia to Indonesia, then up through Japan to Kamchatka - and that's just the half of it. From there it cuts across to Alaska, down along the west coast of North America and continues south through Chile. Seventy-five per cent of the world's volcanoes sit around this ring, 452 in total. The highest concentration of them pokes up from the Kamchatka Peninsula like pimples on a pumpkin. We were flying over the hot spot of hot spots.

The largest of Kamchatka's volcanoes, Klyuchevskaya Sopka, is the highest active volcano in the Northern Hemisphere. After three hours rattling around in our chopper, we set down at the base of this behemoth. Volcanologists have called Klyuchevskaya the world's most beautiful volcano. It is a perfect cone shape and certainly a majestic looking mountain, but I'm afraid that's all a bit lost on me.

It's a horrible confession to make, but there's nothing I hate more than a big mountain that needs to be climbed. They're great to look at, and I don't mind walking down some of them, but the up bit just isn't for me. I even hate hills. When the New York Times asked George Mallory why he wanted to climb Everest, he famously said, "Because it's there." To me that's a good reason not to climb; it's there, I'm here - why ruin a good thing? I might also point out that in 1924, a year after that Times interview, Mallory died on Everest, and his body was not found for another seventy-five years.

I was all in favor of our helicopter dropping us off at the top of Klyuchevskaya but, with a summit at 15,000-feet, our heavily laden flying tractor would never make it. Instead, we were deposited near a stream on a treeless plain with a clear view of the clouds whisking about the volcano's crater - far, far above. Once those clouds cleared it would be a five or six-day hike up and hopefully back.

I say *hopefully* back because at least seven people had died on the perilous slopes of this volcano in recent years, mostly Russian volcanologists who fell or froze to death when the weather suddenly turned bad. One of our guides summed it up best: "This mountain is a live mountain," he told us. "It is only stable in its danger." Even if I wanted to go, it was clearly no mountain for an amateur. That's why I had climber/cameraman Pat Morrow.

Pat Morrow loves mountains even more than I hate them. He was the first person to climb the highest peaks on all seven continents; over nine years he did Everest, McKinley, Kilimanjaro, and all the others. He'd long been established as an excellent photographer and he joined this mission having just added video shooting to his repertoire.

Pat's wife, Baiba, was a newbie as a sound recordist, but their new career path allowed the two Canadians to work and travel together, which had long been their dream. Pat told me the key to his success in mountain climbing was always to hike just a little slower than his normal pace. I couldn't think of anything more torturous. Can you imagine struggling up from base camp, step after painful step, desperately sucking back the thinnest of oxygen, bundled in enough clothing to keep the Michelin Man happy yet still freezing your bits off, then, finally, when your goal seems to be in reach, what do you do? You continue to walk a little slower than what you can already manage. In the unlikely event I ever got that far, I'd race to the finish as fast as I could, get it over and done with and kiss that mountain's ascent goodbye. But Pat is a patient and meticulous planner, methodical in his approach to all things. He's thoughtful and prepared and the exact opposite of our carefree still photographer, Carsten Peter.

We unloaded the chopper and seemed to set up in two camps. Carsten with his support team of Franck and Irene were near the river along with Eric Dufor, a paragliding pioneer, here to supervise the flying machines. Camera crew Pat and Baiba set up closer to an old friend, our chief Russian guide Fedia Farberov (known as Feodor).

Feodor's parents were both volcanologists during the Cold War. Because they were government scientists they were allowed a rare privilege - access to shared copies of National Geographic magazine. Articles on Russia were always cut out by the censors but, by reading what was left when his parents brought the magazines home, Feodor saw the rest of the world through the yellow rectangle. He had grown up with a sincere appreciation for the tradition of National Geographic and an ingrained respect for Russian bureaucracy.

National Geographic magazine writer Jeremy Schmidt, associate producer Nancy and I pitched our own tents in the middle of these two camps. Our porters set up near us - half a dozen local teenagers who all seemed to be named Sasha - as well as two Russian volcanologists earning some extra rubles by serving as camp manager and camp cook. The standard government wage was only about fifty American dollars a month, so our trip represented a big bonus for all our Russian crew.

We awoke the next morning to see nasty weather around the peaks of Klyuchevskaya, but it was calm enough in our sweeping valley to break out the flying machines and give them a test whirl. A motorized paraglider is not much more than a parachute over your head and a giant fan attached to your back; your legs are the take-off and landing gear. The pieces resemble a child's construction set, except for one major difference: paragliders can kill you. I'm not talking about a nice plummet-to-the-earth death, but much worse. These machines can chop you up into tiny bits. Or they can chop you up and not quite kill you (not necessarily a preferred alternative).

The assembled round metal frame of the paraglider motor houses a fairly open propeller that straps to the pilot's back. In flight, the propeller spins at around 700 revolutions a second, so fast it can't be seen. Unwittingly stick a piece of body in there - say a hand or arm or head - and you won't see it again in any recognisable shape. And that's just the danger factor while you're still on the ground. Start taking off and landing and flying around a hundred yards up and a whole other array of potential disasters await. In the US alone, thirteen people had died while attached to para gliders in the previous four years, and more than half of the injuries happened in flight.

I find the only rational thing to do when confronted with a dangerous activity such as this is to calm oneself with some improbable logic. In this case, I figured most people in the western world die of clogged arteries from a lack of activity; therefore, any activity must be safer than doing nothing. In other words, let's be safe and go fly a rotating guillotine around some high mountains three days from the nearest hospital. It may not make sense, but it works for me. At least paragliders come with their own parachutes - better than the Russian choppers.

Eric ran the normal tests on his motors, found a flat spot for take-off and managed a pretty smooth first flight. He soared to about 500 feet and landed safely. He strapped Pat onto his own harness for a quick tandem flight, which was again impressive given the light breeze. Wind for a paraglider is like water for a boat: the biggest motor or sail in the world won't help if you've got nothing but sand under your keel. And by the time Carsten was ready to fly the second machine, the wind had dried up. Pat and I were both filming and everyone else had gathered to watch. Curiosity drew some of the Sashas close to where Carsten tried again and again to get up enough ground speed for a take-off.

The conditions weren't improving, what little wind there was kept changing directions, and the sixty-pound motor on Carsten's back began to wear him down. At one point he went from a near take-off to a ground-shaking face-first crash. As he came down, the blade hit the dirt and kicked up rocks and dust. He damaged the blade but Eric was able to quickly replace it and, ever-determined, Carsten revved up his engine once more.

This time a light breeze filled his chute and lifted it nicely over his head. He ran as fast as his legs would carry him - but it wasn't enough. The wind died again and he began falling forward, but this time he overcorrected and started to lean back. Still unsteady on his feet, the nearest Russian porter raced up behind him to help in an impulsive action, as kind as it was stupid. We held our collective breath as Sasha reached out for the frame, not even seeing or thinking about the blade inside that was still spinning at 500 to 600 cycles each terrifying second, and so loud he couldn't hear our warnings to stop. Carsten was equally oblivious to the fact that a porter was near and fully exposed to the spinning blade.

We heard a spine-chilling thwack and a scream of pain, then Sasha reeled backward grabbing his left arm. From where I stood it was impossible to see the damage but Feodor, our head guide, was closest and at Sasha's side in short order. The poor boy hadn't gone to the ground but seemed frozen on his feet, looking down at his injured limb.

Carsten had heard the whack and the scream over the sound of the motor on his back and was shutting down, but he was too tethered to his heavy machine to offer any real help. By the time I got there, Feodor had Sasha's arm and was telling him that everything was going to be okay. By some incredible stroke of luck, he was right. The blade had somehow struck just one of Sasha's fingers, and while it had banged it hard it was not severed, nor had the skin been broken. None of us could work out how he managed to escape so lightly. The bruising and the swelling became something to behold for a week or so, but life and limb were intact.

Beyond the physical damage to Sasha, our head guide, Feodor, was angry. These machines were strange and dangerous, perhaps even foolish. We'd had no safety briefing and one of his charges was hurt. Ever the diplomat, he kindly suggested we stop. But as he did, the wind picked up and beckoned the flyboys to try again. Carsten and Eric checked on Sasha, who was embarrassed, and in no way wanting to ruin anyone's plans for flight.

Carsten soon managed to take off and do a test run around the valley. He circled up to a 300-feet or so, snapping off pictures as he went. Despite the mishap, Carsten felt ready to test his wings from the top of the crater. The clouds were clearing from Klyuchevskaya and tomorrow they would begin to hike.

In the supply-deprived years of communist Russia, Kamchatkans learned to get by with few luxuries. Feodor was proud of his improvisations and certain that some of them were better than anything the west would have developed, and this was especially true when it came to hiking equipment. He insisted we all wear a style of footwear superior to anything money could buy. Forget your rugged high-end brand names, Feodor had carpet underlay for us to wrap around our feet. He promised this would provide comfort and protection against blisters. With it snug around our feet, we were to then force our lower limbs into oversized rubber boots; there were many waterways to cross and gumboots would keep our feet dry. Feodor was so certain and forceful in his assertion that this was the best option that we all put our regular hiking boots to one side and gave it a go.

I hiked in, filming the first few miles of the trip before leaving the experienced mountaineers at the first feature that resembled a hill. Though unusual for me to bail out at this point, I was not unhappy to be underqualified for the technical climbing that lay ahead. I wished them luck and filmed them heading up into the wild blue yonder, expecting to see them again in less than a week with tall tales of alpine adventure. I was looking forward to several days at base camp, lazing around in the endless fields of blueberries, maybe doing some reading, or perhaps some time-lapse photography for the show. Hence my dismay when I saw our brave troops trudging back to camp less than twenty-four hours later.

Things had not gone well. The streams had been gushing from summer snow melt, and those unlucky enough to step too deep in a creek found their boots holding water in instead of out. The carpet underlay bulged in the wrong places and was far from sock-like, but that was really the least of it. The weather up high had turned nasty. There had been debate about whether to go on or return, and the mood was sour. Franck had tried to inject some humor, but instead of slapping the imagined mosquito behind her head, Irene slapped Franck.

Word was out too that this was Carsten's second attempt at climbing Klyuchevskaya. The first time, five years earlier, had nearly killed him. On that trip he had gotten separated from his group and had spent a freezing night on the mountain, without food or shelter, before dashing down in record time, narrowly avoiding injury. This was not the sort of approach Pat or Feodor wanted to repeat.

As it turned out, they returned to camp just in time. One of the most incredible storm fronts I've ever seen soon sped across the valley and a giant vertical wall of grey and black swept in and engulfed our entire camp in a matter of minutes. It then settled in like one settles into a nice hot soaking bath, with no intention of moving for quite some time.

We broke out our Marsat satellite phone to see if we could get a weather report, which brings me to another confession: if there is one thing I hate on an expedition as much as hills it's phones. There are few times in life when we get to experience the thrilling sensation of true isolation. Imagine standing solo like some warrior caveman or early pioneer, in your domain and fully responsible for your own destiny without outside influence. You live in a bubble where, for a short time, you have no concerns of family, friends, employers or the world at large. A giddy sense of freedom accompanies your ability to focus solely on the mission in front of you, and nothing else need matter - then the phone rings. Nothing can pop that bubble faster and, alas, such isolation is now a rarity.

Feodor had experience with satellite phones in this valley so he knew the only place to get a signal was from high up on the mountain behind us. "Mountain?" I asked. "Are you sure?" He was certain. It was not Klyuchevskaya, but it was a considerable hike and about a four-hour return trip, three hours of which would be in my least favorite direction - up. There was no passing on this job; as project leader it was unarguably my duty to handle communications, get weather information, and even negotiate with our helicopter pilots should we decide to abandon camp and go for an early pick-up. I had to deal with a phone and go up a mountain - double bummer.

Nancy, Feodor and I started on up, but this time we left the rubber boots behind and donned our regular hiking shoes. After our three-hour climb we set up the phone and got through to aides in Petropavlovsk. The call only lasted five minutes before we lost our satellite link, long enough for us to get bad news: weather not going anywhere; no helicopters available; climb mountain tomorrow and call again for an update.

This went on for several days, an insanely long and expensive time not to be shooting. To top it off, Feodor said he'd once been fogged in like this for two entire months. The answers to our radio questions, as interpreted for us by Feodor, were always the same, and standard answers for almost any question you ask a Russian.

"Will the weather get better?"

"Mozhet da, mozhet nyet." Maybe yes, maybe no.

"Can we get a chopper to lift us out early?"

"Not possible."

After four days of this routine, I noticed that the angle of our satellite receiver paralleled the angle of our mountain. I suggested to Feodor that if the phone worked high up here on the mountainside, wouldn't logic say it should work further down, if the angle of the phone had a clear shot to the satellite above? "Not possible," he assured me. He had been here and attempted this many times with different phones, and it would not work further down. Not convinced, I insisted we give it a go, so we climbed about halfway down and tried again. It worked. From this new spot we could save about two hours hiking a day.

Feodor was very surprised. "Well, if it works here," I asked, "why not in a direct line down at the bottom?" This would be a walk around the mountain from our camp, maybe an hour return trip, but not up the bloody thing.

This time Feodor was less certain. "Mozhet da, mozhet nyet."

We took a new route straight down to the bottom, but with a clear view up to where we'd been trudging, and hopefully up to the satellite beyond. It worked again. Feodor gave a nervous laugh and apologized for his miscalculation. I was more elated than angry, and thrilled that our daily hike would no longer require such a climb. Buoyed by this success, I thought I'd try something different. The next day I called Feodor over. "Let's try it from here."

"Where?" he asked.

"From here. By the flap of my tent."

"Ha," he laughed. "Not possible."

I fired up the phone and gave it a whirl nothing to lose. I thought I saw a signal but it was hard to tell for sure. I dialled a number and waited, but nothing. Feodor gave me an "ah, well" kind of look just as the ring tone came through.

Someone answered. "Zdravstvuy?"

"Feodor," I said, "it's for you."

This time when we were told an early pick-up was not possible - from the comfort of my own tent - I questioned Feodor further. What exactly did that mean? It turned out, once again, that "not possible" did not mean "not possible". It meant that the Mi-8 choppers couldn't get to us with such bad weather, but a more powerful MIT helicopter could.

The MITs look exactly like the Mi-8s only they have twice the engine power, so it would mean an extra cost of about US$1,500. Feodor had assumed this was too expensive and for the last four days had translated that into "not possible". I was beside myself with disbelief. On any shoot, time is your most precious commodity and we'd just burned up a ton of it; our gear rental alone for just one of these lost days far exceeded US$1,500. Of course, Feodor wasn't to know any of this, but he wasn't being totally forthright with all the facts either. We ordered in an MIT as soon as possible and abandoned the Klyuchevskaya summit. Carsten was disappointed that the mountain had defeated him yet again, but he too knew we could waste no more time.

The bus driver who picked us up from where our MIT landed was the first person I ever saw drink the juice from a pickle jar. This, it turned out, was part of a standard and highly recommended hangover cure, and after a few days by himself waiting for us, he was in dire need. Once I learned why he was swilling pickle juice I understood why there seemed to be some confusion about which side of the road we should drive on. We somehow managed to get back into Petropavlovsk safely, and it was time for some serious business. We were halfway through our expedition yet Carsten barely had a photograph, we had no real filming done, and there was no sign of a payoff for our documentary. Something had to change.

Our outfitter in Petropavlovsk was an American who'd married a Russian; Martha Madsen had been living here for a decade and understood the commercial realities we faced better than anyone. Martha was in charge of supplying people and equipment to ensure our expedition had everything it needed to run smoothly. Martha's Russian business partner, Yelena Yarovaya, was out of the room making other arrangements when all twenty of us sat down for a meeting. I led the way.

"When you tell us something is not possible", I explained to Martha and Feodor, "you are making a decision for us. We don't want anyone making any decisions for us. Instead, tell us what it will take to make something possible and we will make the decisions. If we need a chopper and there are no pilots available around here, please find the nearest pilot. We could fly a pilot from Moscow, for example, but you must let us make that decision. Please, no more "not possible"."

I explained in more detail how sometimes you have to spend money to save money and that if we returned without a story, we would be more than $100,000 worse off and in a lot of trouble. The nods were solemn, even embarrassed. But everyone got it, Martha especially. "What do you need?" she asked.

Carsten and I laid out a new itinerary that would allow us to cover a lot of ground in short order, but it meant a lot more chopper time. Acid lakes to the northeast, geysers and fumaroles to the west, ice caves and lava to the south. As we laid out the plan the mood changed. The new mission an - aerial survey of this volcanic landscape - fired everyone up. It was bold and exciting. Yelena had just finished her business in the office and joined us in the room for the first time.

"Yelena," Martha said enthusiastically, "our group will need their own chopper full time for the next two weeks."

Yelena scoffed. "Not possible."

Everyone laughed, confusing Yelena no end. Martha gave Yelena a personalized version of my pep talk and they set to work. To do what we planned was going to cost about $5,000 more than we had on us. Banks in Kamchatka were charging forty-five per cent for wire transfers into the country so that was not an option. Instead Nancy and I combed the city for an alternative.

It's tough to find anything in Petropavlovsk. Even ten years after the collapse of the Soviet Union, there were no commercial signs, billboards or shopfronts. All the buildings of this former secret submarine port had the same gloomy, square, rundown appearance. The giant tubes running all over the city, carrying heat from a centralized furnace, were another sign of the communist era, but there were also odd indications of change. Western television had crept in and influenced fashion in the strangest of ways. Women, in particular, were keen to modernize their wardrobe but they had a lot of catching up to do. The sudden exposure to MTV styles gave them a glimpse at how to be hip, but no context or sense of appropriateness. It was not uncommon to see conservative young ladies trotting off to their bank jobs in stilettos and fishnets. I happily followed one of these employees into a rundown block of rust. It turned out to be the only bank in town that would advance us money on our credit cards. We got the chopper money we needed without the cost of a wire transfer. The next problem was a little harder to tackle.

Our arrival into Petropavlovsk coincided with a most unusual turn of natural events: the lava at all of Kamchatka's active volcanoes stopped flowing. This was hard to fathom. What sort of volcano documentary doesn't have lava? And how could this be? This is the most volcanic place on the planet. What are the chances the red-hot gooey stuff would stop just as we got going? We had no choice but to press on with real questions about what we could get and how we could salvage this expedition.

Our first stop involved another one of Carsten's wild, arguably harebrained, ideas. When a dormant volcanic crater fills with water it becomes a lake. Sometimes that volcano will continue to emit toxic sulfur directly into the water. The result is an acid lake. There are eighty-five acid lakes like this in the world and Kamchatka has three of the most toxic.

The acid is not unlike what you get from a car battery and it will burn with similar results. Someone going for a quiet swim in such a lake would soon find themselves blinded, their swimsuit disintegrating and, before long, their skin would peel off. A slow and horrible burning death would ensue. This was right up Carsten's alley. He was fascinated by these lakes and wanted to photograph them in a dynamic way.

On the surface a lake is just a lake, which can be visually dull. So to add a sense of scale and adventure, he talked Irene and Franck into a boat trip on one of these lakes in a rubber raft. He brought along two inflatable boats, but the tricky bit was guessing how long his support crew could be on the lake before the rubber would melt, instantly deflating their raft and sending them to the smouldering depths below.

We flew to one of these remote lakes and parked our chopper on the rim. It was a rough rappel down for Carsten, Feodor, Franck and Irene, with lots of loose rocks threatening to bounce off an unsuspecting head. Franck and Irene did most of the rigging of the rafts and ropes with Pat, on the rim Feodor taking a back seat. There was nothing about this he liked, and Feodor was convinced he was standing by for a rescue mission. To them this adventure didn't smell any better than the sulfur that oozed out of the ground around us, making the whole place reek of rotten eggs.

We were on a tight deadline to get this done and be onto our next destination before dark. The chopper couldn't fly after sunset and spending the night here was not an option. The flight crew warned us they would leave in short order whether we were ready or not. Down by the water, Carsten and Franck hit a snag when the air pump broke. Franck proceeded to inflate a raft by mouth, and Feodor was kind enough to lend a hand. It was exhausting, but somehow they got it done. They then wrapped the boat in plastic, hoping that this would prolong the inevitable acid holes.

Franck and Irene cautiously paddled a little way out onto the lake and the boat seemed to hold, but it wasn't good enough. As the sun was setting, the shadow from the crater's rim seemed to race across the lake. Shooting from the bank, Carsten desperately needed more sunlight for his photographs and shouted across the water, "Out into the middle, farther into the sun. Quickly!"

Franck and Irene exchanged a look. It was not so much the mission they minded, but this was no romantic sunset cruise and they didn't want to splash each other with acid water. But they continued, now at maximum effort, with each paddle from the shore increasing their chances of springing a leak.

They managed to row a good way out onto the lake and into the sunshine. With only minutes of good daylight to spare, Carsten snapped some unique photographs and the French duo scurried back. They raced up the crater and clambered into the chopper with a sigh of relief and we immediately took off. Once again we'd escaped without loss of life or limb - somehow even the rafts survived.

Next we headed to the Valley of Geysers. This is Russia's equivalent of Yellowstone but far less well known. Boiling-hot thermal pools bubble away, mud pots belch gas and more than half a dozen geysers shoot up water, some that could rival Yellowstone's Old Faithful. Guaranteed good photos - but still no lava.

Tensions reached their own boiling point within camp at our next location. Feodor had constantly ordered the Europeans in our group not to go anywhere without him. He was legitimately concerned for their safety, for which he felt personally responsible, but Feodor's requests often fell on deaf ears. He'd lost some credibility with the adventurers, and just the expression of his concerns soaked up valuable time that they'd rather use exploring.

It didn't help that Carsten's smiley devil-may-care demeanor gave the impression that he was reckless. Pat told me, in the harshest of words, that he thought him a complete idiot. Only after several expeditions with Carsten do you realize how much thought and planning he puts into his trips. He wouldn't bother to tell you, or explain this to anyone, but his risks are indeed calculated. For example, one of the acid lakes we found was leaking out water from the side of the mountain and through a giant glacier. The result was the rarest of formations - a glacier melting from the inside out. The acid stream had created an ice cave, perhaps a mile or more long, and you could see where the entrance to the cave would now and then collapse. Carsten, of course, wanted to explore the depths of this extraordinary mousetrap. He followed it back, under a myriad of spear-shaped icicles, skipping back and forth across the toxic stream, to a thirty-foot-high acid waterfall. Again, extraordinary photographs of a place never before seen.

I asked him later, "Mate, wasn't that a tad dangerous?"

"Oh ya, yes a little," he explained, "but that's why we left at four am." Venturing in during the coldest part of the day meant the ice was more sound. Carsten figured this would dramatically reduce the chance of a roof collapse. Everyone else thought he just wanted to get an early start. By normal standards, though, he was a risk-taker, and even if Feodor and the others knew of his mental preparations, I'm not sure they would have thought him any more sane.

The final straw for Feodor was in Uzon caldera. We landed in this large thermal area and moved our gear into an old volcanologists cottage. I followed Carsten, Franck and Irene off to explore. We were about 400 yards away when Feodor realized we'd gone without him and he shouted at us to come back. Returning could have meant missing some good light for shooting.

I asked, "Should we go back?" But I already knew the answer.

"No, I think we should go on," said Carsten, and we ignored Feodor's pleas and continued over the ridge and out of sight.

Feodor's fears were well founded. This, like much of Kamchatka, was bear country. To the human eye, the brown bears here are indistinguishable from the famed giant grizzlies of North America, and potentially just as fatal. Just four years earlier, Michio Hoshino, another well-known photographer, was here to take snaps of bears, as he had done often. Michio was from Japan and his bear photographs had been published in National Geographic and many other magazines. As the story goes, late one night Michio left the safety of his cabin where his Russian companions were overindulging in vodka, and snuggled up in his tent for some peace and quiet. It was the last thing he did. He quite possibly smelled of food, or maybe even had some with him. Whatever the case, something attracted a brown bear to his location and, before he could unzip the fly to his tent, he was mauled and killed.

Just two ridges away from where Feodor had been calling us, we found our own fine specimen of brown bear, probably half of a ton and just a few hundred yards away. A brown bear can cover that distance in less than twenty-three seconds, much faster than any of us, but this one seemed content to sniff around the volcanic vents and have his photo taken.

By the time Feodor trotted up behind us he was letting off more hot air than the fumaroles below.

"What are you doing?" he chided loudly.

"Shhh," pleaded Carsten as he continued taking photographs, "we don't want to scare the bear away."

"This is dangerous. I called you back. Did you hear me?"

Irene chimed in. "Yes, we heard you."

"You cannot do this - this is not safe. You must listen to me."

"Let's talk later," suggested Carsten. "You are scaring the bear."

Back at our cabin we surrounded a large table to hash out pent-up tensions. I asked Pat to film the meeting; you never know what will wind up in a film or on the cutting room floor, but the rule of thumb is to record first and decide later. Feodor started.

"Today we are very angry because of your behavior."

Irene was having none of it. "I don't think we need a lesson - you tell us once, you tell us twice and three times and we are getting very angry; we are not a child."

Feodor shot back, "But you behave like a child."

"I am not a child," she spat, "and you are not my father."

Pat was not comfortable with the tension. He turned the camera off and swung it away, certain this would not be part of a film on volcanoes. I tried to signal him to keep rolling but he didn't get it. Finally I had to shout across the room, "Pat, keep rolling." No one could have cared less that the camera was on.

Feodor continued, "I don't want to disturb your filming but you put yourself in danger."

Irene countered, "Always you say everything seems to be very risky, always always very risky, potentially very dangerous - and it's not always like this."

Carsten felt the problem was more of numbers. He found it hard to move and to work with so many people. "If we are maybe three or four persons it is not so bad, but if there are ten people . . ."

Feodor explained that the rules he upheld were not his own. "It's also a problem of law, you know - I can be in big trouble."

Carsten pressed on Feodor that photography and filming needed to be more of a priority and that he, Franck and Irene were not his normal tourist group but experienced adventurers. He pointed out an impressive list of past accomplishments, plus the fact that Franck was not only a professor but also a highly qualified diving instructor with enough first-aid credentials to drive an ambulance.

In the wash-up, Feodor was not happy, but he saw that perhaps he could relax a bit and he agreed to be less doting. We all agreed that we would act with more care and would carry two-way radios, but we would ultimately be responsible for our own actions.

At our next stop, an enormous non-acid lake to the south, Feodor allowed Carsten, Franck, Irene and myself to take off in a small power dinghy with nothing but a local bear guard. We all felt a great sense of freedom as we zoomed across the lake, beneath volcanic mountains, in search of thermal activity, leaving behind Feodor, Pat and the others.

The great irony here is that we were more scared of the bear guard than the bears. He only spoke Russian and either didn't understand or ignored our pleas for him to stop using his rifle as a walking stick. He regularly tapped his weapon on the ground in front of him, barrel up, to test the firmness of his footing. Perhaps it was unloaded but I somehow doubted it.

We came to shore by a small creek and happily left our guard to mind the boat as we headed upstream. Before long, the waterway was bank-to-bank full of salmon on their annual spawning run. These were the fish that were being sacrificed to feed the Russian mob with black-market roe. There are so many fish, our guides told us, that they usually cut the eggs from the salmon and throw the carcasses back in the water. The thought of this pristine environment being ravaged, especially in such a wasteful way, was disturbing.

I was standing in the middle of the stream filming Carsten as he played with the fish when an extremely large brown bear appeared along the water's edge. He came
straight over and eyed us from the bank while Carsten snapped off pictures and I filmed over his shoulder. At least I wasn't on the frontlines, but we were both just ten-feet or so from this guy as he began to sway from side to side; he seemed agitated and was preparing to make some kind of move.

When attacked by a brown or grizzly bear, the advice is to play dead. That would be extremely hard to do for long facedown in a stream without it becoming the real thing. What happened next tested our nerve and my camerawork. The bear pounced into the water and toward us; I felt about as helpless as the fish around our feet and all we could do was take a feeble step back.

The bear splashed down further into the stream - and stopped. We quickly realized he'd lunged, unsuccessfully, for some salmon. Food was plentiful here so this bear felt no need to supplement his diet with either German or Australian cuisine. We backed up slowly and watched as the bear retreated to the bank to try again; this time he came up from the water with a big red juicy fish.

We turned our focus back on our story to film some giant pumice stones. Pumice is a volcanic rock that starts as a liquid, deep down in the earth, under pressure. As an eruption throws it into the air, the pressure is released and it expands, fills with air bubbles, and then cools. The result is a rock that can float. Some of the pumice rocks here were more than three-feet across, so to see them floating on the lake was quite something.

We choppered into our final volcano with hope in our hearts. Mutnovsky volcano is the most active of Kamchatka's volcanoes; if lava was flowing anywhere, it'd be here. That hope was short-lived.

A quick flyover told us we were out of luck, but we landed and hiked to the rim nonetheless. Toxic gases continued to pour from one side of the crater, and Carsten and Franck put on gas masks to descend into the wasteland below. Another questionable mission for sure, but this time they took a two-way radio. From the rim we watched them descend to near the bottom, but just as they got there the wind changed in a most concerning way. The air pocket they'd followed down became inundated with fumes and we lost sight of them.

Their masks could only protect them if there was at least some oxygen to filter, and it looked to have entirely disappeared. We heard some coughing over the two-way, then nothing. Feodor tried to raise them on the radio but without luck. It would be foolhardy to send someone down to search for them, but how long should we wait? The wind changed once more so we could finally look down into the crater again, but we could see no sign of them. They'd completely vanished.

The nail-biting minutes ticked by, then a familiar German accent came over the two-way: "It is incredible down here, *just incredible.*"

Almost at the moment the fumes engulfed them they'd found a secondary crater and slipped down - out of radio contact, but to relative safety. There they found a large rainbow-colored wall, oozing fumes like a smoke-breathing dragon with rocks stained bright red and yellow by volcanic chemicals. Carsten's photos captured a sight as rare as it was spectacular.

Having gotten through another misadventure, we turned for home for the last time and, as we did, all the tension lifted from Feodor's shoulders. He and Irene even managed a laugh and a hug. I think it's fair to say that cameraman Pat still thought Carsten one of the stupidest people on the planet, but all that was behind us now.

The challenge for both Carsten and me was to salvage our volcano stories knowing we did not have lava as a payoff. Our solutions ended up being similar. I repitched our TV story with a new title: "Beyond the Lava." After all, any halfwit can get lava, right? That's the obvious bit. Our film became something totally novel: a tale of the extraordinary forces at play *around* volcanoes, even when lava is not present. Fumaroles, acid lakes, ice caves, geysers, even pumice stones and, finally, a giant never-before-seen technicolor wall of toxic fumes. This was all part of a landscape so new that it wasn't yet finished. Carsten's array of sensational photographs provided the magazine with a similar story.

We all gathered for a farewell night of fun. At least, that's what I tried to convey to the extended team. It turns out there is no word in Russian that means "fun". By using the closest possible translation, I made it clear that we were going out to enjoy generous amounts of celebratory vodka. I suggested to Feodor that we get the pickle juice ready. And perhaps, after all, this home remedy has some merit.

About the same time we sat down to tackle our boozy last meal in Russia, back in the United States, the Philadelphia Eagles football team had some pickle-related tackling of their own to do. The Eagles were, right at that time, feeling the heat in a game against the Dallas Cowboys. It was forty-two degrees, no doubt even hotter inside an American football helmet, and players faced the constant threat of dehydration and cramp. Forget other risky and possibly illegal performance-enhancing alternatives: at this point some of the Eagles started to swill pickle juice.

Where they got such an idea is anyone's guess, but maybe it wasn't so crazy. Like a hangover sufferer, a heat-affected footballer experiences dehydration and a loss of electrolytes, which can cause cramp. Dill pickle juice, as it turns out, has electrolytes and other naturally occurring antioxidants, salts and minerals. In what became known as "The Pickle-Juice Game", the Eagles won forty-one to fourteen and credited the juice, at least in part, for their spectacular victory. What further anecdotal proof does any hardcore drinker need?

"No need for pickle juice," Feodor told me. "Tonight we drink Istok, the *really* good stuff."

"Good stuff?" I asked. "What have we been drinking?"

"The stuff we've had is not so good in quality. It gives you a hangover. The good stuff doesn't do that."

This was a revelation that seemed to be coming about six weeks too late. When it comes to alcohol and hangovers, congeners are the bad guys. These impurities, created during fermentation, give alcohol some of its taste, but you can also blame them, beyond just dehydration, for much of your hangover. There are three things that can reduce the amount of congeners in vodka and all of them require some expense.

Firstly, the more an alcohol is distilled, the less congeners it will have. Secondly, vodka alcohol is mixed with water and filtered; if it's a good carbon filter it will get rid of some congeners as well. And, finally, the initial fifteen per cent through your still will be rich in congeners, as will as the last fifteen per cent. So good vodka makers will throw this part away, or use it for something else, and just bottle the superior middle seventy per cent. It was now clear that the vodka we'd been drinking, up until this point, lacked any or possibly all three of these factors, and was congener rich.

"Couldn't we have taken the expensive stuff with us on our travels?" I asked.

"Not possible."

"I didn't like where this was going. I felt compelled to inquire, "What's Russian for déjà vu?" but instead asked, "Why not?"

"It's too expensive. The cheap bottles are only forty cents US."

Impressively cheap indeed. "How much for the good stuff?"

Feodor did some rough conversions in his head. "In US dollars . . . about ninety cents a bottle."

"What?"

"Yeah, very expensive, about ninety, ninety-five cents."

Expensive maybe for a Kamchatkan, but still cheaper than a bottle of water for a westerner. I was floored. I drank lots that night and, sure enough, no hangover. I was so clear-headed, in fact, that once I got over my incredulousness, I was struck with an idea. I could take six or seven bottles of the good stuff without raising any eyebrows and share them with my colleagues back home.

And what if my workmates did the same on their travels? On our last day in Kamchatka I splurged. I spent a full $6.65c on the best vodka and stashed it away as hand luggage. The Exotic Booze Club was born.

The first ever invitation to the Exotic Booze Club went out on October 13th, 2000.

The Exotic Booze Club

Dear National Geographic Colleagues and Fellow Drinkers,

What does it take to make a Russian consume a large amount of juice from a jar of pickles? You're invited to my office tonight to find out.

Drink of the night: Istok vodka.

Russians drink more hard alcohol than anyone else in the world, and if they can afford it, Istok vodka is what they drink.

Kremlin monks invented vodka in 1503, initially as an antiseptic. They soon found they could down copious quantities of their magic potion with impunity if they took a few precautions to prevent hangovers. Here's what the monks advise:

1. *Don't sip - take a full shot at a time.*
2. *In the name of Rasputin, don't mix vodka with anything else, especially sweet, sugary liquids. (Goodbye, Red Bull.)*
3. *Eat a couple of boiled potatoes, slurp up a raw egg and down a tablespoon of olive oil one hour before doing shots.*
4. *The morning after, get up at five am, drink a small bottle of beer and go back to bed.*

And, finally...

5. *When you get up for the day, drink a glass of brine from the jar you keep pickles in.*

Therefore, to answer the initial riddle, if you see a Russian throwing away pickles and swigging the juice, you know it's because he's had a full night of vodka shots. So make like a monk and come join me for a drink - raw eggs optional.

Bar opens at five pm. All welcome.

Cheers,

Brian

Chapter 2

CAMEL COWBOYS:
Victoria Bitter

The crowd for the first night of the Exotic Booze Club was small but appreciative. I'd just left my door open, with the vodka on my coffee table, and kept working until people dropped by. About a dozen came, mainly to see if I had been joking. Alcohol in a National Geographic office was, apparently, against company policy and not something you sent emails about.

That all seemed very unAustralian and adhering to such rules has never been my strong point. I felt I had to follow up with another meeting in relatively short order to let people know I was serious.

I dug through my hidden supplies and found half a dozen cans of Victoria Bitter left over from a previous shoot. Although not at all exotic for an Aussie, VB is not sold in the US, so I figured it'd qualify. The reason these tinnies had lasted so long requires another shameful confession: I'm actually not much of a beer drinker.

I can trace this dysfunction to early childhood and the fact that my parents were teetotallers and I never saw either of them touch alcohol. Other kids around my home town of Marong, near Bendigo, acquired a taste for beer after a hard day at kindie by sipping from dad's glass. I, on the other hand, missed out on this important stage of Down Under development. By the time I desired alcohol, my arms were much longer and could reach straight up to the top shelf. Out of habit, that's where I've kept reaching.

At long last there was a plus side to my condition - some leftover exotic beer for the Club's second meeting. The cans were the favored flavor of a colleague who, unaware of my affliction, had left them in my care as a sign of gratitude: I'd given him work and he'd been thankful for the experience and, mostly, for having survived.

We'd shot the expedition responsible for this stash immediately prior to the Russia trip, before I had the idea for the Exotic Booze Club. This story began one memorable day when my boss saw me in the corridor and said, "Brian, we have some holes in the schedule. Why don't you pick a place in the world you want to visit and find a story there?"

"Will do," I said matter-of-factly while pinching myself. Who is ever given instructions like that?

I sat at my desk counting my blessings and pondering, "Antarctica? Cuba? Mongolia? Hmmm . . ." In the end I went with my first impulse, and that was to visit home. I'd been away for a year and I wanted to embrace the land closest to my heart and the birthplace of my wanderlust.

We never travelled far as kids; there were always animals on the farm that couldn't be left without a major hassle. But I never knew or felt like I was missing out either, at least not until I received the simplest of gifts on my ninth birthday: my parents gave me a two-man A-frame tent and unleashed a hidden desire for travel and adventure.

One afternoon when my mother and father were away for a few hours, a mate and I decided we needed to make backpacks to go with this tent, so we searched my dad's farm for suitable materials. We twisted some wire to hold apart pieces of PVC pipe and thus made two frames, then tied on hessian feed bags and cut seat belts from an old car to make shoulder straps. Into these uncomfortable arrangements we loaded the tent, matches, heavy cans of food, mum's good cooking pot and a box of cereal. We left a note that said "Gone north - camping" and off we ventured.

We hiked at least a thousand miles - or maybe it was two. In any case, it was a grand exploration into the wilds of our neighbor's paddock. We forgot the milk for our cereal so the next morning we tried to catch a sheep to milk. When our mustering skills proved inadequate for this challenge we turned home, a lot wiser and hungry to discover what may lie over the next horizon, and the next.

While I love to travel the world, the big sky and boundless plains of Australia will forever be my favorite destination - plus I speak the language.

I had a few stories in mind that could take me back Down Under, but before I could start development, two other Aussie ideas landed front and centre. The first story waltzed into my office with boundless energy and a big smile. Ashley Hoppin was an outside producer, a fast-talking

Manhattan babe who'd pitched a story on Australia's wild camels, the last place in the world where dromedaries run free. Ashley was an unknown talent, so Geo executives said they'd only green light her idea if she agreed to have me as her co-producer. The big grin shining through my doorway told me she'd agreed.

The second idea was courtesy of Boyd Matson, host of the long-running documentary series National Geographic Explorer. Boyd is one of the best presenters you could ever hope to have on your team and the rarest of TV beings: a savvy and highly professional host with no ego. Years of live television, including a stint as co-anchor of NBC America's *Weekend Today*, polished his skills. He is an extremely confident ad libber who always carries with him the nicest possible demeanor - as long as you adhere to one condition.

Some TV stars may need private dressing rooms or make-up and hair ladies and the like, but Boyd happily foregoes all of the above as long as he gets his regular dose of action-induced adrenaline. I once spent ten days filming him on the world's toughest non-military survival course: no tents, no sleeping bags, no backpacks, no running water and no food - a week and a half in the West Australian desert without a scrap to eat. We each lost twenty-three pounds. Despite the stresses, he was a gentleman the entire way. He's lost toenails from the strain of ultra-marathons, broken bones crashing motorbikes, fallen from endurance horses, jumped out of planes, and played with lions and tigers and bears. At those times, he couldn't be happier.

This time Boyd was set on an adrenaline fix on the Great Barrier Reef, where he was to help test a shark repellent. Knowing Boyd, he'd find some way to get in with the sharks and use himself as bait. For that he might possibly need a medic, but would definitely need a producer to make sure it was all caught on film. Again, as the only Australian producer on staff, I was the obvious choice for the mission. The shark-repellent story was short and we arranged to do it first. This would allow Boyd to join us for some of the camel shoot as well, before other host duties pulled him away.

We landed in Cairns, the closest access point to the Reef. When I say close I mean that in the Australian sense of the word. Much to the delight of locals, first-time visitors to the Great South Land often fail to grasp the distance between points on an Aussie map. It's like a national joke that endlessly amuses those in the know.

Australia takes up about as much of the planet as North America's lower forty-eight states, except in Australia there are only have six states and a couple of territories. I like to think that this was a deliberate design by some scallywag to throw off Joe Tourist's sense of scale. Some foreigners arrive in Cairns thinking they can swim out to the Reef for a quick snorkel. There are three reasons why this is a bad idea: a) they won't make it, b) they'll likely die trying, and c) a lot of Australians will laugh at them.

The closest patch of reef is about twenty miles from Cairns, and to reach the more popular dive spots usually takes several hours in a large boat.

We boated off to Osprey Reef about 100 miles away, a favored location for the sharks we'd attempt to repel. Our team included Matt Stewart, a talented dinkum-Aussie cameraman based out of Sydney, and West Australian sound recordist Jeremy Ashton. Jeremy is a wise soul with a mischievous smile, not so much a sound guy as a fellow producer who happens to hold a microphone and a mixer.

Both of them would also be on the camel shoot. The repellent to be tested came to us courtesy of a South African team; James Nasbury was the brains behind the invention, and Naas Hartzenberg was the businessman hoping to make a killing - in the figurative sense, of course.

Once we anchored, James brought out a dive belt with a small blue waterproof box attached and a single yellow button in the middle. When you push the button, the box emits an electrical pulse designed to repel sharks away from divers, surfers, swimmers and any other tasty morsels who happen to be wearing one.

It is a demonstrated fact that sharks can detect electrical impulses; it's their sixth sense. A gelatinous substance called the ampullae of Lorenzini sits in their snouts and picks up minute electrical signals from the stressed muscles of fish or even panicked swimmers. In short, fear attracts sharks, but if you find yourself in the middle of a shark merry-go-round, good luck staying calm. These apex predators can pick up five-billionths of a volt. To them, your pulsating anal sphincter alone would ring like a dinner bell.

James and Naas were banking that a more intense impulse, still undetectable by humans, would act as a repellent. It would be like a dog whistle that can attract your canine or, at a more disturbing pitch, send them running. With a shark, you just needed to be sure not to get the two mixed up.

This was a mere fifteen-minute story so we had a simple plan. Boyd and James would suit up and jump in the water in a shark cage, where Boyd would use bait to attract sharks and start a feeding frenzy. He would try to pull them close to the cage, then James would hit the magic button and see how the sharks reacted.

Paul Wooly Wolstenholme also joined us to shoot the underwater action. I'd worked with Wooly doing news for Channel Nine in Western Australia years before. He is a quick and reliable cameraman on terra firma, and under water he excels. Wherever he is, he has a thirst for adventure. Once, returning together from a news shoot, we saw a new sign that said "Safety Ramp Ahead".

"What's that?" I asked Wooly as he drove us down a steep hill outside of Perth. He had no idea either, but ahead we could see a dirt road that led up and off to one side. "Ah," I said as it dawned on me, "it must be a road to slow down runaway trucks."

A manic look overcame Wooly's face as he hit the accelerator and veered off to charge up the ramp. Both he and I had failed to realize that this ramp was not so much a road as a pit filled with millions of tiny round pebbles designed to bog out-of-control forty-ton semis.

We skimmed across the top for a few fleeting but glorious moments, then sank deep into the trap. In above our hubcaps and hopelessly stuck, we sat for a moment absorbing our predicament, then Wooly conceded, "I guess that wasn't too smart." We called a tow truck to pull us out, and while it was the joke of the newsroom for a while, I know Wooly thought it worthwhile, just for those few nanoseconds of off-road adventure.

As he prepared now to enter the water, Wooly had that same manic look in his eye and a plan that seemed equally not so smart. For the best angle on the action, Wooly wanted to be outside the cage and close to the feeding frenzy.

One of the boat hands threw chum in the water and within a few minutes the empty void beneath us filled with dozens and dozens of sharks. There were easily a hundred directly beneath our hull. We dropped the cage in the water. Boyd and James double-checked their scuba gear and shut themselves in their aquatic prison cell. Wooly, true to his word, hung outside the cage and tried to stop himself from generating any stress-based electronic impulses.

Boyd had a large mass of fish on the end of a rope and he fed it through the cage. The sharks took the bait, one at first, then several darting in and out trying to snag a full bite. As the sharks worked themselves into the frenzy Boyd had hoped for, he signalled James to hit the button on his belt. Nothing happened. The frenzy continued unabated.

The two surfaced for a debrief. James immediately suspected that the metal cage was interfering with the electronic impulses. Boyd could not have been happier with this assessment. To truly test the device, Boyd and James would have to leave the cage, bait in hand, and join Wooly on the toothy side. Adrenaline assured.

Boyd replenished his bait and they tried again. This time the feeding frenzy, just an arm's length away, dragged Boyd into the depths. He was trying not to let go of his rope, but the constant attacking and jerking of the bait on the other end pulled him deeper and deeper. James had little choice but to pursue his dive buddy and the attached frenzy. Then, just before James hit the button, the sharks disappeared.

It seemed the extra water pressure at depth, induced by Boyd's shark-propelled plunge, was forcing the button to come on by itself. But had the subsequent release of current scared the sharks away? Or had they just finished with their fish? It was hard to tell. The divers would have to try again.

James tinkered with the repellent device over the next few days and Wooly filmed Boyd playing shark rodeo over and over. When the electronics were on the sharks seemed to react and wouldn't come near the bait, but once they were in a frenzy it seemed little was going to stop them until they'd devoured their meal.

We gave the device a mixed review. It showed promise, but it needed more work. It would also have to prove its effectiveness on a range of shark species, and that could take years.

We wrapped up our onboard filming and headed to shore for some tropical cocktails. The next adrenaline hit was a few days away and the challenges there looked to be substantially greater. This wasn't just any film on camels we were doing but the largest camel round-up ever.

We went south to pick up a couple of shark interviews in Sydney, and there Boyd and I met up with Ashley and our camel round-up associate producer David Shadrack Smith, better known as Shady.

Shady had lived in China for seven years but was born in Brooklyn and had a strong Jewish heritage. The combination left him, at all times, one-third patient (in a soft-spoken Asian kind of way), one-third New York artsy neurotic, and one-third guilt-ridden - perfect ingredients for a great associate producer.

Despite this, when we met in Sydney it was clear that something was wrong. Shady was a great shooter and an established producer who was happy enough to take a step back in title to get in the door at Geo. But now he began his first job as an AP with a heavy heart.

The long-term girlfriend Shady lived with in China had just dumped him and he'd crumpled at the news that she would not be following him

The Exotic Booze Club

on his new exploits in the United States for National Geographic. We all felt somewhat responsible for his rehabilitation, so we took him with us for our final shark interview at Manly Beach where we deposited him on the sand and let him soak up some sun. Sure enough, in short order a cute bikini-clad Aussie surfer chick took sympathy on this downtrodden soul and struck up a little tête-à-tête. Knowing Shady as I now do, I have no doubt that he would have confined the conversation to something ridiculously intellectual, but perhaps that was for the best. Something worked, though, and by the time we collected him several hours later, his ego had been boosted and his spirits were noticeably higher.

We boarded our plane for Alice Springs and I warned my American colleagues of the vast empty spaces we were about to encounter. I suspect that central Australia has long been a great challenge for mapmakers; you could hardly hand your boss an outline on a blank sheet of paper and say, "Here, done." As a result, some cartographers fill the void with a network of obscure geologic features and disused mine sites just to justify having made a map.

The problem comes when tourists use one of these overly descriptive references to carefully plan their driving or bike route:

"Honey (pant pant), I thought for sure we'd get water here at Breakyaback Ridge."

"Dang, George, it's nothing but red dirt."

"Not to worry, dear, it's just another, ah, 276 miles to Dead Man Valley."

Poor folks. Though it's good for a laugh down at the pub.

We wasted no time and immediately drove out to Uluru to shoot some introduction pieces with Boyd. After then kicking an Aussie Rules football around for a while to stretch our legs, we headed to camel central. Our home for the next two and a half weeks would be 100 miles south of Alice Springs, in the back country of Henbury cattle station.

When I left Bendigo High School in Central Victoria after year twelve, I ventured to the Northern Territory and was a jackaroo – what American's call a cowboy. I worked for a season on Wave Hill Station – what American's all ranch. With its adjoining sister property, Cattle Creek, Wave Hill made a nice little parcel of some 1.8 million acres. It wasn't unusual for us to spend thirty or forty hours a week on horseback just to work up one paddock, almost always mustering with the support of a helicopter. Henbury was also an impressive spread of about 500,000 acres and being there felt like I was home again.

Ashley had lined up all the contacts out here on a previous trip, and we rolled in to meet the owner of Henbury, Big Ross. Ross Morton is born-and-bred outback, a soft-spoken yet undeniably strong man who looks like he eats half a cow every day for breakfast, and a case of beer for lunch. The washing of clothes appears to be a futile exercise long ago abandoned by Ross, with dirt and oil stains deeply embedded in his outback uniform of khaki shorts and a dark green shirt with the sleeves cut off at the shoulder. Countless packets of cigarettes wear holes in Ross's top pockets, and the broad brim of his Akubra shadows a cheeky grin.

Like many station owners, beef isn't only in his belly, it's in his blood - he's a third-generation cattleman. But when we met Ross, this adventurous entrepreneur was branching out to add something different, camels.

In the mid 1800s, 10,000 to 12,000 camels were imported to Australia to help Europeans explore and settle the outback. In the 1920s and 1930s, trains and trucks replaced them, and the old Afghan handlers who could no longer get work released their herds into the wild. This was like letting ferrets loose in a henhouse. These biblical beasts felt right at home in their new land, and they went forth and multiplied without any natural predators to control their numbers. Now an estimated one million dromedaries run feral in outback Australia.

The very first hour-long documentary I made was called *Camel Outback*. It was a home-made production that marvelled at these bizarre creatures: the revolting football-sized bladder that bubbles outside the bull's mouth when they're feeling frisky, the horrendous smell that accompanies this rutting stage, their ability to drink a third of their body weight in one sitting, their backward-facing penises, and their out-of-control breeding. The government funds culling programs and some cattle owners shoot camels on sight. But not everyone sees them as vermin.

More recent studies show that camels may actually help cattle. They eat plant species cattle won't touch, and at waterholes they may spread useful bacteria that help cattle digest rough foliage. Ross saw camels as very big steaks with humps. He'd had some success in selling camels on the meat market and was ready to scale up his operation.

Each animal yields about 450 pounds of meat, earning Ross around $350 per camel. The only rule: no slaughtering males while they are in rut. The rank odor they produce at this time permeates the meat, rendering it unfit to eat. This was not a big problem as they only rutted once a year and there were plenty of other sweeter-smelling camels ready for the taking. Ross laid out an ambitious plan to round up 500 wild dromedaries, the largest ever muster of its type. We would need lots of supplies - it was time to grog up.

We called into a small one-camel town about an hour down the road and purchased all manner of important alcoholic produce. At this crucial point in our expedition, sound recordist Jeremy called to me, "Hey mate, you tried Wild Turkey?"

I had certainly heard of this Kentucky bourbon, but hadn't tried it. Jim Beam was Australia's most popular bourbon, but Wild Turkey had recently gained ground. Jeremy added several bottles to our order. We'd instructed Shady to treat both our team and Ross's. With some demanding days ahead, we'd need all the goodwill grog we could bestow. We also loaded up with cases of VB and Melbourne Bitter. Shady was a bit shaken by the frenzy, but we now felt adequately prepared for the shoot.

An older, fun-loving larrikin named Paul James was one of the men we were buying for, Ross's veteran stockman. Rarely seen without a beer in his hand, Paul's pouch of roll-your-own tobacco smelt suspiciously more green than the law would condone. Their other team member, Troy Wareham, had done a few seasons with cattle, but this would be his first camel round-up; he and Boyd were the rookies. Each of Ross's men had his own beat-up Land Cruiser, primarily filled with spare tyres, and each was equipped with giant roo bars that ran around the entire front end of the vehicle. It was our first hint of the hazards ahead. Rounding up wild camels, in cars, promised to be a bumpy affair.

Ross knew there were some camels on his neighbor's place so we headed out. This wasn't a jump over the back fence but a drive of several hours. When it got too late we spent the night by a dirt road, sharing a fire with an old-timer known as Popeye. A wiry loner, Popeye was charged with grading the roads. It's a thankless job that involved towing his small camper behind a giant grader, setting up home, grading smooth the dirt roads for a week or so around his new address, then moving further down the track and doing it again, and again, and again. Then, around December, the monsoon rains come and wipe out all his hard work, and in March he starts again from scratch. Not surprisingly, Popeye was keen for a chat and he made a good dent in our supply of VB.

The next day we arrived where our first muster of our big round-up would take place, a paddock that measured about twenty-five square miles. Ross's neighbor was more old school - he didn't like camels and had planned to shoot them - so Ross had stepped in and offered to herd them away instead. We unloaded our camping gear at a suitable spot near some stockyards and charged off, keen to get the chase underway.

We were about 200 miles from the nearest town in a landscape void of mountains, barely even a hill. The red soil of the Centre invaded every nook of our belongings and every crevice of our bodies, but its rich, sweet fragrance immerses you in the experience of being outback.

This welcoming aroma was all the more pervasive after some recent rain. The showers seemed to have calmed the land, making the air crisp, so sound travelled clear and far. You would think, under such conditions and in such habitat, a ten-foot high animal would be easy to find - but no.

We came across an area of flattened sand; a mob of about twenty camels had laid down here not long ago. Ross examined damp patches where some animals had urinated and he knew they must be close. Despite this promise, hours ticked by. Finally Ross spotted a flash of sand-colored hair through the scrub and Boyd, beside him with a Handycam, recorded the discovery on tape. The action was about to begin. Cameraman Matt jumped in with rookie Troy. Shady jumped in with the more seasoned Paul. The rest of us crammed in wherever we could, and the high-speed circus began.

Ross put his foot flat to the floor and zoomed around to face the camels. Immediately they darted. Paul whizzed by in a spray of dirt to head them off, but it wasn't that simple. These giants of the bush had little co-ordinated movement as a group so it was less like mustering cattle and more like herding cats. Individuals split off and charged away. Troy, the rookie, went after one, and Ashley and I bounced around like rag dolls in the back of his Land Cruiser. We had no seatbelts - in fact, we had no seats. Troy's vehicle was an enclosed tray top with old windows that were jammed open. We slammed into branches and bushes doing fifty or more miles an hour and shattered entire trees into pieces. Large wood splinters rained on us through the windows. With the sharp turns and doughnuts that followed, it's amazing he didn't roll the vehicle.

Troy managed to turn the wayward camel back toward the herd but, before getting there, the beast split off again and made another dash for it, this time with a camel accomplice. Ross kicked his truck into reverse to block them and nearly hit Paul instead. He screeched to a halt an inch or two from Paul's rear fender, and the escapees slipped around. Then Troy was off to get them back with us feeling every bump like a sledgehammer up the backside.

It was total madness, but it was part of a plan. Cattle, for the most part, will readily yield to a vehicle or horse, and politely follow each other like a group of good British tourists. Camels, according to Ross, need some training. They have to learn that there's no escape, and only then can you control them and push them where you want them to go. We were engaged in a round-up school for wayward camels, and they all deserved detention for lack of understanding.

We burned through the scrub for hours. Just when we thought the camels were getting the idea, a different camel would split and make another dash for it. Ross's was the first car to get a flat tyre. He pulled out a giant jack and changed it in a matter of minutes, like an expert one-man pit crew. It was a sight we saw often as more and more tyres popped after a high-speed encounter with a low-lying mulga bush, a sharp and brittle wood.

If a mulga spear jabs a person instead of a vehicle it's a serious issue, as pieces readily enter and poison the bloodstream. A local Aboriginal elder had warned us that such an event could be fatal.

Paul brushed past another hazard when the arm he had leaning out the window hit a plant covered in itchy grubs. (Ochrogaster lunifer, also called processionary caterpillars for their habit of following each other around on the ground in a chain; sometimes more than a hundred grubs will form one long walkabout wagon train). These grey hairballs, about two inches long, cause a reaction on the skin that makes poison ivy feel like a gentle loofah. The resulting skin rash can last for months and is easily infected. It's also been blamed for causing short-term psychotic episodes, and new evidence suggests that the hairs of this grub house a pathogenic bacteria that causes mares to spontaneously abort their foals. Nasty stuff. Paul employed typical outback emergency first-aid treatment: he ignored it as best he could, rolled a cigarette with one hand, and kept chasing delinquent camels.

These animals were smart. They resisted sticking together and we filmed them trying to evade us with all sorts of splitting-up combinations. No matter how much we chased, they never seemed to slow. Troy crackled over the two-way, "Jeez, they've got a bit of go in them." At full speed, a camel can hit forty miles an hour.

"Trial and error," said Paul. "Right now more error than trial."

After a long day of chasing/training and about eight flat tyres, Ross's camel school was still full of reprobates and our entire story was confined to a single paddock. It may have been a big paddock, but that still didn't sound very Nat Geo. If the camels ever yielded enough for us to get them out, we'd need lots of daylight to run them up to the nearest stockyards and it was already getting too dark. We had to stop and plan to start again in the morning from scratch.

Ross remained optimistic. "They'll get sick of us turning them and pushing them and trying to tell them what we want them to do," he told Boyd.

Boyd was a tad concerned about the lack of progress. "Well," he said, "after eight hours they weren't sick of it today."

Ross shot back, "Well, after another eight tomorrow they will be."

It was the patience and stubbornness of an outback cattleman versus an animal so naturally combat-hardened that a battalion of them was recruited as mounts for frontline soldiers in World War I.

We headed back to set up camp. Ross didn't do things by halves and had a mountain of equipment, including a large four-wheeler motorbike. We used this rugged little Honda vehicle to select toilet spots away from camp, and for general zooming around. My co-producer, Ashley, took to this toy like a wide-eyed little kid. Her hand seemed glued to the accelerator and I don't believe she ever bothered to work out which bit was the brake.

Ross also set up a full kitchen with giant coolers, large iron hotplates to put over a fire, dishes and trays, a generator, tables and chairs. Ashley had brought some camel steaks for us to sample and Ross cooked them on the fire. The meat was lean and slightly grey, but otherwise hard to distinguish from the average beefsteak. Maybe a little tough, but nothing that couldn't be fixed with a nice bourbon marinade.

Sound guy Jeremy poured me a sample of eighty-proof Wild Turkey and I was instantly hooked. It is a delicious bourbon. I've since tried their 101 and their Rare Breed, but I find the cheaper eighty proof has a peppermint essence that excites my tastebuds. Not that I'm a purist about it. To be honest, I most often have it as Jeremy does, mixed strong with Coke. The Turkey generates a nice buzz, and the Coke keeps me awake longer to enjoy it. Turkey and Coke quickly became my go-to drink, and I've since spread the word to other teams I work with throughout the world. Either they like it too or perhaps they enjoy that I love it so much, but it's common now for me to be picked up from the airport by a local crewmember with a bottle of Wild Turkey sitting in the centre console awaiting seduction.

We set up a tent to protect our camera equipment from the dust and rolled out our swags - an iconic Australian roll-up bed, usually with an outer layer of canvas. Some of ours came with fly nets over the top. That night I slept with one eye open in case Paul went into some itchy grub induced psychotic episode. It didn't happen, but we did marvel at the red blotchy rash that now covered most of his right arm and shoulder.

Alcohol, amply applied orally, was the only treatment he wanted, and we happily provided the medicine.

The next day we headed out early, only this time Ross had called in reinforcements. A Bell 47 helicopter buzzed overhead and quickly found the herd. "Can't get any flat tyres up there," Ross said with glee as he cut open the fence so they could herd camels through toward the stockyards.

We surrounded them with Land Cruisers and, with the chopper's help, drove them to the hole in the fence. What followed was an incredible stand-off that demonstrates the true tenacity of a stubborn camel - either that or they had no idea that the fence behind them was open. But they refused to budge, despite the fact that we were so close with the cars we could reach out and touch them.

We backed off and let the chopper swoop in. It made a hell of a racket and kicked up dirt and dust all over the animals; the daring pilot couldn't go any lower without chopping off some heads. In desperation, he even tried pushing a camel with the skids of his bird. It was fast action and high drama but the indignant animals *still* wouldn't move, turning instead to face the flying machine in defiance.

This was way harder than Ross had ever dreamed, but finally, one of the camels slowly and tenderly took a step in the right direction. Once one worked it out, they all followed. Free at last. It was getting to be an expensive exercise: these twenty animals had burned up more chopper time than anyone had predicted, a good two hours. The pilot finally headed for home and we surrounded the camels again with the cars. They did seem to respond better than the previous day and, after several hours, with minimal fuss and only another four or five flat tyres, we pushed the camels into the yards and Paul shut the gate. "The best bit of the whole day, I reckon," he declared. Then added, "Now I just feel like a beer."

Ashley and I couldn't believe our luck. There is a general rule on expeditions called "Last-Day Payoff": you always get what you really need on the last day and never before. No matter what it is, no matter how long the shoot, it's always the last twenty-four to forty-eight hours that really count. That's what made this so extraordinarily different as we were only a few days into this one. With Boyd's little Handycam included, we just had a five-camera shoot on some incredible drama - and the payoff was in the yard.

It was still far from the biggest round-up ever, but the rest would be gravy. It was also perfect timing for Boyd, who had to leave us in a few days for another shoot. We'd be fine without him; we figured we were a good ninety percent shot with only three days down and ten days still to go.

Ross wasn't as elated. Apart from the unexpected time and expense so far, he had mechanical problems and needed some downtime to put a new engine in one of the Land Cruisers. I was impressed that they were just going to pull up to their own shed and swap out an engine. These were handy guys to have around. They left us to fend for ourselves for a few days. We filmed introduction pieces with Boyd among the camels and I loaded up the car for the long drive to take him to the airport. By the time I got back we'd be about ready to continue the round-up, adding more and more wild camels to the current herd as we drove them towards Henbury Station.

Cameraman Matt jumped onto the four-wheeler for a morning pit stop and tried Ashley's trick of all-gas-no-brake. Away from camp, his toilet roll flew off the back. He was either in a terrible hurry or pumped by the speed of his ride, but when he jumped off the bike and bolted back to collect his lost toilet tissue, he rammed his left leg hard into a piece of mulga bush. I can't imagine the force with which he did this, but he now had a brittle piece of death-bush in his body. I'm uncertain if he finished his business, but I wouldn't have blamed him if he'd gone in his pants right there and then. He returned to camp, an alarming shade of green. The local advice that such an event could be fatal rang in our ears.

We sat him down, took a look, and tried our best not to appear startled. It would be terribly understated to describe what we saw as a 'splinter' - it was a stake big enough to slay a vampire. The spike, about the size of my index finger, had jammed deep into the front of his leg, its full length parallel to his shinbone. We gave no thought to filming this kind of drama. I merely got out my Leatherman pliers to see if there was any hope I could pull the wood out cleanly. Ashley held Matt as I made a solid grip on the end of the stake and gave an almighty tug. It didn't budge in the slightest. There was nothing for it but a trip to the nearest emergency room, several hours away.

Jeremy and Shady took Matt to a clinic in one car, while I took Boyd to catch his plane in the other - for all of us, an overnight trip. We left Ashley with a camera and the camels, ready for when the jackaroos returned to restart the roundup. The doctors at the clinic had seen it all before and knew exactly what to do. They cut open Matt's leg, cleaned it out and stitched him up in no time. Not only was he going to live, he would soon be ready to continue shooting. Matt limped out, lit a smoke and grabbed a can of VB. He was ready to turn his attention to a more pressing matter.

We'd just discovered that Shady had made a severe miscalculation. We thought he'd loaded up our second car with alcohol at the drive-through liquor store, but no. Shady thought he'd purchased enough for two weeks, but - with a little help from our friends - we were nearly dry after just four days. We took the opportunity while in town to replenish our supplies, I got Boyd to the airport, and now we were ready to continue the roundup. Twenty camels down, 480 to go.

By the time we all met up again at a truckstop the next day, the entire game plan had changed. Troy drove in with Ashley on the back of his Land Cruiser and she was shaking her head in disbelief.

"You re not going to believe this," she said, trying to contain her amusement. "The camels are gone. All gone." After we left, Ashley had filmed the jackaroos as they moved the animals out of the yard and down the trail. Stopping to make camp after a while, they used rope to construct a temporary holding pen. During the night a cracking thunderstorm came and spooked the camels, who burst through the rope yard and escaped amid thunder and lightning.

Ross wanted to waste no time in heading out to recapture the camels and get them back down to his station. He too had fully restocked and added some extra company, a friend's teenage daughter and one of her girlfriends. They'd visited us at our other camp, and now they wanted a real taste of some Nat Geo adventure.

The thunderstorm that spooked the camels was now directly overhead. Rain continued to come down in buckets and turned the road into a river. The water fell so thick on the windscreen that the wipers were useless. We pulled over until it eased, and charged off again in convoy.

Ross led the way with rookie Troy beside him, stock hand Paul drove our crew and the girls in the second vehicle, and I drove with my co-producer in third place. We followed a remote fence line, sloshing through the outback toward our runaway camels. It was now dark and all of us were relying on headlights to warn us of the many giant puddles that randomly engulfed our path.

We slipped and slopped down the dirt road, which grew more perilous by the second. The only thing that kept us going was speed. If any of us slowed down at all, the loss of momentum would likely see the mud suck us down to a dead halt.

What happened next occurred in just a few crucial seconds. With little warning, Ross hit water so wide that he couldn't see the other side.

Trying to accelerate through it only got him deeper in trouble and within moments he was seriously bogged, with the suction of the mud ensuring he'd go no farther. There may as well have been a sign saying "Safety Ramp Ahead".

Ross shouted a panicked warning over the radio: "Go around, go around!" Paul pulled left, trying to follow this directive. I watched him head out farther and farther in an attempt to circumvent the water. In the glint of his headlights, I saw a force to be reckoned with - the newly formed Lake Gunnagetcha.

I had to make a split-second decision. If Paul didn't make it and I was following him, we could have three cars stuck days from help and unable to pull each other out. I decided to do a one-eighty. It meant slowing down - maybe too much. The mud gripped at the tyres and tried to suck us down. I threw it into reverse and the wheels spun, then first again. I couldn't get out but I kept repeating the gear change; this constant rocking motion was the one thing that kept our car moving at all. It was only a few hopeless inches, with lots of spinning, but if I stopped, the mud would quickly bury our tyres.

Maybe I could keep it up long enough for Paul to come back and help. Just then Paul crackled over the radio. "Ah, shit," he said. "We're done." He'd gone about 300 yards out from the fence line, but finally met the same fate as Ross. My measly rocking motion now carried all our hopes for escape.

Ross crackled over the radio with uncharacteristic alarm, "If you get out, go to high ground, go to high ground." It was touch and go and I didn't like the responsibility at all. If there weren't a bunch of girls in our group to try to impress, I may have given up. We slipped and slid and revved and reversed and drove, virtually on the same spot, for the next five minutes. Finally, we were facing back the way we'd come, then suddenly the tyres took hold and we surged out of our bog. I screamed back along the road with enough panic and momentum not to get stuck again.

In a flash of lightning, Ashley saw a roadside hill and I accelerated hard off the trail until I reached the top. It was a large mound, about fifty feet high. I turned the engine off to let it cool, and we all sat in silence to digest the situation.

Ross crackled over the radio. "Did you make it?" He wanted to be sure.

"Yeah," I said, we're here. "Whatcha reckon?"

There was a long pause. "Give us a moment."

"No worries."

We weren't going anywhere tonight, maybe not even tomorrow. The real question was about the camels. These troublemakers had cost Ross a lot already and I knew he must be wondering if he should cut his losses and call it quits.

After a long while, Ross trekked up to the top of our mound with a solemn look on his face.

"Well," he said in a hushed tone, "I think we might be done." It was the logical decision. I think his real concern was letting us down. We'd come all the way from America for the world's largest camel round-up and wound up with twelve flat tyres, no camels, and a mud hole to wallow in.

"Well, you know," Ashley said, "we can probably make a pretty good film with what we've already shot."

Ross was cheered by the news and he continued, a little more upbeat. "We're never going to catch em now," he said "not with all this." He looked up at the dark clouds that flashed with lightning.

I confirmed for him that as far as the story went, we would be okay. The first few days had yielded more than enough drama. The documentary may be a little clunky around the end, but we had enough to create a compelling and informative piece.

"Okay then," he said, "looks like we re here for the night and we'll see what we can do in the morning."

I got on the radio to Paul and crew. "Hey fellas, you there?"

"Yep. Where else? What's the story?"

"That's a wrap."

They clicked on the two-way so we could hear their cheers and whoops. "What's more," I added, "we've got the makings of a great wrap party. We have music, dance partners, and we've just stocked up on a week's worth of food and grog."

We agreed to converge on the high ground - our car had the music. There was still rain and Jeremy, worried about the lightning that cracked around us, was not thrilled by the idea of trekking up to our car in an electrical storm, but we needed him to bring us some alcohol. "Don't worry," I told him over the radio, "fear attracts lightning, so just don't be afraid." He found my advice memorable, but unhelpful. Now he was afraid of being afraid, which made him even more afraid that the lightning would be attracted to him. Before his brain could melt down, he loaded up with VB and bourbon and made the dash. He came in soaked and grumbling; I thought it one of his finest hours.

Despite the weather, or indeed because if it, we indulged in a very unique outback wrap party, after which we spread out to sleep, in and on the cars. For a while, we forgot our predicament. To call upon an old news clich, "daylight revealed the full extent of the tragedy".

We tied a long chain between my car and Ross's and I reversed at full speed, hoping to jerk his vehicle free from the suction of the mud. The violent jolt on the chain, again and again, caused a gut-wrenching impact, but not much movement, so Ross resorted to calling in the chopper to deliver shovels and jacks and longer chains. Eventually we got out and drove back home.

We cleaned up at Ross's place and had a barbeque feast. These men were used to steak for breakfast, corned beef for lunch and steak for dinner, with a VB for dessert, but the all-meat-no-veg diet had worn thin on us outsiders, so Ashley cooked up a huge batch of frozen spinach. I don't think Ross or his men had seen anything so green in a very long time and they gobbled it down. The rain lingered as we said our final farewells. It would be months before Ross could try such a roundup again.

Back at Geo headquarters in DC, with the help of what little alcohol survived the camel shoot, the Club had its second meeting. This time I had lots of visitors. I had to ration the supply of VB so everyone got a taste, and I purchased some much-less-exotic Fosters to supplement the general drinking.

Word of the Club was getting around and I realized I needed to set some ground rules. Not only that, I knew I also had to get an okay from higher up. Nat Geo was serious about its anti-alcohol policies, and while I could keep the Club underground in general, my boss was going to find out sooner or later so I needed to get him on board.

The man who hired me, the very one who told me to "pick a place in the world you want to visit and find a story there", is a cheerful and energetic Brit with one of the greatest editorial minds in television. But he is also afflicted with a most unfortunate case of perpetual soberness that earned him the nickname "Earl Grey".

Earl once flew a friend of mine, TV presenter Scott Bevan, out from Australia for a job interview. Scott is an extremely gifted writer, and Earl was keen to recruit him as a producer. Earl took Scott to lunch on Friday afternoon and before they got down to business they assessed the menu, Scott perused the wine list carefully.

In Australian media, like with many Aussie businesses, alcohol at a Friday lunch is obligatory. But more than that, coming back to work sober, if you come back at all, is virtually unheard of. The TV networks

I worked for in Australia provided free alcohol in the boardroom for news staff from six pm, not just on Fridays but every night of the week. I'd dare say that this is where our best ideas were conceived. I think it's fair to say that alcohol is the grease that keeps the wheels of Australian business turning.

As Scott settled upon the best bottle of red for the task at hand, the waiter came by and took the boss's order. "Earl Grey, please, with some lemon on the side." Scott looked up and closed his menu. It was a deal breaker. Scott chatted politely for an hour or so, then returned home to a more understandable culture.

This sobering sobriety was what I faced as I sat in Earl's office and told him my plan for the (already underway) Exotic Booze Club. Rather than appealing to any latent desire he may have for a drink, I humbly appealed to his sense of culture and adventure. He thought for a long while and said, "Very well then. As long as you can be sure that no one leaves your office too drunk to drive with car keys in their hand." This seemed a very thoughtful and understanding response. It wasn't an official okay as far as the Society was concerned, but we'd be overlooked as long as no one in human resources found out. I was thrilled. Now I just had to work on the supplies.

I bought a popcorn machine so we'd have a cheap, reliable snack and began to lobby travelling producers, associate producers, presenters, explorers and cameramen to return with samples of exotic booze. On average, we had about three shoots going out every month, most of them overseas. I figured that would be ample to get the Club going.

I also had one bottle from an expedition that preceded the Club; it seemed as though it had been waiting for the right occasion to come out. I was ultimately glad I'd hung onto it: it was soon to be perfect for the most solemn and sobering toast in the Club's history.

Chapter 3

COBRA HUNT:
Burmese Toddy

It's rare for an expedition to come ready-made for TV. It helps if you're exploring a faraway exotic land. Watchable characters are a big plus too. But above everything else, you need a mission with a good, tangible and, preferably, visual goal - a payoff.

This is what I searched for in my first conversation with Dr. Joe Slowinski, from the California Academy of Sciences. It was the winter of 2000 when Joe finally accumulated enough grant money for a six-week survey of reptiles and amphibians in remote Burma (Myanmar). My job was to go along and make two separate half-hour films of his trip. It was an extremely dangerous assignment - remote travel in a developing country handling highly venomous reptiles - but I brushed aside the many disaster scenarios these factors may conspire to create. As always, my foremost concern was to find a worthy storyline for each show.

"Was there anything from your previous trips to Burma?" I quizzed Joe. "Some investigation that needs furthering? Even if it's not related to the survey."

"Well, yeah," he finally replied. "There are these guys, they remove snakes from villages. Really nasty snakes like cobras and vipers."

"Like snake busters?" I asked.

"Exactly, but here's the weird bit. They apparently do it with their bare hands and the villagers say they're protected from snakebite by their tattoos."

"Sorry. I thought you said tattoos."

"I did."

Burma has some of the deadliest snakes on the planet. Using a tattoo to protect you from their venom would be like trying to deflect bullets with a ping-pong paddle. Joe had interviewed one of these snakebusters before and he knew the town where they were supposedly located. He readily agreed we could take a few days to follow up where he left off. We'd try to find their base and film them doing their business. Story one down.

"For the second story," I continued, "what about a new species - anything you're after?"

"We'll be finding lots of new species. The areas we are going to have barely been touched by scientific hands."

"Great. But is there something in particular, something you've heard about, like the snake catchers. A mythical serpent?"

Scientists usually don't like the suggestion of searching for anything mythical but Joe got what I meant. He slept on it and called me back the next day.

"Actually, there is this one thing. We collected this specimen a year or so ago and our guy in London has only just gotten around to taking a closer look."

"I love it already. What is it?"

"If he's right, it's a new species of spitting cobra. It looks like a monocled cobra with a circle on the back of its neck, but it can shoot venom out from the front of its fangs. We'd have to find some more to confirm."

Bingo.

A few years earlier, Joe had identified a Burmese cobra new to science - the first new cobra since 1922. *Naja mandalayensis* was a spitter and even Joe thought it a once-in-a-lifetime find, but now he had strong evidence of yet another.

With some more information from Joe, I wrote up the stories and pitched them for Geographic's Explorer series as "Clan of the Snake Catchers" and "Cobra Hunt." Both were no-brainers.

Despite our collaboration on the pitch, I didn't get to meet Joe until we landed in Burma. It took about two seconds to recognize a kindred spirit: a clear lover of life, a mischievous smile, a dislike of formality and a drinker. A tall, blue-eyed blond, with an endearing gap between his pearly white front teeth. His mouth is ringed by ginger facial hair that he strokes often in times of deep thought. He'd been working religiously on developing a beer belly which, on a shorter person, would have made Buddha proud, but for now his lofty frame was able to carry it off fairly well.

At the age of thirty-seven, Joe had risen to be assistant curator of herpetology at the prestigious California Academy of Sciences. Good work for a guy whose entire career nearly ended before it began. In his first year of graduate school, Joe decided to ship a diamondback rattlesnake to a colleague in Colorado. He silenced the reptile's rattle with tape, put it in a pillowcase, packed it in a box, and fatefully decided to send it via bus. By Omaha the box had ripped open and an unsuspecting coach captain was alarmed to find a writhing pillowcase thrashing around his cargo bay. Joe narrowly escaped being charged for the offence, a fact that some say saved his career.

Joe's US team included the academy's collection manager, Jens Vindum. Jens, heavy-set with a Santa-style beard, moustache and glasses, could have been described as Joe's right-hand man, but I thought it more apt to call him Joe's straight man. Whether Jens intends it or not, about half of whatever he says is worthy of laughter. It's mostly soft-spoken, self-deprecating humor, and, at its best, delivered with a surprise double negative, such as, "My dick may be skinny, but it sure is short." Jens hated everything about having a TV crew along, but for Joe he put on a slightly less grumbly face than usual.

Joe also had two students to help him out, both budding young male scientists, plus Heidi Robeck, a frog expert from Harvard, and his sister Rachel, a photographer out to see her brother in action.

Joe had made several previous trips to Burma and was captivated by its seclusion and the promise of a new species behind every tree. He planned to make Burma the focus of a long-term herpetological survey and had managed to get the support of the government - no mean feat. The military had ruled Burma since 1962, with an official policy of strict isolationism.

The drive to our hotel began to reveal the nature of the regime. Giant billboards by the road told the 45 million citizens of Burma what they really wanted and how they should behave. The signs read:

PEOPLE'S DESIRE

Oppose those relying on external elements acting as stooges holding negative views.

Oppose those trying to jeopardize stability of the State and progress of the nation.

Oppose foreign nations interfering in internal affairs of the State.

Crush all internal and external destructive elements as the common enemy.

This Orwellian mission statement would be humorous if it wasn't so tragic for the vast majority of Burmese. The interpretation of who is "the common enemy", and who needs "crushing", was in the hands of the junta. The military leaders had assumed dictatorial powers in 1988 and kept the democratically elected leader Aung San Suu Kyi under house arrest for most of the past twenty years.

We had to watch out for clause three of the above national dictum. It was Joe's well-fostered contacts, and Nat Geo's policy of being apolitical, that allowed us to enter the country in the first place, but as outsiders we were not to be trusted. We were warned that our phones would be tapped and that our conveniently positioned taxi drivers would be spies. We were also assigned a minder to ensure we were true to our mission and not in Burma to work with "stooges holding negative views". U Soe Thein, an employee of the Ministry of Information, was our keeper and held the power to shut us down at a moment's notice. Please, lord, let him be a drinker.

On the Nat Geo side, I was working with co-producer Nancy Donnelly again and cameraman John Catto. John is a self-sufficient, wind-up human mule, and I mean that in the nicest possible way. All you need do is strap a forty-pound camera to his back and point. He'll take care of the rest whether rain, hail or shine. John also has the notable distinction of resembling Chuck Norris. People regularly run up to John and ask for his autograph, particularly in Asia where Chuck has a large following. John usually signs his own name, which only adds to the confusion of the autograph hound. You can see them read the name and watch the internal cogs churning: Odd signature it doesn't say Chuck. Is this Chuck? Is this not Chuck? Must be Chuck incognito. Big smile, bow of appreciation. That's what I'll tell wife. Chuck incognito. Then out loud, "Thank you

Chuck. You good fighter."

"Right," John would say. "I'm John."

"Yes, understand. Thank you, Chuck."

The other crucial person on our team was Dr. Brady Barr, Geographic's resident reptile wrangler and our on-camera talent. Geo has a large stable of experts and grantees it draws from, but few have been as regular, reliable and prominent as herpetologist Dr. Barr. Think Dog Whisperer, only where each and every dog can kill you. I could write a whole book on Dr. Barr, but to give you the headlines now: probably the best gator/croc wrangler ever, the luckiest individual I've ever met, a college friend of Joe Slowinski's, and not a big drinker - at least compared to Joe.

Back when the two were studying and in the field together, searching for reptiles in the Everglades, Joe told me Brady would always go to bed early. Joe, of course, and others, would stay up drinking beer and take great delight in throwing their empties at Brady's tent. This would wake Brady up with a start. The best thing, from Joe's perspective, was that the time it took to finish the next beer was exactly the time it took for Brady to get back to sleep. Just as Brady's slumber seemed sound, another empty would come crashing against the outer wall of his tent.

"Hey. What the? Hey. Don't make me come out there."

This, according to Joe, would go into the wee hours with Brady trapped in a horrible twilight zone - never quite getting to sleep, and never quite emerging from his tent. In this way Joe would ensure that everyone was on an equal sleep-deprived footing.

Joe and Brady had bonded over a love of adventure and reptiles and stayed in contact over the years, and it was this connection that sparked the story. Brady has colleagues all over the world doing cool stuff with snakes and crocs, and Joe had called him up to see if Geo would be interested in his expedition.

The catch was that these had to be Brady stories – he was the star. We had two shows to do and I didn't want them to look too much alike, so I asked Joe to play only a very minor part in the *Clan of the Snake Catchers* film. Just enough to give him due credit, but not enough to think you were watching the same buddy-film twice. I know it was an unpopular decision with Joe, but he seemed to understand and was gracious enough to let it be.

Our first task, after getting to the hotel in Yangon (formerly Rangoon), was to change money on the black market. This was a cash-only country and we needed local currency. The official rate was one US dollar to about seven Burmese kyat, but no one uses the official rate. On the street, one US dollar can get you closer to 900 kyat.

Nancy disappeared with handfuls of hundreds, amounting to US$12,000. She came back a Burmese millionaire. We had more cash than we could hold in our arms, a reminder of the country's impoverished state. Under British rule, before the military took over, Burma had been the wealthiest country in Southeast Asia. Now it is one of the world's most corrupt and impoverished.

It's remarkable, then, that many will spend what little money they have on gold leaf, as an offering to Buddha. We visited Shwedagon, Yangon's famous three-hundred-foot-high gold-plated pagoda, built in the tenth century to house eight hairs from the head of Gautama

Buddha. Ever since then, pilgrims have been rubbing it with gold leaf. It's now estimated to weigh some forty-five tons, with a crown of diamonds, rubies and other precious stones. No need for armed guards because in this faith there is virtually no crime. Still, now that we were human cash machines, we hid the money all over the place and prepared to head north.

Joe's survey was to take place in remote Alaungdaw Kathapa National Park west of Mandalay, about a week-long drive. Here, or along the way, we'd hopefully find a new species of spitting cobra. As we passed through Mandalay we loaded up with supplies and marvelled at more gold-plated icons.

The people of Burma are devout without being the least bit belligerent. They are a welcoming race, blessed with genes of great beauty. It's almost impossible to tell how old anyone is but most likely they are older than they look, despite the harshness of life here. They are often tall and always slim, with black hair and smooth golden skin, which the women often decorate with streaks of yellow powder harvested from a local therapeutic plant. Their smiles are broad, but in their eyes you can see glints of great sadness, no doubt from decades of oppression.

We had collected the Burmese component of our team, which included a half-dozen reptile catchers and an interpreter assigned to us by our local outfitter. But something wasn't right and soon two unique problems emerged with our interpreter. The first was that he was not camera friendly. On these kinds of shows, the interpreter plays a pivotal roll. They speak on camera for everyone who doesn't speak English, so they need to be engaging, well spoken and easy to watch. Our interpreter was none of the above, and even more significantly, problem number two was that none of the Burmese men in our group would talk to him.

Just as we were trying to work out what was going on, we happened to meet a local man who called himself Nikki. He was teaching English to a group of students and had deliberately staked out a tourist spot so they could practice conversation with foreigners. I won't try to guess Nikki's age but although his black hair had turned silver, he was still very spry, with a thoughtful expression and an ever-present smile that made him a delight to engage with. We recruited him immediately to be our on-camera interpreter - a lucky find. Nikki eventually conveyed to us that our first interpreter was "not a real man"; he was gay.

In Burmese society, if you sit down long enough, some guy will put his arm around your waist, his head on your shoulder, and go to sleep. They are very cozy people with little or no sense of personal space. Either in spite of this or perhaps because of it, being homosexual is strictly taboo. Once we understood what was going on, we westerners felt bad for interpreter number one - an outcast in his own country and no hope of ever leaving - but by then his fate was sealed. He realized it was not going to work, and once we had Nikki, he conveniently found a reason to leave us and return home.

We moved on from Mandalay toward the area Joe wanted to survey. The location was still several days away but the search for our mysterious new species of spitting cobra began immediately. Joe and Brady used a tried and true method of investigation: they asked people. Most Burmese work close to the land, so they know which snakes are around and who has been bitten and killed. Joe would draw a picture of a cobra and ask villagers if they had seen this type of snake. If they said yes, he'd ask them to draw the pattern they saw on the back of the hood, and if he got a match there he'd ask them if the snake spat venom.

Interview after interview drew blanks but often revealed surprises. Many villages had a teenager or two who, like a young Brady or Joe, collected snakes. Others captured reptiles to sell them illegally on the pet or meat market. Some men, who can afford it, buy these reptiles in the belief that snake blood acts like Viagra; they lop off the heads and drink the blood straight from the tube.

One of the village snake collectors produced a large heavy sack with something moving inside. Joe looked in and his face lit up. He reached in and, with Brady's help, pulled out a giant yellow and black striped snake, thicker than my wrist and almost seven feet long. "Goddamn," Brady exclaimed. "What is it?"

"This," said Joe, "is a banded krait."

"Are you kidding me? And we re handling it?" Brady's surprise was well founded. The Bungarus fasciatus, a close relative of the cobra, was one of the most venomous snakes on earth. A krait this size would pack enough punch to kill you in about thirty minutes.

Joe explained, "We've seen these in villages before. Children play with them. They don't even know they're venomous because they so rarely bite. They are very docile."

An amazing animal, but not the spitting cobra we were after. What these interviews did do was spread the word that we were interested in cobras. At one stage we were duly directed to a type of zoo where we were assured we'd see a large cobra. There was no harm in looking, we thought. We ended up on a kind of construction site. Workers around us were busy building: women carried the bricks balanced on their heads ten at a time, and the men would lay the bricks.

We were directed to the front of an open-air stage where we set up our camera and waited. Soon a man brought in a basket and a beautiful nineteen-year-old woman followed him. Marla Win was carefully attired in a long royal blue sarong with white wavy patterns and a matching long-sleeve top. Her hair was tied back and ringed by large pink flowers. On her feet she wore nothing but white socks. What we were about to see was an age-old fertility ritual, carried out by women when they needed more boys to be born in the village. And you had to really want those boys.

Marla tapped her basket and up shot a 14-foot king cobra, the largest venomous snake species known to man. The cobra tried to take off, so she whacked it on the tail. Immediately this giant beast swung around, raised itself high off the ground and flared a spectacular hood. It looked her straight in the eye and she stared back at it, calm and collected, constantly moving her arms in a waving motion in the snake's peripheral vision. This was some woman.

As we filmed, she began a dance that had us all entranced for the next fifteen or twenty minutes. Slowly she'd inch closer and closer to this snake. When she got too close, the snake would lunge at her and she would deflect it by quickly running her arm up the snake's approaching torso.

Some snake charmers remove the snake's fangs, but this one was well armed, and even a few drops of venom could kill. When the snake tried to escape, Marla would slap it again, and again the cobra would swing around to face her and she would try to creep closer. Bit by bit, she manoeuvred in until the snake's nose was just an inch from her own. Then, in one sure and steady motion, she moved forward and kissed it on the top of the head. Her job was done. And the next child born in the village had better bloody well be a boy.

Brady and Joe were psyched. They got permission to hop up on the stage and try some dancing themselves. They were too smart to try the kissing, but it's not every day you get to be face to face with a serpentine legend. I preferred to remain seated.

It seemed the further we looked, the more dangerous our encounters. Another local snake hunter took us to a hole in the ground and dug up two Russell's vipers. These are exceptionally lethal reptiles. While other snakes will try to get away from you like the king cobra, every Russell's viper we came across would shoot straight toward us.

To put this in context, in Australia we share our extended backyard with one-third of the world's venomous snake species. I grew up in the bush where tiger snakes, black snakes, taipans and king browns were not too far away, and all potential killers. When I was four I used to stand on a piece of corrugated iron and watch my father swim his racehorses in our large dam; it was good equine exercise. One day my teenage brother saw a snake shoot under my particular piece of iron, so he and Dad went and got some snake-killing devices. My brother got a shovel while Dad preferred a homemade contraption, three strands of thick wire braided to about four-feet long. Why this was better than a shovel I can't recall but if nothing else, the thought and effort spoke to the fear and hatred most Australians have toward snakes. The only good snake is a dead snake was our mantra.

When Dad lifted up that piece of tin, wire poised, ready to chop off a snake head, he got the shock of his life. There was not one adult snake in there but five, and at least two different species. In the massacre that followed, my platform was rendered safe, but I don't think anyone ever stood on it again.

I would have followed in my father's snake-hating gumboots but for my job. Working for Geographic requires one to be nice to most creatures great, small and even creepy. Over the years I have made films on more than twenty snake species: cobras, kraits, pit vipers, death adders, boas, rattlers, taipans, sea snakes, even flying snakes (yes, they really fly) - the list goes on. I even ran a series called *Snake Wranglers*, where finding badass snakes was our primary objective. All that changed me. Nowadays I marvel at their incredible diversity and adaptations and am somewhat less phobic, with one absolute exception: the Russell's viper.

When an animal is described as "aggressive", it usually means it's defensive. It's reacting, quite properly, to a perceived threat to its life or the lives of its young. But spend five minutes handling just about any snake and, once it realizes you are not a threat, it becomes putty in your hands. Except for, in my experience, this large, nasty, multicolored beast from Southeast Asia.

Reliable statistics in this part of the world are hard to come by, but conservative estimates put the death count from Russell's vipers at more than a thousand people a year in Burma alone, possibly more than any other snake anywhere in the world. That's at least three people a day, every day. It was enough to have me looking for wire to braid.

As we continued on, we began to get a sense of this place and the connection between the Burmese and their snakes. The local take on

COBRA HUNT: Burmese Toddy

snakes is quite different. For them, Russell's vipers are a regular part of life and, in their philosophy, a valid creature worthy of respect. We visited a pagoda that housed two enormous pythons, the monk in charge urging us to handle these non-venomous giants. On the heads of both reptiles, worshippers had rubbed gold leaf.

We passed by fields of other ageing pagodas and temples, mostly ruins several hundreds of years old, some with Buddha statues inside, unharmed and unstolen. We spent a few of our nights in monasteries - that was the worst. The call to prayer always came before sunrise in the form of distorted music played over giant speakers; it was not the quality of the audio that mattered but the volume. Various chants, backed by random cymbal clanging, came blaring across the courtyard several times a day. As special guests, I'm sure they cranked up the volume a notch or two for our benefit in the misguided belief that every distorted decibel would grant us a fuller appreciation of their commitment to Buddhism.

We drove through villages where people had never before seen a white person, a physical state that apparently has to be touched to be believed. And we were served a delicacy usually reserved for the most regal: whole, deepfried sparrows. And I mean "whole". A dozen to a plate, feathers still on, legs up in the air, crisp from their brief dip in boiling oil. While I was trying to convince the servers that we weren't deserving of such generosity, our Burmese colleagues wolfed down the lot, happily leaving us with the more usual fare of oily noodles.

Our gas stations were usually rusting 44-gallon drums sitting beside the road. Children often pumped the drums, and a stall beside them offered a range of local produce, most notably jugs of alcohol - finally, something to take the bumps out of the road. The brew was Burmese Toddy. This is not the English hot toddy that cured your grandma's cold, but a far more potent and less palatable mix made from fermented palm sugar and sap. A dollar could have bought us about a gallon of Burmese Toddy, but after trying some, I insisted on paying a dollar for considerably less. I sampled a range of toddies; some weren't so bad but, being a homemade brew, no two ever tasted the same. It was a worthy drink for the Club, and it had a curious effect on our interpreter: although it had little more strength than a beer, just a glass would put Nikki out of commission for half a day. An interpreter who can't get through a sentence without slurring was not much use to anyone, so we tried to keep him on the wagon until sundown.

At most rivers we had to wait for a barge to ferry us and our vehicles across, each craft worthy of Jens's favorite and ever-accurate catchphrase:

"That can't be safe." Once we came across an actual bridge. It was large and supposedly strong enough to handle our vehicles, but it seemed to be made of little more than bamboo, straight out of an Indiana Jones movie. When we got out the cameras to film the crossing, our information officer raced over. "No film, no film." The concern, we learned from Nikki, was that this structure had some military significance, and they didn't want any external elements filming this wonder of engineering lest it become a target.

Marvelling at such ludicrous governmental paranoia, I tried to explain that the US government would not be scanning our footage looking for important bamboo bridges to blow up, and should the need arise, they'd probably use satellite imagery with precise GPS co-ordinates. My pleas fell on deaf ears and, frankly, it wasn't an important shot, so we let it go and used the incident to earn some goodwill from our minder.

First chance we had, we employed a tried and true method of snake catching called "road running". As the sun sets, cold-blooded animals such as snakes like to soak up the last of the warmth by laying on surfaces that retain heat, like rocks and roads. We were keen to take advantage of this behavior so around dusk we put the headlights on and headed out.

In other countries you'd pick little-used back roads to avoid traffic, but in rural Burma you can go days without seeing a car, even on the major arteries. Joe hit the ideal speed of twenty-five miles an hour and stuck to it - any faster and you'd risk not seeing what's ahead of you before having to name your newly discovered reptile species "Oopsei roadus killus."

Brady sat hanging out the window of the passenger seat scanning the road with Joe. Behind them, Chuck Norris and I sat with cameras ready to roll. We all had headlamps and Joe handed out pairs of protective goggles, big, clunky, industrial safety wear. It often happens on stories that people need to be seen to be taking over-the-top safety precautions because they are on camera. They may look uncool walking around, say,

a playground or a mall in a hard hat, but if it's technically a construction zone, it keeps the boss happy. Problem is, these things always look dorky on camera and sometimes make your characters hard to tell apart.

"Joe," I said, "aren't these safety goggles a bit over the top? We're driving pretty slow, after all."

"It's not for road safety," he explained. "It's for snake safety."

Nasty animals these spitters. They have a tiny hole at the front of each fang where they can shoot out venom with considerable force.

They are deadly accurate to any target within about ten feet, and they know to shoot for the eyes. The venom, apparently, stings like pepper spray, temporarily blinding the victim. And if not properly treated, that temporary status becomes permanent. My safety goggles suddenly didn't seem so dorky. I lowered them over my eyes and away we drove.

When you run the roads with seasoned snake catchers, beware of the currency involved. There's a monetary system that's employed worldwide, no exchange rate required, that is measured in beer. In our case, the only local ale available to us in Burma was Mandalay beer, a brew that even I'd started to enjoy. The system worked like this: Drive, drive, drive - "Oh, what's that? Snake, snake, SNAKE!" Screeeeeeech. "I got it, I got it, I got it - oh. Ah, it's a stick." Anyone wrongly identifying a stick as a snake has to buy a round of beer. At this stage of our journey, we had lots of sticks, and lots of beer, but no cobras.

Possibly the most dangerous animal we found was a pet monkey. It was beside the road wearing a collar and leash and being held by a beggar. We approached out of curiosity and saw the man had leprosy; most of his fingers had been reduced to stumps, and his toes weren't much better off. Nikki, up until that point, had been scared to go near any of the reptiles we'd encountered, but he thought the monkey was cute and went to pat it. The ape opened its mouth wide, revealing sharp teeth with Dracula-like fangs. It hissed, then darted toward Nikki and bit him on the finger, drawing blood. We were horrified. Bitten by a mangy looking leper's monkey - *that* can't be safe. We cleaned and dressed the wound as best we could and moved on.

Finally our convoy rolled into Alaungdaw Kathapa National Park. Don't think Yellowstone or Yosemite, think more giant patch of untouched jungle with few staff and meagre facilities. This would be our base camp for a couple of weeks as Joe's team set about their business of capturing everything that moved, amphibian or reptile. Joe was also running a course here; as part of his agreement with the government he would teach and help local rangers further their own science. Including those coming in for the course, our group now numbered around twenty people, an insanely large number to co-ordinate.

The interest of TV was not, of course, on the classroom, but on anything that resembled a new species of spitting cobra. We'd visited the area where the species identified in London was captured, but the landscape had since changed: it was a delta, and was now flooded. Instead of filming Brady and Joe hunting snakes, we filmed them paddling around

The Exotic Booze Club

in canoes. The national park was now our best option to find something extraordinary.

Almost immediately upon arrival we realized we had a problem. It hadn't rained in weeks, and when it's too dry, amphibians don't come out that much. And when amphibians aren't moving, neither are the snakes that eat them. Joe taught his courses during the day and we despaired at night. The collecting was not going well at all. Rather than sit and twiddle our thumbs, we got creative.

Alaungdaw Kathapa is named for a famous thirteenth century bodhisattva (a Buddhist saint) called Maha Kassapa, or Kathapa. He was interred in a cave in the park and was about the only reason anyone ever came here. We decided to take a look at what attracted the faithful and, at some point, maybe shoot some scenes for a pilot program Brady was working on, a kids show about nature's gross side. The working title was *Yeck!*.

We hiked several miles along a jungle trail to a temple manned by a lone monk. We were instructed, in accordance with custom, to remove our shoes and socks before passing through. Another trail took us down into a canyon. We crossed a primitive log bridge over the canyon's river and walked barefoot to the entrance of a large dark cave. It looked pretty gloomy and smelled a bit rank, but nothing special from the outside. A few steps in, it got a lot worse.

The muddy bottom of the cave squished up between our toes in a most unpleasant way, and a strange smell became overpowering. We moved in deeper, seeing only what we could illuminate with our headlamps. That's when Joe called out, "Hey guys, this mud is moving." We all looked down. He was right. But what was it? We exuded collective groans of revolt and disgust, suddenly awaking the inhabitants of the shrine.

Hundreds and hundreds of bats streamed out of the cave, flying low over our heads and showering us with urine and faeces as they swooped and screeched by. We didn't know where to turn. Around then we took another look at our toes and all at once realized we weren't standing in mud but guano, a few inches of defecation accompanied by a myriad of squirming maggots, no doubt feeding on the occasional dead bat. Gagging at the stench and our predicament we had the impulse to run, but at the back of the cave I noticed something shiny.

"Quick," I called to Brady, "take a look."

Brady gave me the "are you shitting me?" look, but he didn't want to make this a wasted experience for the film. He raced back with Joe and found the cave's back wall covered in gold leaf, just like the pagoda in

COBRA HUNT: Burmese Toddy

Yangon and other religious sites. How devoted is that? Somehow, without breathing, Brady did the world's quickest piece to camera and we bolted out.

Without saying another word, we all raced straight out of the entrance and jumped into the river, clothes and all. Even immersed in a flowing stream we could not remove the stench from our nostrils. Back at camp we applied liquid soap by the handful, but the odor still stuck with us. It remains one of the most disgusting experiences of my life, equalled only by what happened next.

Back at camp John approached me and I knew something was wrong. He was looking a lot less like Chuck Norris and a lot more like someone Chuck was about to pummel as he said simply, "I got some baaaaaad news."

John had just completed a tape check and it turned out, in all the chaos and mayhem of the bat cave experience, he had not switched on the audio, thus rendering the images useless. In the wealthier days of television we would have had a dedicated sound person, but no more. I broke the news to Joe and Brady; it didn't go down well. If they had have voted not to go back I would have understood, but Brady knew that we were unlikely ever to return here and it was probably worthwhile to do it right. Plus, until it rained, there wasn't much else to occupy our time.

For some reason, our return visit the next day was worse; I guess our tolerance for the smell and the environment had taken a beating. We raced in, maggots between toes, shitting bats overhead, and tried our best not to vomit. Within less than a minute we got what we needed - the bare minimum - and started to exit. Between convulsive retching, I pushed the envelope just a little further. With John's camera rolling, I shouted, "Hey Brady, quick, say something for the kids, for your pilot."

Without stopping, Brady turned straight to camera and yelled, "Hey kids - stay the fuck out of places like this."

The other shoot we did for Brady's pilot was a lot more civilized. We piled a bunch of nine year olds from a local school onto the back of some elephants and went looking for fresh piles of elephant poo that was under siege from dung beetles. We didn't have to go far. Brady taught the kids to say "oooh yeck" on camera and they loved it. We gave them all muesli bars - which, given their regular rice diet, probably clogged them up for a week - and I made a donation to the school of the equivalent of US$30 in local currency, a huge amount for them, enough to pay the teacher's salary for more than a year. That's when something quite odd happened.

The Exotic Booze Club

Heidi, the frog expert from Harvard, had started to act quite strangely. Over the previous week she'd grown more and more despondent and snarky. And now she began ranting that we weren't paying the school enough, taking out two US$100 bills of her own and waving them about like play money. She insisted to the teacher that she take the cash but the teacher, a shy young woman, continued to politely refuse. Foreign currency was of little use to her out here and, even if it wasn't, imagine someone waving ten times your annual salary in your face like it was nothing. We were all embarrassed by the scene and gobsmacked by Heidi's behavior. It was a warning of things to come.

Around day six in the park, rain finally fell and the entire place came alive. The survey group was thrilled with the specimens that almost jumped into their collection bags. There were strange-colored reptiles and amphibians like I'd never seen: lizards with wings, fish with legs, a snake that glinted in the sun like a rainbow - but no cobras.

Joe decided we should go deeper into the jungle and ordered in some elephants to help us. Burma has more working elephants than any other country; at the time, around 5,000 were being used for everything from logging operations to clearing roads. They are great for lugging equipment and are surprisingly nimble movers, but riding them isn't for the impatient as we moved no faster than a few miles an hour. Still, we had seven elephants and they helped us access a new area with the now few dozen people in our group, including two armed guards sent to protect us from poachers.

After a day of searching there were still no cobras, and an even bigger problem emerged. We'd run out of beer. Our local guide had severely miscalculated how much alcohol a bunch of frustrated filmmakers and scientists would consume, even without refrigeration. Joe joked with them that we were all going to revolt if a beer elephant didn't arrive soon. At least, they *thought* he was joking.

On day two of our elephant expedition we were stopped by a grassy meadow when a guard suddenly called out: he'd seen a cobra cross the path in front of him up on the ridge. We bolted to the spot, but by the time we puffed our way up the hill the snake was long gone. Joe kept searching, ever hopeful, and I'm sure feeling great responsibility for our film to have a good payoff.

About thirty minutes later we got a call from the same guard: "Come quick. Joe has something!" We knew if Joe had something it was either a big-ass snake or a nice cold beer. Either way, I asked John to start rolling immediately and we charged up the hill again.

Brady paused and heard Joe call out, "Cobra!" We doubled our speed and found Joe hovering over a hole on the side of a ridge. Inside sat coiled a large, black, angry snake. I marvel, even today, at Joe's patience, waiting for us to get there with cameras rolling so he and Brady could pull the reptile out together.

The snake came out mad as hell, a stunning six-foot cobra, as black as night. Even Joe was surprised by its size. Forgetting the camera, all he could say was, "Holy *shit!*"

Our hearts thumped in our chests as the snake reared up and spread its hood. It was so black we couldn't make out any markings, so there was no telling what species it was. Joe had its body pinned about halfway down with snake-grabbing tongs, while the dangerous end darted about trying to hit its assailants. Brady shouted, "Is it a spitter? Is it a spitter?"

Joe replied, "It's a spitter . . . I think it's a spitter . . . I don't know what this thing is."

Neither were prepared for the possibility of it spitting, and none of us had goggles. Our snake wranglers covered their eyes with one arm and tried to blindly hold a large, angry snake in place. As Jens again put it, "That can't be safe."

We filmed with the snake for about half an hour. It didn't spit after all, which meant it was probably a very dark monocled cobra. Its DNA would have to be checked, but it was not the new species we were after. Either way, it was a gem of a snake, and a good enough payoff to fall back on to finish film number one if nothing else was going to show itself.

That night we went to bed elated. If it weren't for the lack of beer, it would have been a perfect day. Just as I was putting my head on my makeshift pillow I heard an odd clanging noise, the sound of a cowbell swinging rhythmically and drawing closer. I left my tent to see a lone elephant and its handler enter the camp. As the elephant obediently knelt down on the ground I saw what it was carrying: about eight cases of Mandalay beer.

I couldn't believe my eyes. The Burmese had taken Joe seriously after all and, ever keen to keep their foreign guests happy, had sent for fresh supplies. I yelled at the top of my voice, "Beer elephant! *Yeeeeeeah!*" As team members emerged from their individual tents it became a chant of disbelief:

"Beer elephant?" followed by more cheering. We helped unload this most sacred of beasts; it couldn't have looked better had it been covered in gold leaf. I took a photo and I'd swear the beer elephant was smiling. It was a perfect day after all.

Several days later we packed up, left the park and eventually hit the blacktop again. Our next mission was to track down the clan of tattooed snake catchers, but we still worked the roads looking for snakes.

For some reason, on the road, no one ever just says "Snake!" - it's always an adrenaline-pumped "Snake, snake, snake, *snake*, SNAKE!" Joe made the call this time, and we all leapt from the vehicle before it had fully stopped, charging forward. The snake, about a three-feet long, saw us coming and made a dash for it. Brady and Joe both had their snake-grabbing devices and Joe used his to pull the reptile back onto the road.

"Cobra, cobra!" Brady shouted. "Is it a spitter?" Joe was always quick with his ID, but this time the snake was quicker: it let out a stream of venom straight into Brady's goggles. As we continued to film, it spat again and again. Brady asked Joe some questions on camera. It was not a new species, but still relevant to Joe's survey. The snake continued to spit, even as Brady and Joe carefully dropped it into a cloth bag. With a shout and a cheer, Brady put the snake in the car and on we continued.

That night we stayed near a town call Pakokku at a compound run by the Forestry Ministry where Joe and Brady got the snake out again for some more filming. Once done, we put the camera away and left Brady and Joe with the snake. This time it didn't go so well. As they tried to place the animal back in the bag, it struck wildly and sank a fang deep into Joe's finger. I raced back at the sound of trouble and saw blood flowing from the middle finger on Joe's left hand. "You'd better get John to get the camera - I've been bitten." he said soberly. "This is a bad bite, he got me good." By bad bite we all knew Joe meant potentially fatal; he could die.

In school in Australia we're taught not to tie a tourniquet in case of snakebite but to apply a compression bandage. A tourniquet stops the blood flow, which can cause more harm than the bite, but slowing down the spread of venom with a bandage gives your body more of a fighting chance. I put one on Joe's arm. He was scared, but not panicked.

Cobra venom is a neurotoxin. It attacks the body in a most extraordinary way. The patient remains mentally very aware, but starts to lose the ability to move body parts. It can shut down everything, including your irises, but the mind still ticks. Eventually, if you're unlucky, it stops your lungs and then your heart. If you can keep those vital organs going artificially for a while, there's a bit of a chance your body will process the venom and you'll recover unscathed - a bit of a chance.

The important thing at this stage was to keep Joe relaxed, let him sit quietly and not do anything to increase the circulation of blood (and therefore venom) through his body. The effects of the venom are rarely instant; we had anywhere between two minutes and two hours to find out how much trouble Joe was in. The nearest hospital was days away, and Joe especially had no interest in trusting his life to a Burmese hospital. In the movies they give you antivenin and you're good to go the next day, but that's not how it works.

Antivenin can backfire if it's not administered and constantly monitored by someone who knows what they're doing. Not only that, most antivenin is made by injecting tolerable doses to horses and harvesting the antibodies. Joe, as luck wouldn't have it, was allergic to horses, so antivenin would be a very, very bad idea. Doctors had given it to him once before, after a rattlesnake bite when he was sixteen. His reaction was severe, going into anaphylactic shock and needing even more emergency treatment. He said later that the cure was worse than the disease.

So there we sat, looking at each other, watching the clock. Joe calmly told us what to do should he stop breathing. Just when we felt we'd created as relaxing an environment as possible, Heidi, the Harvard frog expert, leapt onto the scene.

Perhaps a cocktail of malaria medicine, alcohol and the local betel nut, which she d been trying, had overcome her. And who knows what else? She had developed a crush on a guide that we'd left back at the national park and maybe that put her out of sorts. Whatever it was, she was venting.

Heidi sat at the back of our open-sided lounge area and began to heckle. We all clung to the hope that while the snake had bitten Joe, it had not actually injected its venom. Heidi turned this possibility into her own toxic attack with words to Joe that still ring in my ears: "If there's any venom in that, you're dead."

None of us could convince her to quietly leave, so Joe chimed in. "Why are you fighting with me, Heidi? I'm not fighting with you."

Her reply came swiftly. "Because you're not protecting me from these fuckers." She gestured toward our entire Nat Geo crew.

We were all shocked and had no idea what she meant. She further explained that she felt jilted because we seemed to be paying far too much attention to snakes and not enough to frogs. Brady, with his dear friend in peril, took Heidi to task.

"What is your fucking problem?" he asked.

"You're my fucking problem, Brady."

"This doesn't help," Joe said feebly. "This isn't helping. Everybody just calm down, we re trying to stay calm."

Brady added, "We don't need you pissing and moaning, Heidi."

Heidi carried on a little longer, mumbling something about how many cobras she had caught before. Joe awkwardly changed the subject and Heidi soon left.

The minutes ticked by, then an hour, then two. Joe was okay. It seems the cobra had spat out its venom on the road before biting Joe. Or perhaps, as cobras often do, it had withheld its remaining supply. Either way, we were in the clear.

Around four am that morning, Heidi, in tears, rattled Brady's tent and apologized frantically and profusely. She awoke a driver and convinced him to drive her out. We never saw her again. We learned from Joe, though, that shortly after returning to the States, Heidi became very ill and was hospitalized with malaria. It turns out she had not one but three strains, including falciparum, an especially virulent strain that often kills.

Joe was one of those weird creatures who never seemed to be bitten by a mosquito. He said he rarely took antimalaria drugs, and some of his crew followed his lead. It was a mistake, and several members of his team returned to the States with malaria. Later, on Joe's eighth trip to Burma, he also contracted this mongrel disease. He and his crew all recovered with the help of western medicine, but many, many others aren't so lucky.

Despite the deadly snakes and other dangerous animals in the world, mosquitoes continue to kill far more people than anything else - by some estimates, as many as a million people a year. We were later told that one of the park employees who d helped us in Alaungdaw Kathapa had come down with a fever and died from malaria just a week after we left him.

The most dramatic case we experienced was Joe's own sister, Rachel. About a week after Joe's cobra bite Rachel was not feeling well and rested in a vehicle while we all ate at a roadside thatch-hut-cum-restaurant. Halfway though our meal she emerged from the vehicle and walked in. Her eyes were closed and she was muttering, "I can't feel my arms, I can't feel my arms." Then she collapsed on the dirt floor by my feet.

We pulled out the Nat Geo first-aid kit and Joe started frantically thumbing through the manual. Nancy took Rachel's temperature with the thermometer. We'll never know Rachel's true temperature at the point as the thermometer only went to 105 degrees and that's where she topped out. She should have been dead.

The restaurant had little help to offer but a block of ice, but that was key. We held it to Rachel's neck and, with some water, we got her temperature down to around 102. Joe, with a driver, raced Rachel off to a local clinic. It had no drugs whatsoever, nor a doctor, but a nurse of some kind put her on a saline drip, which was exactly what she needed. After concluding that it must be malaria, Joe forced Rachel to hold down tablets of a powerful drug called Fansidar. After two days of rest, she was good enough to travel again, a lucky escape. One of our group had suffered a bite from a cobra, and another from a leper's monkey who knew the worst would be the bite of a simple mosquito?

These dangerous ordeals began to ring like an omen. Perhaps we were pushing the tolerance of our welcome and starting to outlive our luck. But the need for our second story prevailed and we took off in search of the clan of the snake catchers. Joe's research told us we were in the right area, so we began asking around. Our inquiries led us to a well-tattooed man who told us two amazing details: first, that he was a long-time member of the clan, and second, that he'd just been bitten by a cobra.

He turned over his hand and in the middle of his palm we could see a pea-sized hole surrounded by black. Apart from that he looked to be perfectly healthy. Through Nikki's translation, this man swore to us that no member of the clan had ever died from snakebite, and he directed us to where active members of the clan congregated.

We descended upon the compound of thatch-roofed huts like aliens - white guys with cameras - and humbly asked if we could speak to the clan's leader. U Lu Maw was a healthy looking thirty-something covered in strange tattoos, which looked more like tables and calendars than patterns or designs. He greeted us with utmost courtesy and said he'd be more than happy to accommodate our desire to film the clan at work. Our timing couldn't have been better as he had just gotten word of a snake on the loose in a nearby dirt-floor shop. We followed him and one of his colleagues to investigate.

U Lu Maw entered the shop barefoot, spotted the monocled cobra, and grabbed it with his hand like a pro. He constantly moved it like a yoyo, never letting it get enough traction or momentum to reach up and bite him. This was a service the clan offered to all the surrounding villages, essentially for free. It seemed they would accept gifts or donations, but they really only had one condition of employment: that the snakes not be hurt. As part of their Buddhist beliefs, the snakes had to be released unharmed.

We followed U Lu Maw to a field beyond the edge of town where he blessed the snake with water. Before letting it go, he pulled out a jar and milked venom from its fangs. He then invited us back to one of their weekly tattooing ceremonies. That's where it all became clear.

U Lu Maw and several other members of the clan gathered in a hut that seemed primitive apart from one surprising addition - a second floor. They'd made their construction strong enough to have a stairway that led to a surprisingly solid single upstairs room with woven bamboo walls. Sunlight streamed in the open windows and gave the entire room a golden glow. A small altar sat in the middle and here they lit incense and said prayers. A new member was about to be indoctrinated and receive his first snake-protecting tattoos.

As U Lu Maw mixed the ink for tattooing, he reached over to a vial marked "cobra" and took out some crystallized venom. As he mixed it with the ink, the dots in our story were joined: clan members weren't only receiving tattoos, they were being inoculated.

The clan leader took out a brass needle as long as my forearm, dipped it in the ink/venom mix, and used it to tattoo the new member on very select body parts. A dot here, a dot there. With each tap of the needle, minute amounts of snake venom entered the bloodstream, just enough for the new clan member to start building up antibodies. All the ink for the upper body was mixed with cobra venom, Russell's viper venom for the lower body.

Brady asked, "If you came to America, would your tattoos protect you from our snakes?"

The answer: "Only if we used the venom from your snakes."

Clan members knew exactly what they were doing. And with that, we had our second story in the can.

There were only two more tasks I had to perform before our trip home: one was to grab a good bottle of toddy and the second was a little trickier. Our web department had asked me to send in dispatches of short, interesting stories from the field that they'd post on the website with some photos. At first the added workload sounded like a pain in the pagoda, a time-consuming distraction from the real job of making the film. But there were lots of good short stories to tell, and I do love telling stories. I wrote seven field reports and had two good photos to go with each.

The next hurdle was to send these as emails from such a military-controlled state. Back in the city, with some effort, I found the office of a high-class hotel with a sign that advertised, in American dollars, "Local emails $1, international emails $2." There was no doubt these emails would be read and checked by the Information Ministry, but I saw nothing in what I'd written that would offend, so what the heck.

The woman behind the desk was most helpful. She spent an hour loading my dispatches and photos into her own computer and hit send. Then we waited. Time ticked by, no doubt as some information officer looked things over. Finally, after forty minutes, the first email went through. We were both elated. We cheered and I taught her how to do a high five. "Yes," she said, "it great. We give you discount."

"Discount?" I thought to myself. "On a two-dollar email?" Something about that just didn't sound right.

"How much for that email?" I asked. She reached across in front of me and grabbed a calculator and started pushing buttons. I gulped.

As my friend did her sums, I went around to the front of the counter and re-read the sign. Upon closer inspection I saw it. Underneath international emails $2 I read the fine print: "per kb". That's two dollars per kilobyte, and I'd just sent a page of text with two photos, and had six more like it waiting.

"Estimate, with discount?" my friend asked.

"Yes, please." Gulp again.

"In US dollar?"

Gulp, gulp. "Yes, please."

"Comes to $1,750."

"STOOOOOOOOP! Quick, stop the rest."

In a mad panic my friend hit delete, delete, delete, and managed, probably by a narrow margin, to stop any other emails from going through. There was no getting around the first email though; if I wanted to leave the country, we had to pay up.

News of the world's most expensive email, I'm told, went all the way to the head of National Geographic. But gratefully, by the time I returned, Nat Geo had accepted my error as an honest mistake. Plus I had returned with fifty cents worth of exotic palm alcohol to make up for it.

It was exactly a year after the Burma shoot that I finally pulled out the toddy, just after September 11, 2001. On that fateful Tuesday of the terror attacks we were evacuated from Geographic headquarters, just a few blocks from the White House. I was back at work two days later, working through the shock and trying to make a tight deadline on another film, when Nancy came into my edit suite, her eyes red from crying.

"It's Joe," she said, bursting into tears. "He's dead."

My mind began racing. "What was Joe doing in New York?" I thought. Or, like two Geographic staffers leading a field trip, was he on one of the hijacked planes? It didn't make sense, he was meant to be back in Burma.

When Nancy composed herself, she explained further. Joe was back in Burma, on another expedition in the remote jungle. At seven am on the 11th of September, a snake - a foot long pencil-thin juvenile krait - tagged him on the finger. The puncture marks were so small they couldn't be seen, but this time they'd transmitted venom. In their remote location, and with bad weather, Joe's colleagues couldn't get the professional medical attention that may have saved his life.

Joe's body began to shut down bit by bit. In the end he could communicate only by wriggling a big toe. Once for "yes", twice for "no". The loyal women on his team gave him mouth-to-mouth resuscitation for hours before asking Joe if the men could relieve them. Joe wiggled his toe "no". It was the last joke he ever made. After twenty-six hours of mouth-to-mouth and three hours of heart massage, he was gone.

Seven years later, author Jamie James published a full account of Joe's death in his book The Snake Charmer. But at the time, in the shadow of the 9/11 attacks, Joe's passing was barely a blip on the national radar.

A few weeks later at the next gathering of the Exotic Booze Club, we raised our glasses in a special toddy toast to Joe as we felt he'd like to be remembered: a dedicated herpetologist, a fun-loving friend, an avid adventurer and a great drinker. To Joe.

Chapter 4

AMERICA'S LOST MUSTANGS:
Wild Turkey Bourbon

What makes for a successful Nat Geo film? Evidence has long pointed to the ratings-pulling power of the "Big Three", that is, jaws, claws and fangs. Even if your film didn't include one of the Big Three, it never hurt to refer to them somehow. One colleague, working on a volcano show, gave it the working title "It Doesn't Bite, It Blows". It was never used publicly, but it was also never forgotten.

For the most part, travelling with National Geographic means developing-world countries with disease-ridden mosquitoes, bad toilets and animals with sharp implements of destruction. But not this trip; this one was taking us straight to paradise. We drove on through horse country in the southeast of North America's bible belt, our Kingdom of Heaven within reach.

Muslims have Mecca, Catholics have Vatican City, Jews have the Wailing Wall, Hindus have . . . I don't know what. I'm making it all up. The point is that ever since the camel shoot, my Aussie colleagues and I dreamed of attending an unusual place of worship: the Wild Turkey distillery near Bourbon County, Kentucky.

Most Americans are oblivious to this venerable establishment brewing quietly in their own backyard. For some reason I'll never understand, only ten per cent of Wild Turkey bourbon is sold in the United States. A full third goes to Australia, and another third goes to Japan, and the rest to several other lucky countries. To get here on a National Geographic shoot required sheer mastery. To pull it off, I pretty much had to sell my soul.

Our camel film was quirky enough to sneak by, but that was an exception. I wanted to shake things up even more and try something different: I wanted to do a horse film. Judging by the feedback, you'd think I was asking to put half an hour of silent black to air. Everywhere I turned the same answer was echoed: "Horses don't rate."

"But how do you know if we don't do any horse shows?"

"We know. We don't do them because they don't rate."

I wasn't ready to give up so easy.

I grew up on a horse farm and I was well aware of the challenges. Horsemanship is all about nuance. Minor, almost invisible changes can be significant, and that made it bad TV, where the big and the bold is beauty. It'd been about a decade since anything on horses had been done for Geographic Television, but I knew I could make it work. With the right approach, I could prove them wrong. And, mostly, I had an insatiable desire to reacquaint myself with a staple of my youth: I wanted to smell horses again.

A young associate producer, Carrie Regan, was doing some development work at the time and heard of my equine ambitions. She came across something she thought would interest me - though with Carrie, you never can be sure.

Carrie is a renowned practical joker who once convinced a new employee that "tomorrow is Pirate Day and you'd better come to work dressed as a pirate or the boss will not be happy". By extraordinary coincidence, the newbie had previously worked at Club Med and happened to have a full pirate costume hanging in his closet. The story is legendary in Geographic hallways, made even funnier by the fact that once the unfortunate victim realized he'd been duped, he decided to stay in character and wear his outfit all day, hat, patch and all. "Arrrrr, that'll show 'er."

When Carrie called me in to discuss horses, I entered and waited for the punchline. She claimed to have been contacted by a man named Carlos Lopopolo (an unlikely name if ever I heard one) who was trying to find and preserve horses with direct lineage to the Wild West's original mustangs. She suggested I give him a call and she handed me a number in New Mexico.

This bait was too good not to swallow whole. I did some checking and rang the number, and sure enough, one Carlos Lopopolo answered - no joke. Carlos remains an enigma to me. Italian heritage (as is clear by the name), and a complexion to match. Late fifties, I'd say, with a trim grey beard and moustache. He was carrying too much weight, accentuated by gammy joints that threw his hips around awkwardly when he walked. I never saw him when he wasn't wearing a black ten-gallon hat, but he didn't talk like a cowboy. More like a deep-throated used-car salesman with a sinus problem. For all that, I couldn't work out what he was selling or why.

The desire to find and preserve the last of the original Spanish mustang bloodline seemed to have come upon him like a bolt from the blue, which made his motives hard to trust. But the more I looked, the more his passion and his cause seemed to be genuine. My scepticism may have been born from being brought up around racetracks, with all manner of unscrupulous horse folk, but I ended up feeling bad for my doubt of Carlos. At every turn I felt like I was waiting for a moment of "Ah ha! That's why he's doing it". But it never came.

Carlos is something of a freelance historian, and not a wealthy man. His plan, he told me, was to round up some herds of horses he'd seen on an Indian reservation in New Mexico that looked to be the right kind of breed. He wanted to take blood samples, send them to an equine DNA expert, and see if he could find any trace of what amounted to a long-lost equine treasure: the first mustangs. If he succeeded, Carlos would try to raise money for protected rangelands and start a breeding program to save the lineage. He called it "The New Mexico Horse Project".

Carlos had particular reason to be looking for this unique breed in New Mexico. He told me the story of Juan de O ate, a brutal conquistador perhaps best known for hacking the left foot from the Acoma people who resisted him. The king of Spain had just the job for such a good-natured man: he'd ordered Juan to ride up along the Rio Grande and spread Catholicism. While doing so, and shortly after claiming New Mexico in 1598, Juan lost some of his horses in a snowstorm. These were quite possibly America's first mustangs. If we got the green light, I knew this would make for a great snowstorm reenactment, minus the foot hacking.

The whole story was good: it was legitimate, and I would get to smell horses. But it wasn't enough. To sell a mustang story I needed more. I was close to filing the project in the too-hard basket and giving up on the idea, but I put in one more call to Carlos's equine DNA expert that changed everything. I confirmed the expert's willingness to volunteer for the program and, more importantly, discovered that he lived and worked in Kentucky. Now I really had some motivation. The story always comes first, of course, but if I could make this work I'd get to visit Bourbon Central. What an incredible bonus.

Rounding up wild horses and taking their blood could be a tricky business. It could look ugly, and even cruel, if not done right. But buoyed by the prospect of a trip to Kentucky, I came up with a solution. The book and movie "The Horse Whisperer" had been a hit a few years earlier. I figured if Carlos agreed to let me bring in a real-life horse whisperer to work his magic on the herd then I may be able to sell the story. I insisted that the horse whisperer would have to be in total charge of the round-up and the handling of the horses. Carlos didn't like the idea of giving over control on his project but ultimately he saw the value of such a collaboration and agreed.

I worked the halls giving my verbal pitch: I had cowboys, Indians, mustangs, and now a horse whisperer - what else could they want? But I still wasn't getting much joy. The "horses don't rate" mantra was prevalent, but who really knew if it was true? I certainly didn't. In my view, ratings are, at best, based on a statistically insignificant sampling of televisions. About 114 million homes use televisions in the US, but only 25 000 of them are randomly sampled for viewing habits. That means 0.0219 per cent of viewers speak for everyone and 99.9781 per cent of Americans have no input at all.

The Nielsen company collects viewing habits through small TV-top boxes called "people meters", and they distribute daily statistics to the networks. There, people feverishly dissect and interpret this data like mad scientists slicing up a circus freak. They study which demographic watched what, when and why, and then tell you things like, We're skewing too much toward females aged 34 to 52. We need more testosterone. But there are so many things they don't necessarily take into account: yes, the TV may be on, but is it being watched or is the viewer in the kitchen cooking carrots?

I remember one night in Perth, Western Australia, when the Seven Network blitzed everyone else in ratings. It was an unprecedented whitewash, as if no one was watching anything but this one news program. The reason was a very heavily promoted story with promo copy that read like this: "Tonight, the truth behind those people meters that measure ratings - how they determine programming, make and break careers, and sway billions in advertising dollars." Everyone with a people meter turned over to watch, hence the disproportionate ratings surge. According to another legendary report, Geographic's ratings went up and stayed up for a time, even in the middle of the night, all because one man with a meter turned on his TV to entertain his pet parrot, and then went away for a week. Apparently Nat Geo is the number-one channel among male macaws aged sixteen to twenty-four. My scepticism of

The Exotic Booze Club

ratings is unwavering - unless of course I have a show that rates particularly well, in which case the figures are most certainly correct.

What I needed for the mustang film was a pitch meeting, a meeting that would get everyone in the one room so I could sell my heart out. Thing was, this was against protocol. Producers don't call a pitch meeting; that's the job of the development people or supervising producers. While in the back of my mind I knew this, I also knew an extra step may stop the story from getting through to the ultimate decision-maker, that very sober Brit Mr. Earl Grey.

In Australia I would have taken the boss out to lunch on Friday afternoon, sold my pitch over a bottle of wine, and job done. I may not have had to mention horses at all; just the idea of Bourbon County, Kentucky probably would have done the trick. Clearly that wasn't going to work with the Earl. That's when I sold my soul - and I wouldn't recommend it to anyone. I went ahead and organized a pitch meeting such that the development boss thought my supervising producer had arranged it, and vice versa. I happily stayed quiet and let them be misled. It was like being a sneaky kid and saying, "Dad, Mum says it's okay if you say it's okay." Then, upon getting the okay from Dad, going to Mum and saying, "Mum, Dad says it's okay if you say it's okay." Try it kids, it usually works. But don't try it as an adult employee. I was blinded by the promise of great visuals, equine adventure and good bourbon, and I really should have been more respectful of protocol, especially with an employer that was affording me so many incredible opportunities.

Half an hour before the meeting, people started paying attention and I was headed off at the pass. The full-on pitch meeting was cancelled and redirected to a meeting in Earl's office. I walked in and instantly realized that Mum and Dad had been talking. Never a good thing if you've been a scallywag.

Earl started. "Now, Brian, what's this horse thing you've got?" It was no time to step back; I pitched my story like my life depended on it. I knew from our demographic experts that our target audience was males aged twenty-five to fifty-four.

"I'm one of those guys," I said, "and I love westerns, and that's what this is."

"Well," said Earl politely, "it reads like a horse film, and you know, horses don't rate."

Mum and Dad were in the room and I looked to them on the off-chance I could get some help. With one glance I knew I was on my own - they were tight-lipped with icy stares. No lifeline there; swim or drown, it was all up to me.

I bucked up and continued. I blabbed on for what seemed like an age. Because Earl was British, he was too polite to say an outright "no", it was more like a "well I don't think this is going to work for us". But because that wasn't an outright "no", I decided to stick my less polite Aussie foot in the closing door and blab on some more. In short, I wore them down.

Finally, with an exasperated sigh, Earl said, "Ahhhh. Well then, I guess we should just let Brian do his film." It was close enough to an outright "yes" and I jumped on it; it was the best green light I've ever had. Mum and Dad had remained silent, but at least they didn't speak against me. Earl had a lot of pressure to deliver shows that rated, so this was quite a leap of faith. In the end I believe he felt that a half-decent filmmaker this passionate about a subject was going to deliver something worthwhile, even if it was about horses.

Always one to push the envelope a little further, I added another request. I'd like to shoot the whole thing on film. Sixteen millimeter. The world had pretty much moved on from film at this time, but not yet to high definition. It was the tape era, where the format was convenient but not necessarily of great or lasting quality. But film was expensive. I pitched again: "Wild West . . . spectacular vistas . . . mustangs . . . cowboys . . . Indians . . . John Wayne . . . John Ford . . . blah blah blah."

Earl thought for a moment - was he up for another battle? No. "Very well, Brian," he said, "as long as you come in on budget."

That was everything I needed. Great. Thanks. Bye. I didn't walk out, I bolted from the stable. I'd done it, and I wanted to move fast before anyone changed his or her mind.

Life is short, so eat dessert first. We headed straight toward Bourbon County. First stop was the Equine Genetics Lab, an establishment at the University of Kentucky dedicated to creating faster racehorses. Scientist Dr. Gus Cothran was Carlos's volunteer DNA expert, and we wanted to have a segment with Gus before the round-up to establish the importance of our mission. We filmed Gus looking at DNA slides and doing lab work, and we interviewed him about the horses we'd be searching for. Carlos had already sent him samples from some promising mustangs that'd been captured and broken in by a rancher. Gus concluded that "these samples may point to something back in time that just doesn't exist anywhere else". He added, "You need to find more samples like this, or better. Otherwise the breed could go extinct." It was the perfect mission statement to kick off our film.

When one thinks of mustangs, the image conjured is usually a large animal with high-stepping hooves and a proud, bold neckline. Not so. We had to look for small, almost scrawny beasts, a detail I'd conveniently omitted from my pitch. We needed to search for traces of a breed called a barb. The Moors brought barbs to Spain in 711AD, but once there, the Moors mostly traded up to the larger Spanish steeds. Why go to battle in a Mini when you can have a Hummer? As a result, barbs were slowly bred out of existence in Europe, but before disappearing some 500 years ago, it seems they had one last important niche to fill.

When the conquistadors rode across the Americas in search of gold and glory, they were on horses that had to arrive by ship, sailing for a few months at a time. The best horses for that kind of journey are tough and robust but small, hence the diminutive physical characteristics we needed to search for in the mustangs we were to round up.

Gus would do DNA testing for the ultimate verification, but he warned us the chances of finding such horses could be slim. In the past 500 years there's been a lot of cross breeding out in the wild, quite possibly enough to have already bred the barbs out of existence.

This was not good news for a producer who'd just put his ass on the line. If we couldn't find a significant trace of barb blood, it would not be much of a story. It was definitely time for a drink, so we loaded up the gear and headed down the road to Bourbon County. It was a short detour and one we logged under "research".

I had with me the dream crew but, like much in this project, they didn't come easy. One thing I knew I didn't want was a cameraman who knew horses and the subtlety of their motions. I needed someone with an eye for the big commercial picture and yet was able to capture the beauty and the drama of the story. And, most challengingly, I needed a cameraman who could shoot it all economically on sixteen millimeter, without an assistant (our horse film budget was too tight for that).

I scored big-time in getting the best cameraman I've ever known, West Ashton, from Sydney. It was no easy task clearing the way to fly in a foreigner to shoot this very American show, but I sold what little remained of my soul and employed the philosophy of "seek forgiveness, not permission". With that I carefully snuck him past the gatekeepers and kept him hidden until it was too late.

West started in the business in Perth as a newsroom camera assistant. There he learned to be fast; news waits for no one. He moved up the ladder to be a shooter, first for news, then current affairs segments, lifestyle shows and documentaries. When he wasn't shooting for work, he was shooting for fun. He loves what he does and does it with extraordinary cheer and expertise. It's been said that West is not a cameraman but a craftsman.

Though we didn't have a camera assistant, we had a soundman as dedicated to his craft as West is to that of shooting, and perhaps that's because he's West's brother - Jeremy Ashton, of camel shoot fame. You'll recall that it was Jeremy who first got me hooked on Wild Turkey, the brew one reviewer called the "Clint Eastwood of whisky". In my mind: tough, well aged and with enough kick to make you squint your eyes and start talking to the empty chair beside you. It was a long way for the Ashton brothers to come for a shoot, but the promise of a visit to the Wild Turkey distillery was enough to have them promptly accept the assignment.

We pulled into Wild Turkey HQ and kissed the earth in the parking lot. I'd fought hard for this and it was a much-anticipated pilgrimage. We headed straight to the main store to arrange a tour and to buy everything Wild Turkey that we could see. And the first thing we saw was a sign on the door - "closed".

We'd spent too much time with Gus and, at five pm, we were thirty minutes too late for communion. We swore and we cursed. It was a crushing blow. We pressed our faces hard against the window and longingly looked at the merchandise just out of our reach. Our anguish kept us glued there until we heard a voice from behind. "Can I help you?"

We turned to face a man walking down from the distillery, and at least one of us said, "G'day, mate, how ya goin'? Damn, looks like we re a bit late."

"Are you Australian?" he asked.

"Well, yeah."

"Heck, we *love* Australians." The man was none other than Eddie Russell of the legendary and long-lived Russell family - bourbon royalty.

After nearly fifty years, Eddie's father, Jimmy, was still working here, the master distiller. Eddie will no doubt take over one day if he hasn't already, and he's someone who well knows that a third of his income comes from Down Under. He'd finished for the day and was about to head home, but instead he flung open the doors, gave us a private tour of the distillery, tastings included, and sold us all the swag we could carry: t-shirts, jackets, signed labels, bottle openers, a drinks tray, fridge magnets, a couple of flasks - we went crazy. His gesture was not only goodwill for Wild Turkey, it bought me a lot of goodwill with the crew. It would be needed - I was about to put them through hell.

The Exotic Booze Club

We sobered up and flew to our next stop to meet up with our horse whisperer and film some background of him at home. I'd first heard of Pat Parelli when my eldest sister did one of his natural horsemanship courses. This had been a few years earlier, but she showed me a video so dramatic that the images left a permanent imprint. In the video, Pat, a good-looking, wisecracking cowboy with a big hat and a handlebar moustache, demonstrates and explains the magic of his methods. He took problem, traumatized and wildhorses and turned them into docile animals that followed him around like puppy dogs. I was entranced. And best of all, the transformations weren't subtle - they were worthy of a Hollywood blockbuster. I knew from the time I saw the video that one day I'd be working with Pat on a TV show, and that day had come.

There are several so-called horse whisperers around, probably none as accomplished, nor as successful, as Pat Parelli. His courses run all over the world and his disciples number in the thousands. To keep up with it all, he has about forty full-time employees, and one Linda. Linda Parelli, Pat's gorgeous blond bombshell of a wife, is the one who jumps in and cracks the whip when needed. Most importantly, she's Australian. There's nothing an expat Aussie likes more than another expat Aussie. It's like a mafia for mischief - don't mess with us or we'll send the boys around to drink you under the table. Linda had given us the thumbs up and Pat welcomed the project with open arms.

We flew to the Parelli ranch in Pagosa Springs, Colorado to film Pat working with a couple of stallions and interview him about his career. He started as a rodeo rider and realized he'd get a longer ride if he soothed his horse instead of provoking it. He started to experiment with methods, and he entered a mule he'd trained in a high-level equestrian competition. In the snooty world of horsemanship, this was an absolute insult, an unforgivable act of rebellion - how dare he pit a half donkey against ivy-league equines.

Pat and his mule, Thumper, did everything that was asked of them with incredible precision. What's more, they did it all without reins or a bridle. No one had ever seen anything like it. The judges were forced to at least give him and Thumper third place, after which the organizers immediately passed a motion that forever banned mules from the competition.

We left Pat and Linda with a plan to meet up in New Mexico and I took my team to Albuquerque. I immediately identified with the wide-open spaces. New Mexico manages a different feel than every other state around it: more traditional architecture, its own distinct culture - an actual feel of Mexico but with more money and a lot more gringos. Not that there weren't a few unpleasant surprises to come.

As we left the lobby on day one, ready to check out our desert surrounds, a concierge came running up to West. "Sir, sir, sir. Sir, sir, sir!" It took West a moment to register; he was not used to being addressed so formally. "Sir," said the concierge with alarm, you can't take that out there. We all looked West up and down thinking the same thing.

Take what? We'd already loaded the car and the only thing he had in his hand was a bottle of water. And, indeed, that was the offending object. Albuquerque has a law of no open bottles on the street, and apparently they were in the midst of a crackdown. The concierge explained that West could be arrested for carrying his water out to the car.

"But," West said, "we're going into the desert." We were dumb struck. Obviously it had to do with something like reducing the amount of alcohol on the street, but rather than saying no open alcohol the rule is no open bottles. West had long wanted to pitch a show called *That's Bullshit!*, kind of like the old *That's Incredible!*, with the audience shouting out in unison after hearing some crazy story that just didn't make sense. He wrote this event down and filed it away, and we made a mental note to stock up on unopened bottles of water.

We met up with Carlos and filmed him going through ancient archives that traced early horse movements in the west. We then headed out to the Native American reservation that would be our main location and met three respected members of the Pueblo of Laguna tribe, who'd kindly agreed to accommodate us and the horse project on their land. They were good-humored and easygoing cowboys and rangers who seemed endlessly amused by the media invasion. The horses we were targeting had lived on their traditional lands for as long as anyone could remember, free and protected. We drove up to a mesa with binoculars to see if we could get a bit of a look.

The landscape was dramatic: spires and box canyons below giant flat-top mesas, all high-altitude desert. The soil was rich with red and yellow tones and the vegetation was low brush and cactus. It was the wild west of my favorite boyhood movies.

We eventually spotted the horses in the distance and managed to get a few far-off shots. The herd was small in height but sturdy in stature, as we'd hoped. We counted about ten adults and a few young, the mix of paint and palomino colors making it a good-looking group.

As much as possible, we wanted to shoot around dawn and dusk when the light was at its best. That's why I knew I was going to put the crew through hell: sunrise was around five am, sunset at ten pm. Plus, the shooting location was more than an hour's drive from our hotel, so we were in for several very long days. I can deal with the late nights, but early mornings have never been my thing. If I really have to film a sunrise, I usually shoot a sunset instead and just play it backwards. But this was a short shoot and we'd need every kelvin of light we could salvage to film all that we needed.

For our first early start, we needed to get some better shots of the horses in the wild before the roundup so we drove out to a clearing on the reservation and waited for our helicopter to show up. And waited and waited. More than an hour after our appointed time, a small helicopter flew in from Albuquerque with a young pilot named Jacquine. He apologized for being late and blamed the weather, which seemed a strange excuse - we could just about see Albuquerque from where we stood and there was nothing but blue sky. I think we all figured he'd slept in and was too embarrassed to admit it. If he were Russian, I wouldn't have been surprised if he smelled like pickle juice.

The chopper could hold two people and a pilot, a tight squeeze across the one bench seat. West and I went to hop in but Jacquine was quick with a "no". He was concerned about the weight and wanted just one person on board with him. We figured that this was a reasonable request to give him more manoeuvrability with flying, so I stepped out. When it came to helicopter safety, all I knew was to check that any duct tape on the rotors was fresh, and not too frayed. West, on the other hand, really knows his stuff. He had completed about nineteen hours of helicopter pilot training, and he'd been in and out of news choppers his entire career. In this case, though, there was one thing he didn't know.

When getting in a chopper, there are many risk factors, but three in particular that an old hand watches out for: an inexperienced pilot, too much weight, and too high an altitude (at altitude the air is thinner so there's essentially less for the chopper to grasp onto). We've all flown with at least one of these three factors, and West reasoned that for a short flight he'd be okay with the young pilot, but he didn't know we were already over 6,000 feet in altitude. In Australia, when you see desert it pretty much means you're at sea level. New Mexico's mesas are often snow-capped in winter and top out just shy of a nosebleed.

We left West and Jacquine and drove to a high point so we could watch them film the horses. What happened after we left was, without a doubt, the most unprofessional pilot behavior I've ever witnessed. Jacquine was still concerned about the weight at this altitude and wanted to dump fuel to lighten up. That actually could work, but dumping fuel on an Indian reservation would have gotten everyone into a lot of trouble.

He fired up the engine okay, but to gain enough ground speed for a proper take-off he flew a hundred yards or so, just a few feet off the ground and *under* powerlines. Even I know that powerlines and helicopters are natural-born enemies. And these weren't high-up, high-tension lines - that'd be bad enough - but the much lower beside-the-road zappers, still with enough whack to stop you flying and start you frying.

West let out a nervous "whoa" and tightened his belt, but for the sake of the shoot he didn't want to abort. Still not realising the altitude issue, West started telling himself it'd be okay, this was just a short-and-simple preliminary shoot. In two days there would be a *lot* more flying. We planned for West to film most of the muster from the air, as Pat and his men rounded up the mustangs on horseback and drove them into a corral for taming and blood testing. It suddenly became hard for West to think that far ahead as he gripped his seat with white knuckles.

The chopper flew into our view, and within a few minutes they spotted the horses. Dropping down a little to get closer, Jacquine began to make a turn. As he did, the strain was too much for the engine and they lost power and hit the ground hard. Despite the jolt, Jacquine started to take off again, spurring West to finally speak up. "No, no - let me out, let me out." West had already been working on a plan B. "I'll plant myself on the ground and you just muster the horses by me and I'll get the shots we need." It was good thinking, but Jacquine had other ideas. Telling West not to worry, he flew up about thirty feet and the whole rig dropped like a stone.

The tail hit hard and bits of helicopter flew off. They were then thrust forward onto their nose at enough of an angle that West thought they were going to flip. His life flashed before him and he thought these may be his final moments on earth. Rather than flip, the chopper thankfully fell back onto its skids and they sat there in stunned silence.

The accident was out of view from our vantage point, but we saw the horses running off into the distance without the chopper behind them so I knew something wasn't right. I radioed through on our two-way. "You guys okay?"

West's reply was calm. "Ah, yeah, we re okay. But we've had a bit of a mishap. You'd better come over." A quick analysis of West's understated coolness would have revealed what he was really saying: "Holy CRAP! We're alive, but only just. You won't believe what this fucking idiot did. Get your ass over here now."

The chopper was a mess, Jacquine was strangely unapologetic, and West looked to be going into shock. We quickly surveyed the scene then took West back to the hotel. On the ride home the trauma really started to settle in. West was physically uninjured but we couldn't help but worry about him. I was wracked with guilt: devastated that I'd put my trusted friend at such risk, and angry at the inadequacy of Jacquine and his now defunct chopper.

As for the story, the entire muster required a cameraman to be airborne, but West was in no state for it - not now anyway. Our associate producer found a back-up cameraman and put him on standby, in case West wasn't up for any more flying. We had planned to shoot a regular motorbike roundup the next day, to contrast with Pat's more natural methods, but our AP did some hasty rearranging so West could take the day off. That and a few stiff drinks was all we could do for now.

West was resilient. After a full day's rest, he bounced back ready enough to jump back in the saddle of the horse that bucked him off. Long term he ended up feeling too mortal to ever complete his helicopter licence, but he knew he'd have to get back in the air sometime as a shooter, so it may as well be now.

The real kicker was Jacquine later calling me to ask for payment. I couldn't believe my ears. My mind raced immediately to the pilot for the show West wanted to create; I could already hear the audience echoing in my ears, "That's bullshit!" I asked Jacquine whether he wanted to be paid for arriving an hour late, or for crashing the helicopter five minutes into the flight with my best cameraman on board. I'll never forget his reply. "I did not crash the helicopter," he told me. "I was just the pilot when it went down."

I stored that line away for future use. If and when I ever truly screw something up I'll be sure to tell my boss, I didn't set the building on fire, I just lit the match that fell into the gas. If Jacquine lives long enough such bravado may get him places, but it wasn't getting him paid. We exchanged a few more bitter words and I never heard from him again.

We still had a day before the muster, and our AP was charged with finding us the biggest, strongest, safest helicopter she could, with the best, most experienced pilot in New Mexico. We wanted someone with sharp eyes and grey in his hair, regardless of budget. This was not an area to skimp on, even though we were tight on cash. Because "horses don't rate," the money allocation for the project was not all I'd hoped. Film stock and processing was expensive, but I knew West was good enough not to burn up excessive amounts of it. I hoped this would justify the cost of flying him halfway around the world.

It's conceivable that there were US-based cameramen capable of this kind of challenge, maybe even some already in Nat Geo's stable of award-winning freelancers, but would these mere mortals extend the influence of the Aussie mafia? Would they drink Wild Turkey like it was soft drink? And would they have a location-relevant name like "West"? There really was no other option.

As I did some mental maths on where we stood financially, Pat arrived out on the reservation. He and Linda came in style in a giant souped-up motorhome, with half a dozen of his best men, ten of his most trusted horses and a truckload of eighty panels to build stockyards. He'd embraced the project more than I could ever have imagined, and with his generosity of resources he did nothing less than save the shoot. He'd found a sponsor, Priefert livestock equipment suppliers, to provide the portable yards and his men drove to a box canyon and set about making corrals. This is where we'd attempt to drive in the mustangs.

The traditional landowners hit it off with Pat right away. Not so Carlos, who immediately felt upstaged. There was nothing to do about it; Pat had a job to do and he was focused on doing it right. He had no time for ego issues. Carlos had corralled some local volunteers to help with the yards and the muster, but Pat wasn't so sure about them. There was going to be some extremely rough riding and he felt responsible for everything going well.

Pat arranged a basic obstacle course and riding test to see what the volunteers could do, and it wasn't pretty. In the game plan, he positioned the volunteers where they could block off exits if the mustangs went the wrong way, but the hard riding would be left to Pat's tried-and-proven men, plus one other - me. Pat spared me from the obstacle course and took a leap of faith that I could ride well enough. That was a big leap. I'd wanted to smell horses, I hadn't said anything about riding them. He'd made a logical assumption that I wanted to do the hard riding after I had told him that I'd spent a year on a cattle station and that my father was a horse trainer, but I had neglected to mention a few smallish details.

It was true that my father's farm often held as many as forty racehorses, but what I did not tell Pat was that I never rode any of them.

None of us did. They weren't those kind of horses. My dad trained harness horses - trotters. They were trained to pull carts, not wear saddles. And being pulled in a cart requires considerably less skill than riding. I'd been placed on a small pony when I was four: it took off and left me face down in the dirt. The next time I had anything vaguely resembling a riding lesson, I was in my teens. For a laugh, one of my sisters threw me on an old grey mare and instructed me not to jiggle so much when trotting. On the cattle station, some of my colleagues didn't even have the benefit of that advice. We all learned on the job how best to hang on, the primary object being to do so in a way that would reduce the number of bum blisters. And that was nearly twenty years earlier, with not a lot of saddle time since. I still love horses, they smell good and the ones that pull carts are lovely for picnics, but this was no picnic.

Now we were getting close to action time, I thought I should come clean and share all this with Pat, and that's when he brought out the horse he'd trucked all the way from Colorado - just for me. It was a beautiful steed, well groomed with keen eyes that seemed to say, "Hop on, jackaroo." What could I do? For better or worse, I decided to keep quiet; if I managed to stay on, I'm sure my bum would recover. Plus, my role would be a little different. I'd help with the roundup if I could but, more importantly, I was the radio link between Pat and the chopper to co-ordinate shooting.

Jim Sugar, a photographer sent by Nat Geo to take some publicity pictures, showed up. Instantly Jim recognized that what we'd pulled together was something special and visually spectacular. He too was enamored by the backdrop, the cowboys, the Native Americans, the mustangs and the story.

Without telling anyone, Jim hatched an ultimately unsuccessful plan to make this much more than a publicity shoot. He thought if he shot it right he could sell the pictures as their own story to the magazine. Over the next three days he proceeded to take over 2400 photographs, a good proportion of them by getting in our way. If the magazine had commissioned the story then we may have been more tolerant, but this was like someone jumping the queue to steal your favorite dessert. As politely as we could, we explained that the film was the priority, and to please stand back. When trying to shoot economically, the last thing West needed was a photographer creeping into his shots. It wasn't just about saving film - there was much more at stake.

Every night we got back to our rooms around eleven pm, with barely time for a Wild Turkey nightcap. Instead, there was more work to be done. West and Jeremy would spend close to two hours cleaning the dust out of the film gear and reloading the magazines, black boxes that attach to the camera to hold and protect the rolls of film. We had six mags, each capable of recording ten minutes of footage.

Once you shot all of them, in just sixty minutes, it would be an hour-long process to change out the exposed film and reload the mags with new stock. It was a big and responsible job that had to be done in a clean environment so the film didn't wind up scratched or damaged; a single hair or even a speck of dust could ruin a lot of film. I was foolish in not getting West an assistant to do this for him.

We knew that once we started rounding up horses there'd be no time to change out mags. West had to get everything we needed in an hour of recording, with enough left to roll at the end as we got the horses into the yard. In most cases, only about three per cent of what a cameraman shoots is ever used, but we needed this muster to take up about five or ten minutes of screen time, which meant West had to shoot a ratio closer to fifteen per cent, five times the normal. Talk about stress.

An epic all-blue sky had greeted us every morning, and the day of the big muster was no different. It was another 3.30 am wake-up call with just a few hours sleep. We moved around filming the cowboys as they saddled up. The traditional landowners were happy to be spectators, jumping in when we needed advice on routes, landscape and locations. Their reservation was an arid maze of mesas and giant sandstone outcrops. It was too hot to wear jeans, but the low, dry vegetation was too prickly to safely wear anything else. The sweating started at sunrise and continued till sunset, and if you weren't stepping on a cactus you were probably kicking up dust, the latter being a much greater hazard for our film equipment.

The cast of characters Pat brought with him livened up the film in delightful ways. Along with Pat himself, there was an outgoing Aussie named Andy Booth (more mafia) and old Ron Willis, a master horseman who had all the presence, and possibly the age, of Moses. Ron rarely spoke, but when he did, you listened. Every word was well considered and precise. West, Jeremy and I approached him with the camera. "Hey Ron," I called, "can you tell us about this hole here?" On the ground by his horse was a large open hole, perhaps made by a gopher. The hole was hard to see with the desert grass around it, and I knew that hazards like this could cause serious trouble on our muster.

As we rolled film, Ron calmly turned and knelt down by the hole. He cleared the grass away, took a good look, and spoke with ultimate world-wise authority in his slow, deep, gravelly voice. "There's an old Arab proverb that says the rider's grave is always open. A horse that's really galloping can stick a front foot in that, break a leg, kill a man, the whole thing." Jack Palance couldn't have said it better. It was perfect dramatic delivery.

Ron stood up, took another look at the hole, mounted his horse and rode off, at which point I jokingly added, "Aaaand cut." It truly felt as if we were on a Hollywood set.

Our Native American hosts had headed out early to spot the horses. They came back to the yards with troubling news: the horses had moved off the plains and up to the top of the mesa. There was a way we could drive our cars and floats around to the spot, but it would take too long to muster the mustangs down that same route on horseback. There had to be a short cut, but no one knew where it was.

The mesa stuck up from the ground like a layer cake, its sides vertical and probably 500 feet high. We transported our muster horses up to the top to try our best. Pat and Ron were sure that if we drove the mustangs along the top they'd show us the short cut down and we'd have to follow. It was the only plan we had.

Our AP had done well on the new helicopter and pilot. West had no gyro system to help him steady his shots (could I possibly make this guy's job any harder?), but with the new pilot and a twin-engine JetRanger, West felt confident he'd make it work. My only concern was how much the chopper would influence the herd. It was there for filming only, but the horses would likely shy away from wherever the chopper flew, adding to the challenge of the riders on the ground. This notion had been troubling me for some time, but I couldn't think of any way around it. Somehow it all just had to work.

We unloaded the horses on the top of the mesa and mounted up, Pat, Linda, Ron, six of Pat's most trusted riders and me. West got a few final shots as we took off to where the mustangs were last seen, and then he boarded his chopper. I stuffed my radios into my shirt and followed Pat. We spotted the mustangs within minutes and circled wide around them, but they were onto us immediately and dashed away. The chase was on. We bolted through the desert dodging giant jumping cactuses and a wild array of holes and obstacles.

Pat had taken great care of me. My horse had a delightfully smooth gait, so when I held on tight it was as if we stood still and the world galloped by us and my blister-free bum. I was all at once on my horse and in heaven.

West was above and to our left. The wind from the chopper combined with the wind from my ride blew off my old Akubra hat. This would normally be a serious casualty as it can take years to break in an Akubra: you have to wear holes in the top, stitch it together with hide, accidentally run over it a few times, stain it with sweat, the dog has to chew on it and the cat has to have kittens in it then it's ready for a big muster. Despite such time and effort, the loss of my hat became secondary to the fun I was having. Nothing short of serious injury could spoil this moment.

Despite its proximity, the helicopter seemed to have no influence on the mustangs at all. I couldn't work out why but it was good news, and I charged on. After twenty minutes or so we caught up with the herd as it ran along the edge of the mesa. One of Pat's men spotted what looked to be the short cut, so we circled the horses and pushed them toward the path. Once there, at Pat's instruction, we backed off a little but kept the wild herd surrounded. They were still together, twelve horses, but all were reluctant to step down off the mesa onto the path. It's unclear why but they dug in their hooves and refused to budge. I began having camel déjà vu.

Pat's preferred horse-moving apparatus is a long stick with a plastic bag on the end; you shake it, and the horses move. Normally it works exceptionally well, but not this time. Andy, the other Australian, had a whip he was cracking, but that made no difference either. The mustangs proved themselves every bit as stubborn as an outback dromedary.

We had the chopper move behind us, but not even that helped. The trail was a one-horse-at-a-time deal, and we knew if we pushed them too hard we'd risk sending some over the edge to their deaths - and that, aside from everything else, would be bad TV. We had to be persistent but patient. That's when West came crackling over the radio.

"Hey Kimosabe, it's West here, you copy?"

"Roger, Tonto."

"I hate to tell you this," he said, "but we've got less than five minutes of fuel left before we have to bail."

Crap. Getting the horses off the ridge was now clearly a major part of the roundup and thus the film. It was also a one-off deal: if West missed it, editing would be very difficult. It'd be like watching an Olympic event where you see the start of the big race, then suddenly cut straight to the medal ceremony.

"Understood," I replied, trying to hide my stress. "Give it as long as you safely can. We'll do our best."

We nudged and nudged as the chopper circled above. Kids and animals - never work with them. Why the horses were being so stubborn we'll never know, but suddenly one of the mares, a brown and white paint, took the hint. She pawed a little at the trail and cautiously started heading down. The others followed, as did we, and just in time. West filmed the start of our descent and they flew off. The pilot dropped West at a good position by the corrals and headed for home.

It was rough and dangerous heading down the short cut. The mustangs managed it in short order, but we all had to take our time. We eventually hit the flat and charged off again. The mustangs overshot the box canyon where the corrals waited, but Pat's men managed to flank them in good time and, with his expert hands, it was not hard to turn them for home. The horses ran straight into the wide-open gates of the corral and we shut them in. Life was good.

West had just enough film left to get some back slapping and cheers, and went in for the all-important smooch shot to cap it off: Pat giving Linda a big celebratory horseback kiss. As West started to roll, Jim, our trigger-happy photog-rapher, jumped into frame again, not just once but twice. I duly threatened to strangle him with his own camera strap but, that aside, it was a job well done - especially by West, who made it with just seconds of film to spare.

They were good-looking horses, and remarkably adept at handling the terrain. We spent the next hour pulling cactus needles from our horses legs, but the mustangs had not a one. West reloaded his mags inside the shelter of the motorhome, and Pat turned his mind to how he'd get blood from these horses in the gentlest way possible. Under his orders, no one was to give the wild horses water without his say-so.

We had a couple of small holes to fill in the sequence and wanted a few horses to head down the mesa short cut again so we could film tight shots from the ground. It was hairy enough the first time with giant boulders to step over, but Ron and a few of the others came with us for a quick reenactment. West was ready to roll when Ron piped up for another rare narrative.

"Now listen," he said, "I'm doing this cause Pat asked. But I'm not goin ta kill my horse for no one. I'll do it once, and once only - get it right the first time." If West hadn't previously appreciated the dangerous nature of what we were asking these guys to do, he certainly understood then. And though he knew the film gear was good to go, Ron's words shook him enough to triple check. All went well though and the round-up was in the can.

I discussed with Pat which horse he should whisper to first. He had just a few days to get all the mustangs accustomed to people before the vet came to draw blood, so there was no time to waste. Pat suggested we start with one of the quieter mustangs as a bit of a warm-up. I knew we wouldn't film every horse being tamed, and I knew the first horse would, in the film, represent all of them. It was an important decision, and the filmmaker in me wanted the toughest challenge and the most dramatic transition up-front. The cowboy in Pat has never shied away from a challenge, and this was no exception, so he graciously picked the mare that'd led the way down the short cut. She was not only the leader but also the wildest, craziest, maddest looking horse of the bunch.

Pat's men opened a gate to get her into a separate round yard and, being the leader, she flew in. She virtually chose herself. From one side of the round yard to the other was about 25 feet. The railing was made of horizontal iron bars a couple of inches wide and spaced about a foot apart. The top rail looked to be nearly seven feet high.

The self-selected mare, to the wither, was about as tall as Pat. Her patchwork brown-and-white coat made her quite the specimen, just the type we were told to look for by our equine geneticist.

The horse ran wildly around in circles looking for an escape. Pat is apt to point out that horses are natural-born claustrophobes and this one had never been so enclosed. Pat stood quietly in the middle of the yard with his most trusted horse, Casper. The wild horse didn't know what to do; she could have charged Pat but instead frantically circled him. Pat just stood there trying to let her settle a little, but the mustang had other plans. She leapt up madly and tried to jump the railing, and she nearly made it too, but it was ultimately a daring yet hopeless attempt. She slammed into the top rail, bloodied her nose, and fell over backwards. I began to wonder how on earth Pat was going to calm this thing down - the vet coming to stick this wild horse with a needle would do well to buy some extra insurance.

A wild horse is a bundle of nerves and nuances. It is a creature of highly tuned sensors and emotions that exist beyond the comprehension of most mortals. Every hair on a mustang's body is a trigger that can release uncontrolled panic. All it takes from an outsider is a murmur, a twitch, a glance or even a thought.

Recall the repulsion you feel when a stranger stands a little too close, maybe that guy in your office building with the odd sense of personal space, and imagine that creepy sensation you get when he leans toward you. No touch is involved, but when he crosses a line, alarm bells in your head say "too close, back off". No one teaches you where this line is, no one draws it for you; it's just there and normal people of similar upbringing and culture all share the knowledge of its exact placement. Now imagine this awareness a thousandfold, with the slightest invasion of your space sparking an impulse that makes you run, jump and kick - that's a horse.

Evolution dialled this mechanism to extreme levels in horses as a matter of survival. The sensors live in a multitude of places around their bodies and at a multitude of levels. If the threat invading a horse's space stands behind its shoulder, it will be propelled forward. But if the invader moves up just an inch and looks the horse in the eye, it will swivel to leap off in a different direction. Pat is a master at reading and feeling a horse's personal space; a twitch of an ear, a blink of an eye or the flick of a tail speaks volumes to him. He feels out what a horse will and won't tolerate and he uses this knowledge to communicate with it.

Back on her feet, the mustang resumed her circular gallop. In these situations, Pat normally speaks to a horse with his body language and talks to a crowd of onlookers to explain what he's doing. I asked him to forget the crowd and to talk to the horse. I felt it'd portray a more intimate feel on film to have full focus and communication directed at the mare. It took Pat a moment to get his rhythm doing this but soon he was enjoying it. I sensed that, in general, it was what he'd rather do. There was something very pure about it.

Pat used hushed tones and talked the horse through what he was doing. "I'd like to start a relationship with you and develop a partnership," he said. "I know you are looking for something here that's going to give you security." As the mare ran circles, Pat used Casper as a foil and tried to let the mustang know it had options: she could pull in close for the security of being next to one of her own kind. It nearly backfired when the mustang shot *between* Pat and Casper and frantically swung her hindquarters to Pat. A wild kick from those hind hooves would pack more punch than a dozen Mike Tysons. Pat darted out of range, then got back to Casper as soon as he could. A little shaken, he resorted to his most magical technique to make things safer.

When the mustang turned her hind legs to Pat, showing him no eyes, Pat would slap his leg and make a sharp noise, causing the mustang distress. If she showed him one eye he'd do something to agitate her just a little, and when this wild horse was brave enough to show him both eyes, he planned to reward it. He explained, "I've never been kicked by a horse that was looking at me. The secret was in the reward."

Most humans instinctively relate to horses as we do to dogs - big mistake. Dogs are predators and pack hunters; they like to know their place in the pack and they like attention. Horses hate attention, especially wild ones. When a prey animal like a mustang gets attention, it usually mean it's in trouble and may end up as a predator's meal. So to reward a horse, you give it no attention at all.

After a few minutes of the leg-slapping game, the mare finally tried something new: she looked Pat in the face with both eyes, just for a fraction of a second. In that heartbeat, Pat turned and walked away, rewarding the horse for doing the right thing by paying her no attention. It was a miraculous move. This wild animal suddenly dropped its head to a less defensive posture and began to follow Pat around the yard. The change couldn't have been more dramatic. It was as if he'd swapped the mustang for a trail horse.

Pat picked up one of his sticks with a plastic bag on it and gently used it to stroke the mustang down her side, positioning the plastic so it made no noise or movement. Using a stick was a start, but Pat had to win this mare's trust to allow close human contact behind her head where the vet would need access to draw blood.

For the most part, the horse let Pat stroke it; not tap it like you would a dog, but stroke it like a mother horse licks a foal. Suddenly it seemed too cozy for the mare. She darted away from Pat, and he instantly brought his plastic bag alive and shook it violently. When the horse eventually turned to face him again with both eyes, Pat lowered his stick and walked away. Now, wherever Pat walked, the horse was right behind him licking her lips. The lip licking is international horse language for "I'm thinking", and if you could read her mind, this little horse would have been saying, "Ahhhh, now I get it." She also stopped sweating, a good sign that her stress levels were dropping.

When Pat stopped, the horse calmly walked right up to his back and stood there. Pat let his horse, Casper, out of the yard and swapped his stick for a lasso. Over the next ten minutes or so Pat worked more of his magic, eventually throwing a rope around the horse's neck and using it to ensure she obeyed his commands. He gently pulled on it when she resisted the rope, and quickly released any pressure when she did as he wished. Soon enough, the two were right beside each other, calm and relaxed.

Pat started jumping up and putting a bit of his weight across her body. Forty minutes ago this was a wild animal, trying everything it could to escape, but now, to our amazement, Pat slowly climbed up and knelt on her back. "And . . . cut."

A good chunk of my life has been around horses, and I've never seen anything like it. The Native Americans in our group told me it was like a spiritual experience. They felt they were witnessing methods not heard of since the time of their ancestors.

I learned later that while we had been distracted by the helicopter accident, Pat had chartered his own chopper to take a look at the horses. He used the same techniques with the chopper that we saw him use in the round yard: when the horses faced the chopper with two eyes, he'd have the pilot back away. It was a brilliant move and the reason why the mustangs ignored our chopper during the round-up.

Over the next day or so, Pat and his men performed similar miracles with the rest of the herd. The men carried buckets and were the sole source of water for the horses, making the bond even stronger. With all the horses now manageable, Pat began introducing another technique. He would apply pressure to the top of a horse's head while pinching its neck. The pinch was simulating a needle. If the horse started lifting its head, he'd pinch harder; when it finally lowered its head, he'd release the pinch and stroke its neck. By the time the vet came, the taking of blood was a piece of cake. The vet said he'd rarely had it so easy.

The blood work was sent off to Gus in Kentucky, and we filmed a scene of the horses being released out the gates and back into the wild. Some of Pat's men even rode a couple of the horses bareback out onto the reservation. "When I came here," Pat said, "I knew I loved horses, but these horses didn't know that they'd like people, and that is a fabulous feeling looking at them right now."

Carlos had arrived and helped the vet, but by this time he was feeling so sidelined that he didn't want to interact with Pat at all. It was childlike, so I talked to him about it, assuring Carlos that this was still his project and it wouldn't have happened without him. He finally agreed to one last scene and walked out with Pat as the herd returned to the wild. But after that, Carlos was done. If you ever see the final sunset-silhouette shot, it's not Carlos up there on the ridge by Pat but the closest Carlos look-alike we could find.

We'd jumped almost all the hurdles with just one to go: the blood test. Now it was all about the genetics and it'd be six weeks before we'd learn from Gus in Kentucky if these little horses were descendants of the original Spanish mustangs.

We headed for home, exhausted from three extremely busy days with a total of only nine or ten hours sleep. Back at the hotel I counted up the film rolls then counted again. Something didn't seem right. We only had twenty-two rolls of film, which amounted to less than four hours. To put that in context, for a half-hour film, it would not be unusual to come back with forty or fifty vital hours of tape. Either something was missing or West had just managed the most incredible shoot ratio National Geographic had ever seen. Thankfully, it was the latter.

We shot another roll doing a conquistador reenactment and started putting it all together. The only shots not usable were the ones where our photographer had jumped in the way - everything else was art. We had ample footage to work with and even dropped a scene or two. Despite all that good news, this story represented the last of the film days. As far as I know, this was the final television documentary from Nat Geo that was shot a hundred percent on sixteen-millimeter film.

I wanted someone special to narrate, someone who loved horses and who could tell a story with passion. The head of our post-production department told me that the former captain of the Star Trek Enterprise loved horses. Patrick Stewart was doing a show on Broadway and I contacted his agent. Stewart has a wonderfully rich voice, British, but with a richness that would allow Americans to oversee this shortcoming of heritage. The message came back: "Patrick would love to do it, but he's not really into horses." Turns out, much to my embarrassment, I had the wrong Star Trek star; William Shatner, the original Enterprise captain, is the horse fanatic. I listened to Mr. Shatner's voice more carefully and, although not as commanding as Patrick Stewart's, it was, I felt, an even better match for this very American film that we (mostly Aussies) had created.

Captain Kirk agreed. We called the film "America's Lost Mustangs" and I flew to California for the recording session. When Mr. Shatner started to read the script it was slow, like a man drowning in treacle, the kind of pace that Geo documentaries had in the sixties - possibly the last time Mr. Shatner had seen one. One of my supervising producers, Jon Goodman, had been listening in and I took him off speakerphone.

"Crap," I said, "this ain't working. What do I do?"

Jon's advice was simple: "He's an actor; give him direction. He wants you to get in the ring and box with him." With that, Jon said goodbye and hung up.

I rubbed the stardust from my eyes and started to box. Jon's call was spot on. It was a thrill to tell Captain Kirk what I wanted, then hear it come from his mouth, and with a bit of back and forth I got the exact read I wanted.

When we were done we went back to Mr. Shatner's stable to film an on-camera introduction to the show. He must have liked, or at least respected our boxing, because afterward he took me for a ride on his highly trained reining horses. The slightest move of my leg or my arm and the horse he'd given me would start spinning in circles like an equine gyroscope; this horse was a much better ride than I am a rider. William Shatner, as it turns out, I could direct, but this thing was way out of my league.

When we finally got the news from our genetics expert, the results were good. There was enough of the original mustang lineage in these horses to make them worth protecting and breeding. We could go with our happy ending. My boss, Earl Grey, was so happy with the film that he bestowed a rare honour: a catered party at his home to watch the Sunday-night premiere broadcast on Explorer.

At the Exotic Booze Club the following Friday, I cracked open a celebratory bottle of Wild Turkey, one direct from the distillery that I'd saved for precisely this occasion. Toward the end of the evening, Earl Grey dropped by with a piece of paper that I recognized as the printout of our ratings. I poured myself another shot. There is one reason we put so much into our films and take such risks: because if we do well, we get to do it again. Like it or not, the figures in Earl's hand were my scorecard. Earl went out on a limb for me on this project and a low score could be really bad news.

"Now, Brian," he said, "this horse film."

"Yes."

"I have the ratings here."

"Yes."

"You should know, it did very well for us."

"Really?"

"I may be understating it. It did *very* well for us. Do you have any more like it?"

He seemed to have totally forgotten what it took for me to get the initial green light for *America's Lost Mustangs*, but I was okay with that. The party and the ratings were the ultimate compliments.

I didn't have any more shows like it, but I did have an idea. We shot another ten minutes of Pat demonstrating his methods on a domestic horse, dug up the left-out scenes, and extended the half-hour show into an hour for our home video department. That too sold very well.

During the mustang shoot I had been a little concerned about supplies for the Club. Although I was thrilled to get to the Wild Turkey distillery, it didn't really qualify as an exotic alcohol. I need not have worried though bottles poured in as Geo's field teams returned from their global assignments. Other producers and cameramen had embraced the exotic alcohol mission with fervor.

Some of the actual bottles were as intriguing as their contents. Rather than throw out the empties, I came in one weekend and quietly erected a 14-foot long shelf, high up on my wall, for our spent trophies. Only one bottle never made it there because, no matter how much we drank, it was always full of Georgia moonshine. It seemed to many that this vessel had magical powers, not only because it was always full, but also one editor swore her eyesight improved with every drop.

I kept our moonshine provider secret at the time, but I can now reveal the source. One of Geographic's contract office cleaners used to stop by before our Friday meetings; I'd shut the door behind him and let him try whatever we had on offer. In return, he'd pull out a gallon jug from the bottom of his cleaning trolley and top up our moonshine bottle with his uncle's homemade brew. It was great stuff.

From a few shoots in South Africa came a Kalahari liqueur made from local herbs and bulbs that was served in a gourd. Also from South Africa came a bottle of Amarula, a creamy liqueur made from a bean that reportedly causes psychotic episodes in elephants. Every country seemed to have a drink with supposed aphrodisiac qualities and often these concoctions, especially those from South America, had traditional uses in rituals and ceremonies. Around all these bottles and our meetings a sense of global community emerged.

I brought back bottles from my other shoots, too, everywhere from Paris to Panama, Sicily to Singapore. We learned to pace any stockpile so there was always something new to sample, because you never could tell when a shoot would take you to one of those tragic places where you'd really be in danger. I'm not talking about jaws, claws and fangs now; I'm talking about real peril: counties and even entire countries that are sober.

Chapter 5

INTO THE TORNADO:
Don Julio Tequila

I headed out on the worst kind of shoot for the Club: one that was Stateside and did not include Bourbon County. I'd be spending four weeks chasing twisters in a stretch of middle America known as "Tornado Alley". Hence, I faced a great double challenge: find and film a tornado, *and* find an exotic alcohol worthy of the Club.

Our headquarters would be Boulder, Colorado; no tornados in mountainous Boulder, but plenty for us to film on the plains directly to the east. And, more significantly, Boulder was the base for our collaborating scientists from the National Severe Storms Laboratory or, as I renamed it, the National Storms Laboratory for the Severely Afflicted.

If my alternative sounds strange then you probably don't realize that storm chasing is an addiction, and this laboratory is like a bad-weather Betty Ford clinic for the worst reprobates: people who manage to turn their addiction into a career. Only thing was, no one was looking for a cure. The mission was to get under the weather and stay there. We planned to piggyback on the work of these poor obsessed souls as they combed the country for tornados to study.

We rocked up to our rented pad in Boulder and settled in. Where possible on long shoots, I prefer to rent a house rather than hotel rooms. The price usually works out around the same but there's more room to spread out the gear and charge batteries. Meals and cocktails can be made at home both more cheaply and healthily, and it keeps the crew together and bonded. It also makes departure times more certain.

Rich Scholtz, our main cameraman, lived in Denver and had a strong background in news. The latter meant he'd be fast, which was crucial on this kind of shoot. He's also blessed with a patient, easygoing nature that would be a plus on the long tornado-searching drives we anticipated.

Shady completed our film crew. If he could weather the camel shoot, he should be able to weather this one. He was now on staff as a coordinating producer and he'd long been a great shooter in his own right, another much-needed skill for the mission before us. I felt lucky to have him on board.

This shoot was another collaboration with Nat Geo magazine. The primary assignment was to take the first photos and footage taken from *inside* a tornado. Many had tried before and failed. Few daredevil photographers would volunteer for such a risky mission, but one relished the task: Carsten Peter from our Russian adventure. The magazine assigned the Coca-Cola-loving German and he was happy to give his much-loved volcanoes a rest to pursue a whirling phenomenon instead.

Carsten was teamed up with Tim Samaras, an engineer and master storm chaser. Tim had fitted out his van to the max. He set up wireless links to live weather reports and radar, and mounted cameras on rigid monopods, which he could point toward an imminent twister at a moment's notice while continuing to drive. Tim is an educated and articulate self-confessed weather geek with a passion for severe storms. He often travels solo, but for this mission he agreed to join us and the team from the Severe Storms Laboratory.

Our first call was to meet Dr. Erik Rasmussen, a legendary addict who started chasing storms as soon as he got his driver's licence. But this time Erik would be chasing from the chair of his home office. He'd look at radar and satellite images and a mountain of the latest weather data and, from the comfort and safety of home, he'd guide us via mobile phone into the path of some of nature's most fearsome forces.

Erik looked to be in his late forties, but with the grooming and fashion sense of a distracted child. His bowl haircut portrayed the image of an endearing but single-minded mad scientist. I checked that his shirt buttons all lined up with the right holes and we got some shots of Erik in his office. Then we got more outside as he jumped up to work on a storm-chasing car, wearing cut-off denim shorts and sandals over his pulled-up white knee socks. We also set up a small camera by his computer so Erik could roll video on himself while communicating with the field team. Most of our filming was going to be with Erik's road crew and meeting them was next on the agenda.

We arrived at the Severe Storms Lab base in Boulder to find the addicts preparing their mobile weather stations, two hail-dented sedans with an array of apparatus on top. The instruments gave an impression that the cars were wearing novelty hats, the goofy pyramid kind with windmills whirling. The objective was to drive these roving laboratories back and forth near the storm so the instruments could collect atmospheric data. They hoped that this kind of research would lead to a better understanding of why tornados form and allow forecasters to give communities more warning of when one is about to strike.

No sooner had we rolled up than the project coordinator for the scientists, Anton Seimon, raced out to where some of the crewmembers were working on the cars. A storm was brewing and he was in a bit of a flap. Tornado chasing is pretty much confined to five months, from March through to July, so time is precious.

"What's the status of the vehicles?" he asked, wanting to leave immediately.

Anton's question was directed to the man who calls the shots in the field, Al Pietrycha, known to his fellow addicts as "Al Nado". This boss man looked too tall to be crammed into a sedan for hours on end and carried an I'm-too-cool-for-the-camera air about him, often grimacing awkwardly when speaking with us. I got the impression that it wasn't his idea to have TV cameras along and he wasn't too happy about it; perhaps that's why he also seemed unimpressed by Anton's awkward sense of urgency.

The cars were ready enough, though, so there was no excuse not to go. Off we raced on our first attempt to actively find and jump in front of a funnel of death. Our convoy headed to Lamar, Colorado, about 200 miles away. The storm that looked promising on radar had produced a "supercell", a thundercloud with a large area of rotating air called a mesocyclone. Supercells can be twenty miles across and twice as high as Mt Everest. Only one in a thousand thunderstorms creates a supercell, and about twenty percent of these spawn tornados.

Lamar is on the western edge of Tornado Alley, the loosely defined area of about ten central prairie states in a strip between Canada's cold mountains and Mexico's warm gulf. Streams of air from these very different regions meet and mingle in the middle to spawn the supercells and, hence, twisters. Tornados occur all over the world, but nowhere more than the United States, which produces around a thousand every year. About half of those touch down in the alley.

This was a crash course in tornados. I was learning fast, but I didn't like everything I heard. It so happens that almost all tornados occur within an hour or two either side of sunset. When news of a supercell forming way over the horizon comes in, if you can reach that destination a couple of hours before dusk you may get lucky enough to film it. The truly tragic news is that this timing clashes with every cocktail and happy hour known to man. I'd only been on this shoot for a day but already I didn't like it. I should have done more homework - or at least brought a cooler.

Carsten was far more on the ball. Not only did he have a cooler full of Coke, he'd spent months developing a device to help him capture the first-ever images from inside a tornado. To construct this apparatus he had to descend deep into the bowels of Nat Geo headquarters and seek help in the shadowy, secretive realm of the "Wizards," a consortium of rarely seen creatures that inhabit closeted, windowless rooms behind secure metal doors. Hunched over giant metal workbenches and surrounded by precision instruments and strange-looking leftovers from their previous travails, the Wizards are photographic engineers.

These masters of machinery conceive and concoct devices that traverse land, sea and water to snap unique images of nature and wildlife. Think 007's master inventor Q, only with even less humor. When you ask the Wizards to use their creative powers to assist you with an assignment, their collective answer is always the same: you tell them what you need, they hover over plans and calendars for a while mumbling something about "bubble, bubble, toil and trouble", and then one of them will emerge to pronounce,

"There's not enough time." Sometimes they'll even skip the Shakespeare and go directly to telling you that the deadline you've given them is impossible to meet. Then they promptly set about meeting it anyway.

For Carsten, the Wizards created a solid 95-pound metal device about the size of a large kitchen sink and resembling a small stealth bomber. Borrowing from another tornado-related wizard, the Wizard of Oz, they called this device the "Tin Man". Tin Man held two still cameras and three video cameras, which aimed out at different angles through tiny windows. With a push of a button they would all start recording the still cameras snapping photographs at regular intervals hopefully as a tornado swept over them. The senior Nat Geo Wiz put the hopes for a successful deployment in perspective: "On one hand you laugh to yourself and say, This is not going to work, but hopefully, you know, in the process, we get an image. We just need one, and a few seconds of tape. Ten seconds flying around inside a tornado on tape could be pretty hot stuff."

The Exotic Booze Club

Putting this photographic gizmo in the path of an oncoming twister was Tim and Carsten's job. Tim also had several disc-like shells to put out, which were called turtles; they had no cameras but were crammed with scientific measuring instruments. He laid out the plan for me with a glint of childlike excitement in his eyes: "You have to drive into the path of the tornado, you have to wait there for a period of time so you know you are right on the money, and at the last possible moment, you make the decision to go ahead and deploy."

This was akin to playing chicken with a freight train - only more dangerous. A train sticks to the tracks; tornados change direction like, well, like the wind. Tim and Carsten may get as close as a hundred yards from an oncoming tornado before dropping the Tin Man and turtles and making a run for it. At that range, fast-flying debris could quickly end their dash for safety. Carsten's only protection was a bicycle helmet; how ironic, I thought, if he used it to headbutt a flying bike.

After nearly four hours of driving we reached the plains near Lamar where our storm was brewing. Where we stopped we had a clear view to the distant horizon, and what we saw was spectacular: not a tornado, but an enormous cold-weather front.

We often use time-lapse cameras to speed up cloud movement but there was no need here. We watched this cold front scream in at an estimated 75 to 90 miles an hour. There was no mingling with the warm air from Mexico - this chilled air forced out the warm with an almighty shove and swamped us like ducks in a deluge. The weather was now way too cold to produce a tornado, and if this impressive front turned out to be too big, our operation could be shut down for some time.

We turned for home through torrential rain and hail. It was well into the night when we finally pulled back in to Boulder. This was the end of June, the beginning of summer, hence our surprise when we woke the next day to find deep snow covering the ground. It was a freak occurrence that no one could ever have predicted. Tornado Alley was now Snowball Lane and the front that caused it was continuing to Mexico, which meant no hope of any twisters for at least a week.

Suddenly we had downtime on our hands and I immediately began searching Boulder for any exotic or boutique booze for the Club. I was out of luck. Boulder is, however, the home of Celestial Seasonings tea, so I grabbed a box for Earl Grey.

We decided to take Carsten on a drive to Hoisington, Kansas so we could film him photographing some tornado damage that would be good background for our stories. Just a few weeks before we started chasing, a man had been killed in Hoisington and hundreds were left homeless after the town was hit by an F3 tornado.

Experts measure the severity of a tornado using the Fujita or F-scale, and now the Enhanced Fujita scale. The scale effectively runs from F0, a modest twistette, to F5, a raging mega twister with winds around 300 miles an hour and possibly gusts faster than the speed of sound. The original system, developed at the National Severe Storms Forecast Center in 1971, is largely calculated with a complicated engineering-based assessment of the damage left in a tornado's wake.

To keep things simpler, you can also use my very own personalized alternative. It's easier to work out and remember and, perhaps best of all, you can calculate the rating before the damage is caused. It's called the expletive scale; storms are rated by the number and quality of the expletives evoked in confronting it. An F1, for example, would be greeted with "Oh, fuck, let's get out of here." An F2 would be a louder and more urgent "Oh, fuck, fuck, let's get out of here now." And so on for F3 and F4. An F5 is just one big, loud expletive, stuck for a while in the middle like a scratched record - "OH, FUUUUUUUUUUUCK!" - and is followed by something matter-of-fact and obvious, such as your untimely death. Some people have lived through a face-off with an F5, but most only have time for the expletive and then it's lights out. I admit this is not terribly scientific but I wouldn't be surprised if it's what Mr. Fujita had in mind all along.

The poor folks in Hoisington had been doing a lot of F3 swearing; the devastation was jaw-dropping. A giant swathe through the middle of town barely left a house standing. A few trees were still upright, but none of them had any leaves. We entered the wreckage of a home that had no roof and only a few remaining walls. A large caravan had tumbled down the street and landed on its side not far from the front door. Carsten wandered around this unsalvageable shell taking pictures. It was a sobering moment for us all.

You always hear about the destructive power of tornados, but standing in the wake of a killer twister suddenly throws it all in perspective. As Carsten put it, "The powers of these tornados are unimaginable . . . I see it now from a different angle. To place [Tin Man] into the tornado, might be a very, very difficult approach."

Carsten thought hard about the safest way to get his Tin Man into an oncoming twister, and we thought hard about the best way to film it. The Lamar storm that produced the snow had been a good dry run for us - a very wet dry run, but a good chance to see how things would work when we got a real tornado.

We drove well in convoy, and when close to the action the scientists would stop briefly to get out and look at cloud structure. That would be our chance to enhance our coverage. When we hit that interval, Rich would jump in with Carsten and Tim, Shady would jump in with Al Nado, and I'd continue to drive our car and look for alternative angles.

After a week of sipping Celestial Seasonings in Boulder we finally had our chance to try our system and charged off through Oklahoma to Texas where, finally, a promising supercell was developing. Problem was, everyone seemed to know it.

These are the states most popular with amateur storm chasers and thrillseekers. There are even tour groups in Texas that take paid customers out to tornado spot. The addiction seems to be contagious. As a result, hitting Texas meant hitting traffic, as hundreds of cars and minivans patrolled the dirt backroads for a good vantage point of a supercell. Al Nado was antagonistic toward some of these "idiot amateurs," but there was nothing to be done about it. I had a brief vision of all these tornado tourists getting together in one big room of shame: "Hello, my name is Bob. It's been three months since my last twister."

One thing we had that most others didn't was a driving need to get into the heart of the storm. We paused by the road and Shady and Rich took up their respective positions in the other vehicles. Our group separated from the crowd and we drove in under the supercell. Huge dust clouds formed ahead - a good sign that a monster storm was in the making - and soon we were in rain and hail. The two laboratory cars started driving back and forth around the storm to collect atmospheric data, while Tim went to the front right of the cloud formation, where tornados concentrate.

Every now and then one of the chasers would get out and start talking storm-speak: "Wow, look at the TCU." "There's a great hook on radar." "It's really wrapping up." "RFD is starting to rap in here." "Tornado genesis is imminent." "Strong rotation backing here, the cyclonic couplets right in here, and there, anti-cyclonic, classic mesocyclone set-up." It was largely gibberish to us at that stage, but now and then something would stand out, such as, "Let's get in the car before we re struck by lightning." That made sense.

There were two pre-tornado storm hazards to watch for in particular. One was the dirt roads we'd likely have to traverse to get into the path of an oncoming tornado. Once these roads were wet, it'd be easy to get bogged, not a good position to be in with a twister barrelling down on your tail.

The other warning concerned lightning. No one actually told us about this, but we noticed that our scientists would often hop out of their cars and stand on one leg in a flamingo-like posture. When I eventually asked what was going on, we learned that this was an anti-lightning technique. It would not protect you against a direct strike, but if the lightning hit the ground nearby the electricity would bypass you. Otherwise it would shoot up one leg and down the other - presumably frying everything in between. Being rather fond of everything in between, we quickly adopted this curious habit.

We were more prepared than ever, but it was another, very wet, dry run. No tornado. Tim wasn't fazed. It was now dark, but he wanted to keep going to see what the storm did. It sounded truly obsessive, but upon following him we saw firsthand the awesome power of even a non-tornado-producing supercell. Mammoth hail covered the road, and we were treated to a lightning show to rival the best fireworks display. Bolts of white cracked above us like giant fingers stretching across the sky. I have never, before or since, seen such an exhibition.

Eventually we all rolled into a cheap Super 8 motel in the middle of Nowheresville, Kansas. It was late, we'd driven nonstop all day and every food place was closed, so we crashed without dinner. The next day, thanks to the super-thin Super 8 walls, I heard the scientists outside getting ready to go early. I immediately went out.

"Hey," said Al Nado as I approached. "Looks good up near South Dakota. We're heading out. You guys will have to catch up."

"South Dakota? The state?"

"Yeah, if we re quick we'll be there in time."

I woke the others and we scrambled. A quick look at the map revealed that we had just over 500 miles to cover before unhappy hour. Al Nado was stopping for no one, and his driver was sitting on 75 miles an hour. We had no hope of catching them, but in any event it was another bust. We met them, late again, at another Super 8.

I'd learned my mistake, and this time *before* going to bed I asked, "Al, how's it look for tomorrow?"

"Maybe back down to Nebraska."

"Where we just came through?"

"Yep. Could even be Kansas again."

Sure enough, the next day we zoomed off on our back-track, only stopping to refuel and grab some junk food at a couple of truck stops. Our exclusive diet of corn chips and beef jerky was getting old fast. Rich took an extra minute to get an ice-cream and it cost us dearly. Although

Al Nado only accelerated away a minute ahead of us, his driver was going so fast that it took us nearly two hours to catch up; we had to be more on the ball or a twister would happen without us. We vowed to treat our future roadhouse pauses like Indy 500 pit stops.

Again, Kansas was a bust. "And tomorrow?" I asked fearfully, standing in yet another Super 8 parking lot in featureless Flatasatacksville.

"Tomorrow," said Al Nado, "looks good for Oklahoma and Texas."

And on it went. We drove endless hours to another non-tornado, stopping for nothing but gas, a speedy resupply of junk food and Carsten's Coke. No time for cocktails and no sign of any exotic alcohol. This shoot was getting desperate.

Each time we had to shoot set-ups, just in case we got a twister. At one point we got creative and used a high-powered suction cup to attach a small camera to the hood of Al Nado's car. We set it rolling as he drove off, but because he stopped for nothing and no one, our next chance to retrieve it was after he'd ventured through torrential rain.

On this run we'd ended up on the wrong side of a supercell, where powerlines and trees already littered the road and water rose above our hubcaps. This is the side where debris makes your top speed around walking pace and the storm easily outruns you. We did get some good footage from our little hoodcam before the water totally destroyed the camera. After that, we chose to mount similar cameras on Al Nado's dash, safely *inside* the car.

Now and then the weather gods would drive us closer to Boulder and we could actually use our rental house. There we picked up some food of a more edible nature and DVDs to watch in the car. Yeah, yeah, I know it's not safe to drive while watching a movie, but we only chose films with little action and no sex scenes, lessening the risk of distraction.

While we picked up supplies for our next multi-state outing, Al Nado collected his girlfriend; she had to ride in another car, but could at least keep him warm at night. Then we learned that Al Nado's driver was his former girlfriend. As we drove the length and breadth of Tornado Alley, we who were otherwise bored senseless found this scenario endlessly amusing.

At the next twister-tourist hot spot, some expensive-looking black four-wheel drives zoomed by with fancy gadgets attached to their extremities. It was a rival research group with a far more polished look.

"Yes," Al Nado spat, "they got corporate funding."

Back in the car, a bolt of figurative lightning hit Shady.

"Oh my God" he said. "We're in the movie Twister."

INTO THE TORNADO: Don Julio Tequila

We rented the DVD next chance we had and Shady was right. This was the 1996 Hollywood blockbuster where a scientist travels around with his soon to be ex-wife, while attempting to keep the new girlfriend happy - all the while despising the corporate-funded enemy and trying to get information from within a tornado. There was also the potential for these silver-screen similarities to go way beyond the personal dramas within it.

When the movie *Twister* came out, it was the laughing stock of the storm-chasing community. Special-effect wizardry had livestock and large vehicles flying through the air, scenes that were well beyond the suspension of disbelief for even the most fanciful of addicts. Then came a day when everyone stopped laughing. That day was May 3rd 1999, when some 140 twisters broke out across a large area centred on Oklahoma City. Included in these was the most powerful F5 tornado ever recorded, with all the destructive power Hollywood had dreamed up - vehicles and livestock *did* fly through the air. Not even words from the expletive scale could adequately describe the carnage. In the wash-up, thirty-six people were dead and nearly10,000 homes were badly damaged or destroyed.

Despite our knowledge of this disaster, as we continued our Midwest tour of Super 8 motels we began to crave such a dangerous twister encounter in a disturbingly lustful and salivating kind of way. We dreamed of a glorious face-to-face meeting with a magnificent force - maybe not 140 twisters, but at least one. Pretty please.

Sometimes we drove past the beginnings of a tornado as it dropped from a cloud and we'd shout at it to form right beside us. We could imagine ourselves outside the car, filming the formation of a beautiful, awe-inspiring funnel and jumping for joy on one leg as it barrelled over us. Perhaps all this time in our car was driving us stir-crazy but, in short, we were joining the ranks of the addicted.

We began to use the jargon as we gazed wide-eyed at the TCU (towering cumulus), cursed the HP (high precipitation) and scanned the skies for cyclonic couplets and the RFD (Rear Flank Downdraft). Even these non-tornado wonders would have made dramatic shots, but now no one was stopping for anything short of a twister. "Average shooting speed," Carsten joked, "between sixty and eighty miles [per hour]."

It got more and more crazy and dangerous. We finally came extremely close to two remote tornados in Oklahoma, but they'd formed on the wrong side of sunset and it was pitch-black outside. The crazy bit was we gave chase anyway. This was insanity. We could have blindly and happily driven directly into one of these funnels without even the benefit of enough light to shoot it. "But it looks good in Wyoming tomorrow".

After two and a half weeks of this we'd clocked up an incredible 15,000 miles, and still no joy. There were dozens of tornados out there, but we always seemed to be where they weren't. I'm sure predicting these things is extremely difficult, and we didn't want to say anything, but it was hard not to question our experts. Tim, the addict helping Carsten, regularly wanted to go in what would turn out to be the correct direction. But he was obliged to obediently follow our team leaders, as were we.

We slowly realized, driving state-to-state, that this section of America all looks the same. I'm sure there are subtle differences between states, but for us, the flat landscape, the crops, the simple architecture, the culture, the pit-stop food and even the tornado-attracting trailer parks all looked identical. We were just thinking it may as well be all one big state when we finally made it to the one exception: New Mexico.

We chased another non-tornado into New Mexico and felt like we were in paradise. The relief from the usual was extraordinary. The buildings were unique and handsome, the plants and landscape different, and it was the first variety in food we'd had since leaving Boulder. Adding to our joy, the forecast for the next day was for a supercell in nearby Texas, so we could actually sit down and enjoy a real meal at a Mexican restaurant. The quesadillas were fresh and never tasted so good. And then I saw it, like a vision in a dream, shimmering on a shelf behind the bar. It was a bottle of Don Julio tequila. After all we'd been through, Don Julio counted as exotic.

Tequila has a rich history in this part of the world. When the Spanish conquistadors first settled in Mexico, they soon ran out of their own brandy. The local Aztecs had long been fermenting the juice from agave hearts to make a beverage called octli, but it didn't have much of a kick. The Spaniards began to distil the agave and thus produced tequila. New Mexico was likely the first place in the United States where it crossed the border.

After we'd bloated ourselves on food, I purchased two bottles of Don Julio plus some shot glasses and jumped into the passenger seat. Rich drove while I lovingly admired the bottles and enjoyed the delay of my gratification. It was the only time in more than 15,000 miles that I didn't sit behind the wheel. Once we reached the luxurious surrounds of our new Super 8 parking lot, I poured us all shots and we toasted our new and more fickle love: To twisters. We'd earned a drink.

The next day was a bust, and the next. Then we zoomed back up to South Dakota and *finally* got a glimpse of our first daylight tornado. Al Nado stood on the roof of his car and cheered at the hint of a large grey funnel off in the distance.

He was perhaps overly excited, given that this monster was at least twenty miles away and impossible to get to. Even for us newly addicted it was the methadone of fixes: somewhat satiating, but not like an up-close experience with the real thing. And certainly not much in it for TV.

We were running out of time. Tornado Alley is generally considered to be ten states and we'd already chased storms in eleven, finally winding up with yet another bust in Iowa. Al Nado told us there was nothing happening anywhere the next day, so we may as well head back to Boulder - only nine hours drive away. It was good timing as Carsten was due to be on a plane the next morning.

We'd finished the storm with Tim's van and our crew car separated from the scientists and had slowly started making our way home. After a few hundred miles, the scientists still hadn't caught up. It was odd, so when we got near enough to a cellphone tower I gave Al Nado a call.

"Hey, where are you?"

"We decided to crash here in Iowa."

"Oh, you said you were on our tail."

"Yeah. We decided to stay."

After our early education, we'd been sticking to our guys like glue. For better or worse, we'd followed them to all ends of Tornado Alley and beyond. I internalized my disappointment that Al Nado had not told me his new plan.

"What about tomorrow?" I asked.

"No, we just checked all the data. There's nothing anywhere."

"Are you a hundred percent sure?"

"Positive. I spoke to Erik."

I pushed it even further. "So there's absolutely no chance you'll be chasing tomorrow?"

"Not a chance. You're totally safe to go back to Boulder. We'll see you there tomorrow."

Al was so positive that I knew for certain we were screwed.

My stomach churned like it was doing somersaults. The rule of Last-Day Payoff was beating in my head: you *always* get the goods on the last day. And tomorrow was, for us, the second-last day - close enough. We immediately found the nearest not-Super 8 hotel and pulled over. Rich and Shady agreed. Al Nado and Erik had pretty much called it wrong every day for nearly three weeks - why would we start trusting them now? Tim decided to continue on to get Carsten closer to his flight, but we stayed. We even talked about driving back to Iowa but that was now several hours behind us, so we just stayed put in Nebraska and would call Al Nado in the morning, or even let them catch up to us and take it from there.

The next day I tried Al Nado early but couldn't raise him. It'd been a rough few weeks and I'm sure very stressful for him; maybe he was sleeping in. I continued to call but no answer. Cell service was pretty sketchy in some of these areas, but I wasn't moving until I heard from him. About ten o clock, I got through to Erik at Boulder headquarters.

"Hey," he said, "we've got a big supercell developing in Minnesota, near the Wisconsin border. Al's on the way there now. Where are you?"

"But . . . what . . . where?"

The storm was way to our north, about six hours drive away. We charged up there and late afternoon I eventually got Al Nado on the phone. He spoke quickly and he said little more than, "Hey, it's on my tail. Gotta go." He hung up without further explanation or apology.

We arrived on the wrong side of the storm. For us it was a bust. But on the other side, the Severe Storm Laboratory cars were in the thick of it. A large twister had formed and turned and was now essentially chasing them. With debris all over the road, they could only go so fast, and the tornado was going faster. They were no longer worried about performing transects; they were consumed with trying to escape unscathed. With little time to spare, they cleared the storm area and zoomed off. The tornado faded away behind them, a close and dramatic call.

I fumed. It was exactly the kind of payoff we needed to salvage the film and we'd missed it. But before I could get too upset, we learned that others had lost much more than a TV show. In the town of Dewy, houses were destroyed and the twister had killed three people. This was a serious business.

We found Al Nado and, without stopping to talk, formed a solemn procession back to Colorado. This time we all headed back because, as it turned out, the word from the lab team on our last day of filming was that "it looks good in Colorado".

We got Rich back to Denver in time for him to pick up the brand-new super-sized four-wheel drive he'd ordered, but before we could stretch out our legs in his giant beast of a car he corrected our aspirations. He parked it at a gas station and we again crawled into our rental; the seats now seemed to mould around our bodies. In the unlikely event we met a twister on our last day, Rich wasn't going to risk his new car.

We finally met up with Al Nado and his team on the road as the forecasted Colorado supercell began to form. Al Nado was unapologetic for his miscalculation and lack of communication, I can only presume out of embarrassment, or perhaps his apparent disdain for television. We interviewed him about the storm in Dewy and he described it as a life-changing experience; it was his first up-close encounter with a twister that had actually caused death.

"After what I saw and witnessed up there," he said with his tight-lipped grimace, "the indescribable damage as it was occurring, there's no doubt in my mind I won't look at [tornados] the way I did before."

We retrieved the cameras and tapes we had mounted on their dashboards for the past two weeks and followed them into one last storm. We chased the supercell around for two hours. It was a good one, lots of hail and lightning, but no tornado, and after dark we headed for home. We lamented about our four-week folly and declared ourselves officially unaddicted.

Having run out of DVDs to watch, we turned on the radio for the trip back. Amid the usual tornado updates was news that the storm had produced giant hailstones over two inches wide. The reports became background noise as we continued chatting about Shady's aching back and if there was still enough tequila left for the Club. Rich piped up with a jolt. "What was that?"

"Tequila?" I asked, "I was just . . ."

"Turn up the radio. Quick."

I upped the dial and a reporter announced that the Red Cross had set up a field station and was treating people injured by hail at Watkins truck stop, about twenty miles east of Denver. Dozens of cars had been damaged. Rich let go an F1 on the expletive scale. That was the exact location where he'd parked his brand-new four-wheel drive.

Rich continued to groan for the hour or more it took us to get to the truck stop. When we arrived, his groaning was not only justified, it was proven to be a severely understated preemptive reaction. He upped his rating to a very repetitive F3.

On the ground, we could still see hailstones well over two inches wide. Rich's car looked like five sumos had taken to it with sledgehammers. The front window and side windows were smashed and there was not a panel unscathed. Even the bumper bar was thoroughly pockmarked.

Poor Rich wandered around in a fog, finally taking some deep breaths to call his wife. I pulled out the camera to film the scene. It was ugly.

"To just be in the exact spot where all this damage happens," he said on the phone, "is one in a million."

Coincidentally, that seemed to be about the same chance I had of making a story out of this entire mess. We had lots of incredible footage of supercells, storm damage and the general wrath of nature, but no decent tornado. And this time I knew no one would be interested in a beyond-the-tornado show. We didn't have enough of a payoff to sustain it.

I was still a bit dazed when I got back to Geo headquarters. I saw Earl Grey walking by, handed him his Celestial Seasonings tea and broke the news that we didn't have a story. My first bust. He took it well and understood. It was always a gamble, and at least he had his tea.

As I recounted our tales of woe at the Club, I became more and more indignant about what had happened. With the twister in Dewy, our story had a grand finale, we just hadn't been there to record it - or had we? I popped in the tapes from the camera that we'd mounted on the dashboard of Al Nado's car. To my joy, I found that Al Nado had the presence of mind to turn the camera on at the start of the storm. He'd recorded the whole drama on tape and had even jumped out to squeeze off some shots of the actual twister - after which he scrambled back into the car in a panic and can be heard shouting "Go!" to his ex-girlfriend. It was exciting stuff and I called my boss.

"Hey," I said, "I take it back. I think we can make this work."

The show came together pretty well. We shot an iceskater doing pirouettes to demonstrate how tornados work. When a spinning skater pulls in her arms she spins faster: that's the way a tornado works as its circling winds draw in closer. It was a well-liked device. On a tape Shady had recorded, Al Nado had given us another gem: "If you want to dance with the devil," he said, racing off to a storm, "you have to get to the party." We took the devil analogy and milked it in the script. We also created a fiddle-filled, Devil-Went-Down-To-Georgia kind of soundtrack to match.

I'm not sure I'd ever do a twister story again, but Rich went out the next season for more chasing, and Carsten's addiction was even harder to shake. After several more years of trying, he and Tim finally made a successful deployment of the Tin Man. An F3 twister sent it flying though some fields in Iowa and it went missing in action for nearly a week. They ordered wanted posters to help find it and eventually retrieved Tin Man from a hayfield. From inside they recovered incredible still shots of life inside a tornado, plus a significant amount of data from the instruments inside Tim's turtles.

Even after that deployment Carsten continued to chase storms with Tim for many seasons. It was just lucky for Carsten that he was not with Tim on May 31st, 2013, for a storm in El Reno, Oklahoma – the chase that was to be Tim's last. Tim, his 24-year-old son Paul, and another seasoned chaser, Carl Young, found themselves in the path of a powerful and erratic two-point-six-mile wide tornado. It sucked Paul and Carl out of the vehicle as it lifted the car from the ground. Tim remained strapped in the driver's seat as the twister tore out the vehicle's engine and sent three of its wheels flying in all diretions. Another chaser's video, analysed later, appears to show their white Chevy Cobalt in the distance falling from the sky. This display of nature's incredible power resulted in an unthinkable tragedy that shook us all – especially Carsten. Twenty-two people were killed by that El Reno twister, including Tim and his two companions.

Previous to his death, Tim had become a lead character in Storm Chasers, a popular Discovery series, but his first real foray into TV was with us and our own devlish brush with nature; Into the Tornado.

By the time our show went to air, the Club was out of Don Julio, so we toasted the turtles with a unique and surprisingly popular beverage. About fifteen people crammed into my office to try absinthe. This is what Van Gogh was drinking when he cut off his ear. It's a bitter wormwood-based green potion with a name from the Greek *apsinthion*. To work around the bitterness you heat it on a spoon with some sugar before swilling.

Absinthe was banned in the US for decades and is still hard to obtain, but Nancy Donnelly had managed to get her hands on some from Czechoslovakia. Club members downed the entire bottle in a night. Like any work-based social gathering, the Club was also a good place to pick up rumors and internal goings on. It was right around this time I heard one such rumor that didn't sit well.

A very reliable source told me that someone in human resources had learned of the Club and was raising questions. Even though Earl Grey had given the EBC a thumbs up, he did not officially have the authority to grant permission. It was still very much against Geographic policy to allow alcohol in an office and I knew this high-level HR murmuring presented a serious threat.

The Club had quickly become a part of our filmmaking culture and experience. It had taken on a life of its own, and when I was away others would step in to open the bar. Losing the Club would mean losing this bonding experience and, more importantly, losing the wealth of stories.

The Club was also delightfully irreverent, and on some level that allowed me to still feel Australian. I hadn't lived at home for four years, and while I loved the opportunities I was finding in America, I was always the square peg not quite fitting into the round hole: I had little tolerance for red tape and time-wasting bureaucracy; I held no particular veneration for executive positions and tended to look out for my staff more than my boss; I usually couldn't speak in my normal accent and be understood; and unlike most of those around me, I didn't go to university or hold a degree. Geo's summer interns, forking out tens of thousands of dollars for an education, hated hearing that. I had been lucky enough to get fully paid on-the-job training as a news cadet and I had worked my way up from there. The EBC was the one non-PC place at work where I could be myself and have a bit of back-home-style scallywag fun.

I looked up at the top shelf where some eighty empty bottles now sat. About twenty other bottles of partly consumed leftovers were in the cupboard with several new bottles ready to open. The thought of having to stop was unconscionable, but I also knew any battle for the Club would have to wait. I had just been handed an urgent assignment that commanded my immediate attention - and *nothing* comes before a good story.

Aging Mi-8s are kept in the air with sheer grit... and duct tape. Packing our gear was like jamming toys in a kid's closet.

Franck (shown here) and Carsten don gas masks and descend through poisonous vapors to capture rare images of Mutnovsky's active crater in far-east Russia.

INTO THE TORNADO: Don Julio Tequila

Our Kamchatkan bear guard liked to use his rifle as a walking stick, making him more of a worry than the bears.

Carsten lands his motorized paraglider, a useful but dangerous way to capture aerial images.

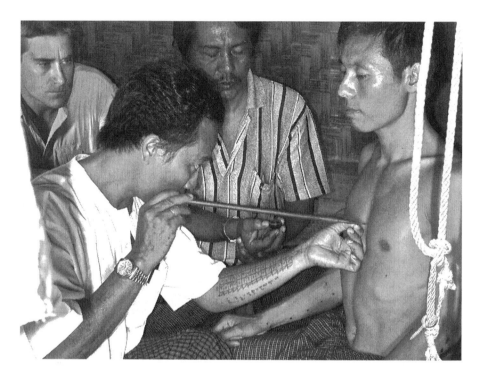

Burmese snake catchers mix venom with ink and create tattoos that 'inoculate' clan members against snakebite.

A Burmese woman performs an age-old fertility ritual, kissing a deadly king cobra on the head.

INTO THE TORNADO: Don Julio Tequila

After a tough day filming in the Burmese jungle, the crew is rewarded with cases of Mandalay beer, delivered by... a beer elephant.

The Exotic Booze Club

One of Pat Parelli's men takes a dangerous ride on a wild mustang fresh off the mesa.

INTO THE TORNADO: Don Julio Tequila

Ever-reliable Aussie cameraman, West Ashton, catches the action. I'm having a ball, despite losing my beloved Akubra hat along the way.

The Exotic Booze Club

With Tim Samaras we chased tornados across eleven states - clocking up 15,000 miles in two and a half weeks. (Photograph by Carsten Peter)

INTO THE TORNADO: Don Julio Tequila

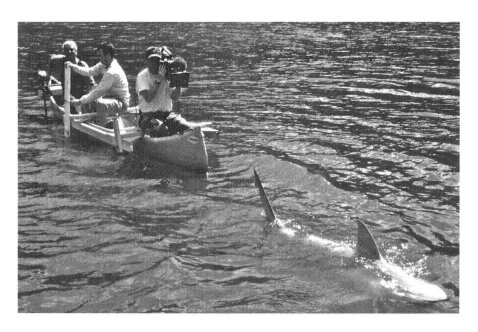

'Sparky', our replica bull shark, helps us reenact the horrific New Jersey shark attacks of 1916.

Naked Man', in Madagascar, is very comfortable with nature in all forms.

Malagasy wildlife.

A mangled steak and fake blood help set the scene for our painstaking reenactment of the 1916 New Jersey shark attacks.

Great results in Madagascar – a new species of tiny primate and a promise from the government to protect its habitat by creating a new national park.

Hannes Botha with a giant Nile croc captured for Brady's Dangerous Encounters. Another great use for duct tape.

INTO THE TORNADO: Don Julio Tequila

National Geographic engineers created pressure gauges so we could measure the comparative bite force of some extremely large predators.

The Exotic Booze Club

A selection of the Club's exotic booze.

Chapter 6

ATTACKS OF THE MYSTERY SHARK:
Indian Archer XXX Rum

Some travellers are enamored of India. They find the vibrant colors, the intense smells and the diversity of culture a feast for the senses. As I walked through the impoverished back alleys of Calcutta, I wasn't being enthralled in the same way. I couldn't exactly put my finger on why. It wasn't the poverty alone, but perhaps it was also my strange perspective. I was walking backwards, as I often do, and if I wasn't careful I'd trip over a beggar.

Deeper into the slums, I continued my backwards walking so I could film Fabien Cousteau coming toward me before this rookie did his very first piece to camera. Fabien, grandson of famous underwater explorer Jacques Cousteau, was my new on-camera talent. The story we were about to shoot was his first big chance to break into television.

Fabien, a blue-eyed, square-jawed 35-year-old, was French born but did much of his growing up in the US. He'd studied economics and had been selling antiques at a high-end store in Manhattan, about as removed from Calcutta's slums as you can get. Fabien was a fish out of water on camera and my job was to make the results worthy of Nat Geo television.

Step one, a warm-up. Rather than talking straight to camera, I put him with one of our guides, Mr. Chattergy, and asked Fabien to talk to him about where we were.

"It's absolutely beautiful your country," he told our guide, "all the colors, the smells." It was a polite thought, but not quite fitting the visuals of our ghetto surrounds.

Behind Fabien and Mr. Chattergy I could see decrepit old buildings with makeshift wiring and crumbling paint. Nearby, someone was selling off-smelling fish from the trunk of a rusty old Fiat. Trash burned in the street and grotty young children, in bare feet and rags, darted around us.

Mr. Chattergy was under no illusion about the state of his city. "No," he corrected Fabien in a thick Indian accent, "the smell is *very* bad. It is a very bad smell." Fabien couldn't help but laugh and it turned out to be a nice moment. Time to try step two, a piece looking directly at the camera.

I wanted to keep it short and simple, making sure Fabien had good presence and attitude, and solid eye contact with my lens. I didn't want to give him a script to read as that always sounds artificial, especially with newcomers. The key was to be spontaneous and natural. "Okay, Fabien," I instructed him, "tell me where we are and what we are doing."

This story began with a box full of research folders and a bunch of tapes. MSNBC was broadcasting Geographic's *Explorer* series and they'd requested a shark story to go up against Discovery's infamous Shark Week. Unbeknown to me, the idea had been wallowing without direction for months. A few things, some shark research, had already been shot - hence the tapes in the box - but there was no sense of a story that could sustain an hour. That's when I was put on the case. The really bad news was we had just twelve weeks to create a show and get it to air. Our normal schedule for editing alone was around fourteen weeks so we'd be editing while shooting - never ideal. Whatever this story was, it was going to be tight.

I spent a day looking through the box and wasn't having a great deal of joy until I came across a new book by a guy from New Jersey named Dr. Richard Fernicola. The book was called *Twelve Days of Terror* and documented a turn-of-the-century spate of shark attacks that bore a resemblance to the plot from Jaws. The book detailed America's startling introduction to the world of shark attacks over twelve days in 1916 when four people were killed by, in Dr. Fernicola's opinion, a great white.

The strange thing about the attacks was that two of them occurred up a New Jersey creek. That's hardly great-white behavior; rather, it's more like the lesser-known bull shark. My mind jumped in leaps and bounds: what if we could prove that *Jaws* was based on the wrong shark? This would be like a shark whodunit.

I barely had to do a pitch: with this sort of deadline, the execs basically had to live with whatever I came up with. But I did need resources. I had an associate producer who loves the water almost as much as I love exotic alcohol. Colette Beaudry had lived in Australia for ten years, mostly to be warm and by the sea. She was really a producer but, like many before her, she had taken this associate producer gig to get a foot in the door at Geographic. At last I had an AP who could understand my accent.

I've given Colette several nicknames over the years. I use Beaudacious often because that just seems to fit, and sometimes I call her Miss. Thank-You-Sorry-Please as she has a tendency to leave longwinded phone messages that say something like: "I'm just calling to say sorry for all those thankyous I left you in that last message. Please, please let me say sorry. Thank you again - and sorry for that thankyou too. [Pause] Thank you. [Pause] Sorry. Bye."

Courtesies aside, Beaudacious knew how to make a film and would be a tremendous asset. I knew we'd need more help, but this was a great start. Together we gathered additional research and I watched a show about the attacks. It had been made a few years earlier by the History Channel and did a good job covering the major points. The first attack was considered a freak event, then five days later a man lost both his legs below the knees, later dying from his wounds. Public hysteria followed - a monster was prowling the Atlantic. Then came the attacks up Matawan Creek, about twenty miles south of Manhattan and eleven miles in from open ocean.

Eleven-year-old Lester Stillwell was taken and killed, then 24-year-old Stanley Fischer was attacked while looking for Lester's body. He also died from his wounds. Shortly after, locals captured a great white in the bay near the creek reportedly with human remains in its stomach. It was a shocking tale, well told in the film. For me the only surprise came at the end as the credits rolled up the screen.

The name of the producer was Ashley Hoppin, the same Ashley who co-produced the camel shoot. Beaudacious and I went to New York to recruit Ashley for our show. Ashley was reluctant to join our team, not least because she was already working on a follow-up and had lined up shoots and contacts. This, of course, made her even more valuable to have on board - with our tight deadline, it'd save a lot of time. She didn't have a broadcaster though and we did, so rather than compete with us, she signed on as a co-producer. We made a shopping list of what we'd need to get this show done:

1. Author Richard Fernicola and a shoot that'd get him in the water to re-evaluate his premise that the 1916 attacks were all great whites.
2. Proof. A great payoff that would solve the mystery of which shark killed the victims of those turn-of-the-century attacks.
3. A killer reenactment of the original attacks.
4. A shoot that showed the nature of the great white.
5. A shoot that showed the ability of the bull shark to go upstream.
6. A host: someone to play the Sherlock Holmes of our investigation and tie everything together.

It was a daunting shopping list. Ashley already had Richie Fernicola lined up and had spoken to descendants of the victims about exhuming one of the graves. An analysis of bones could reveal the kind of teeth - and hence the kind of shark - that did the chomping. It was a long shot, but worth a try. Tick off numbers one and two on the list as things already lined up to film.

Ever-reliable AP Nancy Donnelly joined our team to help with the reenactment, so number three was in capable hands.

From the research box we already had tape of marine scientist Scott Davis tagging great whites off California. Geographic's funding arm had given Scott a grant to help him track great white movements and the footage looked good. In it, Scott sits on the back of a motorboat with a spear-like device in his hand. Circling his craft is a true monster, a sixteen-foot-plus great white. Scott nearly falls in as he reaches over and jabs the shark with his harpoon. When he pulls back his spear, a small satellite-tracking device is left attached near the shark's fin. Scott gives the rest of his team high fives. On tape, we had both topside and underwater coverage as they tagged nine other sharks as well and began tracking their movements. A follow-up interview with Scott and some additional filming of the tags was all we now needed for number four. Another tick.

Beaudacious had been looking for any other places on earth where sharks have been known to attack up rivers. Turns out it's not that uncommon in India. We quickly pulled together an expedition to investigate and recruited a good-looking, easygoing and articulate shark researcher to help. Rocky Strong was also a Nat Geo grantee, and up for the task. He believed the shark responsible for attacks in India had to be a type of bull shark, so he and Beaudacious left in short order to try to catch one. It would be a month-long trip. I would join them in a couple of weeks with a host - which brings us to the final item on the list.

My first call was to the very experienced British TV biologist Nick Baker. He had some other commitments to juggle but said he could make it work. Then, two days before the first shoot, he pulled out. Or, rather, his agent pulled him out to bluster over some contract issues with Geographic. It was quite likely a negotiation tactic but I had no time for such games. It had already been a pain to work around his other commitments, so rather than plead my case, as I'm sure they expected, I told them we would go with one of our other options. Wait . . . what other options? Enter Fabien Cousteau.

Fabien had patrolled the hallways of Geographic in search of a gig a few months earlier, but there wasn't much going at that time. Now that we did have something suitable, I was still reluctant to use a newcomer. I also had a bias against Fabien for another reason: an ordeal I'll never forget with his father, Jean-Michel Cousteau.

After many long months of negotiations, Geographic had reached a deal with Jean-Michel to do several films on the release of Keiko, the killer whale that was the star of the *Free Willy* movies. Keiko was then in the care of Jean-Michel's foundation and I was to spend three months in Iceland covering Keiko's rehabilitation and hopefully reunion with his original pod. I had rented out my house in DC and packed my bags, but was a little uneasy. The day before my departure we still didn't have a signed contract, and Jean-Michel was stalling.

My boss, Earl Grey, called Cousteau on speakerphone and a few of us sat in and listened. The conversation began with Cousteau demanding more rights and conditions and back-end, all of which, with some reluctance, the Earl was able to agree to. But nothing made Jean-Michel happy. Eventually Earl said, "Jean-Michel, am I dealing with someone here who wants to make a deal, or someone who is trying to get out of a deal?" It was the latter. He had been stringing us along.

Jean-Michel finally revealed that he was negotiating a different contract with ABC that would make him unavailable for the Keiko films. It seems he was merely using us as leverage for another deal. Earl put it to him that we do the Keiko films without him. "Ha!" he said. "If there is no Jean-Michel, there is no film." He then conceded that none of us would ever want to work with him again, and so be it. He bid us adieu and left us to untangle months of good-faith arrangements and preparations with dozens of organisations and crew.

Now I faced dealing with the son. Surely the ocean wasn't big enough for two Cousteau egos that big, but that was going to be Ashley's call. She was based in Manhattan where Fabien lived, so we sent her to meet the new generation while I kept looking at other options. Ashley called in and summed up Fabien: "Good looking," she said, "sounds good on the ear. Green. Will certainly need work. He was clearly born with a silver spoon in his mouth, but not a huge ego. I think he'll do." With that, and no other timely options, we threw caution to the wind. Fabien was thrilled with the assignment and the whirlwind began.

A few weeks later, Fabien and I landed in India for the biggest shoot of the film. At that point, Rocky and Beaudacious were well into their search for sharks in the Ganges River but we'd received a message that they needed more bait to chum the water.

"Here we are in Calcutta," Fabien started with his first piece to camera, "but before we can continue our mission, we have to fill up these drums with meat and waste from…"

"Hang on a sec," I interrupted. "We don't need the whole scoop. Let's tease it out. At this stage of the story we'll already know what city we're in, so how about you start with, "Before we can continue our mission…""

"We have to fill up these drums?" he added.

"Yeah, say "with some special kind of chum", and why don't you just add…" I thought for a moment, "And what if you just say and "it smells like we re getting close?""

Fabien liked the idea and gave it a go. He got it in one take with a nice wry smile at the end. Perfect. This might just work.

The piece to camera was no lie. As we followed our noses we drew close to a rare place in this Hindu-dominant nation. Usually cows are sacred and respected animals in India, but we had ventured into a suburb where commerce trumps religion. All around us were backyard abattoirs. For the devout, this was like a grotesque morgue, featuring the butchered bodies and organs of their loved ones. Fly-covered intestines hung everywhere, drying in the sun so they could later be used as sausage casings. We wasted little time loading up several large drums with a revolting mass of cow guts and strapping them to the roof of our van.

Just to make the day entirely offensive, I asked Mr. Chattergy to stop where I could purchase some local alcohol. As well as not eating cows, devout Hindus don't drink. I wondered if it was one of the reasons I wasn't taking a shine to India, but that didn't feel quite right either. After my experience at the backyard abattoir I was ready to become a vegetarian myself, and I'll never condemn anyone - even an entire country - for not drinking alcohol, I just reserve the right to look at them in a strange way.

Mr. Chattergy took us to a hole-in-the-wall store with several choices of really bad alcohol. With Mr. Chattergy as translator, I asked the shopkeeper what he recommended. He smiled and generically waved his arms around. I was on my own. I searched the dusty shelves for what may well be, given the rumors, one of the Club's final alcohols. I became particularly enamored by a small bottle of Archer rum produced by an undoubtedly quality-assured institution called Eastern Distilleries & Chemicals Ltd; I liked the way little bits and pieces floated around the bottom of the bottle. This was a must and I grabbed several versions. We then headed off driving through West Bengal to meet our boat on the Ganges River.

The Ganges runs from the Himalaya Mountains through India, to Bangladesh. It is 1,500 miles long and supports more than 400 million people so, not surprisingly, it has become less of a river and more of a giant sewer. The water is a putrid grey-brown soup, and in some places it has more than 150 times what's deemed to be the safe limit of fecal matter.

Our boat, the *Jungle King*, resembled a small and narrow paddle-steamer without wheels. It chugged down this unsavory waterway for several hours and took us within a few hundred yards of Bangladesh. We were now deep in the Sundarbans in the Bay of Bengal, the world's largest mangrove swamp.

We finally reached Rocky and Beaudacious's camp. John "Chuck Norris" Catto was part of their team and they'd been working aboard the *Jungle King* every day for nearly three weeks. We were eager to hear what they had found.

Beaudacious was thrilled to see a familiar face but was not so happy with what she had to report. They hadn't found a thing. She was full of "sorry, sorry, sorry", but of course there was no one to blame. The river was filthy and overfished and the sharks had to be uncommon, if not rare.

The next day, instead of fishing, we boated out in search of witnesses - people who had seen an attack or been attacked by something in the water. We didn't have to look far as it seemed each village had a story to tell. The survivors we met were mostly women, which made sense since they're the ones who spend much of their time fetching river water, and cleaning in it.

More than that, every day we saw women, and sometimes children, chest-deep in water, walking to and fro near the bank. They dragged large nets and trawled for shrimp larvae. Eight or nine hours of this mundane mission could yield them around fifty cents worth of income. It was a hard way to earn a living, and risky.

At one of our first stops, villagers directed us to a small hut away from the water. We rolled tape as Sumitra Mistri emerged from the dark confines draped in a flowing gold sari; these were probably clothes kept for special occasions, and our visit qualified. Our interpreter introduced us and we bowed our heads in respect. Sumitra was a shy mother of three, with a round face and big sad eyes. She agreed to tell us the story of when she was attacked and she pointed to a shady place where we could sit. As she did so, her left arm emerged from her robes and revealed a stump about eight inches up from where her hand should have been. It was a jarring sight, but it was not the only injury.

On the day Sumitra was attacked, she had been out trawling for three hours. She suddenly felt a bump and a piercing pain in her upper right leg. "It tore off the muscle slowly," Sumitra told us with tears welling in her eyes, "and dragged me underwater for some distance. I pushed the animal and it immediately took off my hand."

Somehow Sumitra pulled loose and dragged herself to shore, where she took one look at the blood coming from where her hand used to be and fell unconscious. Those with her applied the only first aid they knew: they ran from hut to hut, collected sugar, and used it to pack the wounds. Sumitra cried freely as she told us that this attack had happened seven years earlier and she hadn't been in the water since.

Rocky was chief interviewer and he took a scientific approach. He drew a picture of a crocodile and a picture of a shark, and asked Sumitra which one had attacked her. The Ganges is so murky it would have been easy for her not to see the culprit at all, but she was clear. Sumitra pointed to the shark. "*Camote*," she said, the local word for shark.

Sumitra retreated to a private hut where she permitted Beaudacious to view and film the wounds on her leg. A giant chunk was missing from beneath her buttocks, a maze of scars running down the cavity about a foot long and four inches wide. It was a wonder she could still walk.

From village to village we collected the same sorry tales from a dozen or so other victims. Almost always they showed us the same type of horrific injuries: a large piece taken out of their backside or upper thigh, and a hand missing from where they'd tried to fend off their attacker. It was a high price to pay for fifty cents worth of shrimp larvae.

Fabien was concerned that all this was going to give sharks an even worse rap than they already had, so he asked to do a piece to camera. We worked out how to articulate what he wanted to express and he delivered it with a very furrowed brow. "Hearing stories like this is," he said, "to say, at the very least, extremely difficult. And it's sometimes hard to keep in perspective that sharks are neither heroes nor villains, and that this is just part of everyday life, a very, very difficult life." He was perhaps a little too earnest for my liking, but it was working. We'd thrown him in the deep end as a host but, as you'd expect from a Cousteau, he was swimming not sinking.

Now we just had to get our hands on one of these sharks. We recruited a local fisherman who said he could take us to where he'd seen some recently. It was a long shot that he was even telling the truth - he was a fisherman, after all, and this was a fish story - but we were getting desperate.

We tied the fisherman's thin wooden canoe to the side of the *Jungle King* and off we went. After an hour or so, our fisherman disappeared. We found him in his boat bailing it out. We called out for our captain to stop and hopped in to help. His little canoe didn't look like much, but it represented this fisherman's entire livelihood. He was green around the gills, not from the bailing out, but because our boat's exhaust was puffing directly into his face. The *Jungle King* was still going full steam ahead, so again we called out to our captain to slow down but still got no response. We charged downstream, the canoe taking on more and more water. Finally I managed to climb back on deck, marched to our captain and flipped my lid. I slapped him with my hat and shouted, "Stop this fucking thing *now*!" This time he stopped. He didn't understand a word of English, but he'd known what we wanted all along. Then he abused the person next to him, who abused the person below him, all the way down to a cabin boy who got kicked up the backside. Our fisherman's boat was saved and we retied it so it wouldn't take on water.

When we found out why our captain wouldn't stop, what it was about India that rubbed me the wrong way finally dawned on me. It was the caste system. No matter where you fell in this society, that was where you were destined to stay. You knew it, and everyone else knew it. Desperation is one thing, but desperation without hope is truly tragic. There is barely a glimmer of a chance that the impoverished beggars that glare at you in the street, or their scrawny malnourished children, can one day rise above the level of humanity that surrounds them. Our captain hadn't wanted to stop because the fisherman was beneath him.

We further confounded our captain and his crew by going back to check on our fisherman's wellbeing. As I walked back to see him, he took off his ragged shirt to cool down and I was astounded by what I saw. From the lower part of his ribcage down he was missing a huge chunk of flesh. Rocky saw it too and called over our interpreter. "Ask him if this was a shark - did a shark bite him?" Our interpreter started to listen to the man's story - and listen, and listen. He was so engrossed in the tale he quite forgot to translate. After a minute or so we couldn't wait anymore. Rocky interrupted, "So, was it a shark?"

"No," our interpreter finally said. "It was a tiger."

"A tiger?"

Just when you thought it was safest to stay out of the water. Our fisherman had once been a honey collector; these are men who earn *their* fifty cents a day by heading into the numerous mangrove islands to raid wild beehives. According to our fisherman, he was out one day when a tiger pounced on one of his colleagues. Our man grabbed a knife, jumped on the tiger's back and cut a piece off one of the cat's ears. That's when the tiger turned around and took a chunk out of his side. The tiger ran off and left the Sundarbans short of two honey collectors: one was dead, the other, once recovered, traded jobs and started to fish.

Many others still run the gauntlet with an estimated 6,000 families relying on honey collection to make ends meet in the Sundarbans. The tigers are protected, but not the people they now actively seek out as prey. As if we needed further proof, a few nights later a boat full of panicked honey collectors waved us down for help. They'd pulled up to a mangrove and a tiger had jumped into their canoe, hauled one of their team overboard, and took off with him into the night. There was no help to be had, and they knew it. The survivors were fresh from an extremely close encounter with death and were freaked out. We now shared their state of mind but could do little else but give them some food and water before they paddled off. Soon, I thought, they'll all be fishermen.

We finally arrived at the spot where sharks had reportedly been seen. Rocky spent a few hours laying out a shark line with thirty-six baited hooks. Once out, they had to be checked every hour on the hour. We vowed to keep vigil, day and night, until we found a shark.

On the other side of the world, my co-producer was having a much better time. Ashley had brought *Twelve Days of Terror* author Dr. Richard Fernicola to Walker's Cay in the Bahamas. This is a place where they guarantee lots of big bull sharks in clear shallow water, and if you're brave enough they'll even let you dive with them. That was, of course, precisely the plan. Richie is not exactly a he-man; in fact, at the time, he still lived with his mother. When he agreed to follow Ashley to the Bahamas, he quite possibly missed the bit about close encounters with potential man-eaters and was more focused on fruity cocktails. At least, that's where my mind would have gone. The Caribbean is, after all, where the invention of rum was first documented.

The water at Walker's Cay was apparently crystal clear as promised, and with a bit of chum it was soon full of extremely large bull sharks - about a dozen, and all a good six or seven feet long. As the name suggests, these are solid sharks with bullish heads that probably weigh in close to 300 pounds each. Bulls are among the heavyweights of the shark world; almost all shark attacks on people can be attributed to great whites, tigers or bulls.

Richard looked down from the dock at the shark-infested water below. Anyone would have second thoughts about this undertaking, and that's right when Ashley showed up beside him, suited up and ready to jump in. If a woman was game, how could he refuse?

Ashley had also brought Adam Geiger, a fearless underwater cameraman. Ashley and Adam calmly entered the water and lay on the bottom in what was only about four feet of water. Sharks swarmed around them - it is still the most menacing shark footage I've ever seen. Richie, his heart in his mouth, followed; once underwater he stayed as still as possible. Sharks darted around him, over him and at him, sometimes two at a time. As we saw in the Sunderbans, even a nibble from just one of these bulls would be ugly.

In Richie's own words, "I really was not prepared for the immense size, especially of the pregnant female bull sharks; they look like these hulking small trucks." Seeing their incredible power up close was enough to have Richie rethink his great white theory. Once back on the dock, he agreed that the river attacks in 1916 could indeed have been a bull shark.

Had our Geo team stayed another week they would have gotten further dramatic proof. As they flew out, another film crew arrived from the Discovery Channel with naturalist Eric Ritter, an expert from the New Jersey based Shark Research Institute. Maybe Ritter smelled a little more like chum. As he stood waist-deep in the water at Walker's Cay, doing the kind of shoot we'd just done, a bull shark decided to take a bite and effectively separated Mr. Ritter from his calf muscle. The footage became the well-promoted clip for a film called *Anatomy of a Shark Bite*. It was the highlight of the following year's Shark Week. Walker's Cay however was not so lucky. The resort did not survive the publicity and shut down soon after.

Ashley had dutifully purchased a bottle of Nassau Royale sweet coconut rum (in the belief that, somehow, the Club would continue), and she had brought her team home at just the right time.

Meanwhile, in the Sundarbans, no sharks were biting. Rocky said on camera that he'd never fished for so long and gotten nothing. We'd rationed the chum, so as not to use it all at once, which turned out to be a mistake. In the hot Indian sun the chum in the barrels bloated, and one morning we woke up on the wrong side of the wind and found the drums overflowing with flyblown gaseous organs and intestines. The smell was intolerable and it seemed to bubble and burp as if alive. Perhaps worst of all was how offensive this was to the many Hindus on board. It was too hideous for television and there was nothing we could do but tip the whole lot overboard as fast as possible. Rocky and I tackled this thankless task with t-shirts wrapped around our noses.

The odoriferous addition to the Ganges didn't help bring the sharks any closer - maybe the opposite. And the Hindu gods certainly weren't shining on us. After a couple of weeks of trying, the closest we came was a broken hook. Something very large had taken the bait, hook and all, and was gone. The rule of Last-Day Payoff was broken and that never happens.

We had but one stroke of luck before we had to quit when Beaudacious and Mr. Chattergy found a couple of small sharks in a local market. Back on the boat, Rocky and Fabien inspected them. They were newborn, maybe just a day or two old judging by the umbilical marks. Rocky meticulously counted their tiny teeth to confirm that they were indeed bull sharks. It was a good sign they were still in the area, even if we couldn't catch a live one, and the eyewitness accounts painted a chilling picture of bull sharks hunting up rivers.

Rocky put it all in perspective of the 1916 attacks. "If it was a white shark," he told Fabien, "it was an exceedingly rare occurrence. If it was a bull shark, it was an animal doing what it is quite capable of doing and does do often."

"And the reason they might venture up Matawan Creek?"

"Because they can leave all their other competitors behind and be king of the hill up inside an environment they are very good at dealing with, and other sharks just aren't."

Bull sharks are truly special animals in this regard. Other sharks can't handle fresh water because it causes the salt in their bodies to flush out.

Their cells expand and rupture, they bloat, and within a few hours, they die. But the bulls can lock in and re-use the salt already in their system. They frequently hug the shorelines and, if they choose, don't mind a quick jaunt up a brackish or freshwater river.

Great whites are very different. There is no doubt they've taken people just waist-deep in the surf, but they much prefer open ocean. Every one of Scott Davis's satellite tags showed great whites heading way out into open water. There was only one more thing we needed to further our investigation into the Jersey attacks: proof.

We had remained hopeful of getting permission to examine the remains of the boy who was killed up Matawan Creek in 1916. But at the last minute, Lester Stillwell's family politely decided they would not like his grave exhumed. In one way, it was a bit of a relief; I'd thought it an extreme measure for, at best, an unlikely result. But we had to come up with another plan. We pondered as we regrouped, not at Nat Geo headquarters but in Georgia.

It was too cold to do a water-based recreation in New Jersey or even Washington, DC, so we moved the whole production to the sun-filled South. Our location was an out-of-the-way town that had a suitably secluded river and a rail bridge close enough to the kind that used to run over Matawan Creek.

We arrived on a Sunday and settled in before shooting started the next day. We drove around searching for a pub but, in this religious part of the world, all the pubs are closed on the Christian Sabbath. We didn't mind resorting to a bottle shop and taking supplies back to our hotel but even that was not an option; I was horrified to find that alcohol couldn't legally be sold on Sunday at *all*. I longed for the "Sunday sessions" of home - a great pub tradition - and considered that perhaps alcohol was *my* religion. I felt truly discriminated against. This did not bode well for the shoot.

I wallowed through the valley of soberness, then, a sign from the heavens. Our Georgian location manager, Linda Burns, greeted us at the hotel like a burst of sunshine, and in her possession was a bottle of vodka. She'd been burned by this clash of Sabbaths before and came prepared to accommodate mine.

Finally, relaxed and focused, we revised the plan for the next day and mulled over what we'd have for a payoff. There were all the ingredients for a great story, but no final climactic scene for our investigation. It was something to drink on. Although I prefer bourbon, some of my best ideas are revealed with vodka.

"It's a detective story," I said to Ashley. "We need a smoking gun." We stewed on this for a moment then had the same idea at the same time: a tooth.

When sharks attack, they readily lose teeth; great whites can go through more than 50,000 in a lifetime. The ferocity of the attacks in Matawan Creek would certainly have caused the shark to lose a tooth or ten. We decided we'd go back to the site of the attacks and dredge for shark teeth.

All at once, we began making arrangements for a professional excavation as well as getting stuck into our reenactment. Nancy had been busy. You can always get a little extra money for a show that is a fast delivery, and she'd used the extra cash well. Our Georgian location was worthy of a Hollywood set. We had actors in period costume, a steady-cam operator, a forty-foot jib to fly the camera over the set, hair and make-up artists, topside and underwater cameras, and an explosives expert - after the attacks in Matawan, locals took to the water with dynamite, trying (unsuccessfully) to kill the perpetrator.

We also had a life-size fibreglass replica of a bull shark that we dubbed "Sparky". Sparky's makers had a way of attaching it to a motorized canoe so it could slice through the water. To top it off, we had lots of fake blood.

This time we took a real gamble with Fabien: we dressed him in period costume and had him tell part of the story to camera from inside the scene. It was no easy task, even for a seasoned pro, but again he pulled it off. In an incredibly short period of time he'd made the camera his friend. We filmed in alcohol-limited Georgia for three days (thank you, Lord, for a Sabbath that comes but once a week). Then it was on to look for a shark tooth, the last climactic scene of our film.

Dr. Dick Gould, a seasoned marine archaeologist from Brown University, agreed to lead the dig. To picture Dick, think of Sean Connery with an American accent. He was full of enthusiasm and excitement for this challenge, and he came to New Jersey with a couple of guys who had a high-powered underwater vacuum to suck up the material from the creek bottom. Dick also brought several students to sift through the deposits like gold diggers. It was another long shot, a needle in a haystack, but we knew at the very least it would occupy several valuable minutes of screen time to complete our hour.

With the help of Richie's research, we narrowed down the location of the attacks to a relatively small area of about forty square yards. All we had to do now was dig out enough of the bottom to take us back ninety years or so, and sift through the rubble.

I helped set up the excavation, which took a lot longer than expected. We spent a lot of time setting up silt-catching barriers (an Environmental Protection Agency requirement) and making an underwater grid that mapped out the location. I would have preferred to spend the time digging and looking for a tooth, but I'm no archaeologist and we had to do things by the book.

The grid for mapping was made from PVC pipe and it was ultimately about fifty squares, each two feet by two feet. Finally, all the preliminary work was done. I was looking forward to hauling up tons of dirt for sifting and had visions of a small mountain forming from which, if we were careful, we'd have to find something. We were ready to roll on the action when Dick spoke up. "Right," he said, "now for the lottery."

"The lottery?" I asked, having no idea what he was talking about.

"That's where we randomly draw six numbers from a hat and those are the six squares of the grid we dig in."

"Six? What about the rest?"

"That's not how it works in science. The lottery squares represent the whole, so if we don't find a tooth in one of them then there's no tooth out there."

I was flabbergasted. Why couldn't we just dredge the whole thing and start looking? This made no sense to me whatsoever. But no matter what I thought, there was no real arguing with a Brown University professor. This was his gig now: we'd put him in charge, and Geographic would have it no other way. I did make a token protest, I think, saying something like, "But, but, but, but…" and that was about it. I had to whiz back to DC to keep an eye on our edit (which was well underway), but every few miles of my drive I found myself muttering, "Six squares? Six squares!"

After a few days I popped back up to Matawan hoping for a result. So far, six had not been a lucky number. They'd found nothing, and it was their last day. After India I didn't know if the rule of Last-Day Payoff was still in effect, but it was all I could cling to. I picked up the camera and trudged my way around the muddy creek to where Fabien, Dick and the team were still sifting. They'd sucked away enough material to be down to an area that represented 1916, at least in the lottery holes, but nothing yet. With little else to do, I started filming shots of the process that had probably been shot by our cameraman a hundred times over in the previous few days. Then, as I rolled, a voice popped up behind Fabien.

"Hey guys." Laura Ryan, one of Dick's sifters, had found something interesting. She handed it to Dick.

"Oh hey, look at this," he said. "It's a fang, an actual fang, it's not a shark but it is a fang... I don't think it's a shark... oh wait..." All eyes focused on Dick. "We could be wrong - that *is* a shark!"

Before anyone could cheer, Laura piped up again. "Wait, guys . . . Guys, *look*!" Another larger piece was held high in her hand and she squealed with delight.

"My God, look at that!" shouted Dick, pointing to the piece of tooth. "Here's the big one, yes!"

It was all I could do to keep the camera steady. Dick's entire team erupted into cheers and shouts. Altogether there were three pieces of tooth and they fitted together like a perfect little jigsaw puzzle.

There were three astounding elements about this moment that I'll never forget. The first was that Dick and his team had actually found a shark's tooth from an appropriately historic layer of mud - the odds of that were extremely long. The second, with perhaps even longer odds, was that I was filming at the precise moment this happened. The Irish should be so lucky. And the third, and certainly the most confounding element, was Fabien's reaction. During this entire goosebump-inducing scene, he virtually ignored the commotion around him and kept his head down in his own sifting tray. Perhaps he thought it was a joke, or maybe he was afraid of blocking my shot. It'll remain a mystery. We had to cut around him as best we could in the edit suite.

Near the shark tooth, Dick also found two pieces of cylindrical material that resembled bone. "Ashley," I called out to my co-producer, "we need a medical expert to give us a quick read."

She shot back right away, "Ah, here's one."

In all my dealings with author Dr. Richard Fernicola, I'd never really focused on the Dr. part; I figured he had a PhD in literature or history or some such. It turns out that he is a writer and a practicing medical doctor. Richie, or I should say Dr. Richie, examined what we had found.

"Absolutely incredible," he said. "It's hard to say whether it is human but it could be consistent with a young boy, maybe even a clavicle there."

We bagged up the specimens to take to a forensic expert. It was exciting stuff. A mystery nearly a hundred years old could soon be solved and, if so, the answer was in our hands. We finished the rest of the edit and awaited the culminating scene with a final word from a shark tooth expert: was it a great white, or a bull?

At the National Museum of Health and Medicine our experts gathered: Richie, Fabien and Professor Gavin Naylor to look at the tooth, and forensic scientist Paul Sledzick to look at the bone. Paul went first and, after scrubbing off the creek scum, he slowly came to the conclusion that, whatever this pipe-like material was, it was not bone. More likely something man-made.

Next, Gavin carefully examined the tooth. He pretty much knew instantly what it was.

"This came from a shark about five or six metres long," he said. "It's a fossil. It wasn't from a hundred years ago but about sixty-three *million* years ago. It was not the answer we'd hoped for - but what an adventure.

We spent three days with Fabien getting the best narration from him we could, long and hard work for something that would take a professional just a few hours. He wrapped up with his own conclusion, drawn from the bits of evidence uncovered in the show: a great white did the ocean attacks, but it had to be a bull shark up Matawan Creek.

The National Geographic Channel played our final film, *Attacks of the Mystery Shark*, over and over again, and no one seemed to care or notice that the shark tooth we found was a fossil. Ashley entered the program in the CINE awards for filmmaking (something I've always been too busy or too lazy to do) and she won us a Golden Eagle. I mounted our shark-tooth fossil in clear plastic and gave it pride of place on my wall. I hoped it would bring some much-needed luck with any threat to the Exotic Booze Club.

With the shark show wrapped up, I could finally turn my attention to the Club's future, but before I could do anything, it was done for me. The then president of National Geographic Television, Tim Kelly, had been in a meeting with human resources when the subject of the Exotic Booze Club came up. Tim, my boss's boss's boss, had been a fan of the Club from the time he first heard of it, dropping by frequently and occasionally bringing guests with him. He recognized it, as we all did, as a rare place where anyone from an intern to a president could sit in a relaxed environment and exchange ideas, shoot the breeze, and enjoy some adventurous alcohol.

As I understand it, Tim went to bat for the Club. Perhaps he argued that it should be exempt from the no-alcohol rule because closing it down would be bad for morale. Maybe he spoke of its educational value, or the need to have cultural respect for the founder's Australian heritage. Whichever way, it worked. While HR wouldn't change the alcohol policy, it seems they agreed to turn a blind eye. Officially, HR says it never knew the Club existed. That's fine by me. Had they actually changed the policy, I think the Club would have earned some unwarranted legitimacy

- and that wouldn't do at all - but turning a blind eye is something to which I can relate.

The true value of such regular gatherings is hard to calculate. How do you put a price on intangible ideas and invisible bonds? As if to validate our president's intervention, the benefit of the Club's existence would soon be apparent to all.

Chapter 7

KING KONG IN MY POCKET:
Malagasy Vanilla-Bean Rum

A new member of the Nat Geo family came to the Club for a get-to-know-ya drink. Mireya Mayor, now Dr. Mireya Mayor, was made for TV. She was a child actor, a Fulbright scholar, and a rising star in the field of primatology. In between her academic achievements and her fieldwork on primates, she'd also managed a four-year stint as a Miami Dolphins cheerleader. "Cheerleader" always looks good on a résumé, and indeed in real life.

Ashley Hoppin had recognized Mireya's considerable attributes when she happened to meet her in the wilds of Madagascar. Apart from Mireya's Cuban-acquired good looks, her brains and a flair for television, she was quite at home roughing it in faraway jungles. This was a rare combination to find in one person. Ashley introduced Mireya to Nat Geo and the young scientist's career in television began almost immediately.

Perhaps best of all, Mireya (or Rey, as I prefer to call her) had a great sense of humor and liked a drink. When we first sat sipping some homemade Georgia moonshine (always good for clarity of vision) at her introductory Club visit, she had a few shows under her belt and was juggling her new TV work with finishing her PhD. Rey was about to return to Madagascar, not for a film but to try to find a type of lemur she and geneticist Dr. Ed Louis had captured about a year earlier.

In his lab at Omaha's Henry Doorly Zoo, Ed had confirmed this lemur was a species new to science, and they needed more samples to prove the finding and write it up. Little bells started going off in my head. Still a relative newbie to the TV biz, it hadn't occurred to Rey that this may be the basis of a film. I asked her to tell me more about this lemur. How special was it?

"Well," she said, "it doesn't exactly stand out. It's small. Like really tiny."

"How tiny?"

She cupped her hands together to make a bowl that this creature would easily fit into.

"Wow. That's a small gorilla."

"Yeah, lemur," she corrected. "A mouse lemur. It could be the smallest primate on earth."

"*The* smallest?"

"Yeah, we'll know when we find more. If it's not the smallest, it's probably the second smallest. And maybe even the rarest."

Rey was downplaying it, but she had an inkling that this was quite likely the biggest discovery of her career, and I confirmed for her that it also had *great* potential for TV. I set to work writing up a treatment. There was no time to lose; Rey was booked to leave the following month.

I likened our Rey to the actress Fay Wray, star of the 1933 *King Kong* movie, both beautiful women with destinies linked to strange primates in far-off exotic jungles. A bit of a size difference in the species, of course, so we called our pitch *"King Kong in My Pocket."* It was a lot easier to sell than a horse film, and away we went.

We landed in Madagascar's muggy capital, Antananarivo, better known as Tana. We settled into a hotel and started checking that our gear had survived the trip; Air France, in my experience, is the worst airline in the world for losing luggage. Noticing we were one bag short, I complained to the Air France lost-baggage boss, who summed up his policy thus: "It is not my bag; it is not my problem." It sounds even ruder when you say it out loud with a French accent - try it.

We never saw that case again, so we were down a monitor and our rechargeable camera batteries. We'd get by. We were in for a major expedition so we had disposable batteries along with a lot of camping gear, and we were just grateful Air France lost nothing more serious and that our other twenty-three bags made it safely to Madagascar.

With me on this trip was Bill Swift, an associate producer on his first overseas jaunt for Geographic. Remember the newbie who Carrie, the Nat Geo staffer, tricked into thinking it was Pirate Day? Well, that was Bill several years earlier. Bill had worked on many domestic shoots, but it was as if other producers had collectively conspired not to take anyone overseas who had a pirate costume hanging in their closet. I was happy to assume that risk, even before I found out the other asset Bill had acquired from his time with Club Med: he is fluent in French. Madagascar was pretty much a French colony from 1883 to 1960, and French is still widely spoken as the number-two language.

Operating the camera for me was Jeff Wayman, but you may as well forget his real name now. It's better that you know him as we all do: Naked Man. Jeff has actually been known by many inexplicable names, like Finn and Trip, and then a few names that make total sense, such as Naked Man Up A Tree, the latter coming from his time living primarily unclothed in a tree house in the jungles of Hawaii. By the time I met him, he was out of his tree in a hippie commune, living in a cliff-side yurt that overlooked whales migrating off the coast of Maui.

There are two guarantees when you take Jeff on a shoot. One is smooth, flowing pictures and the most rock-solid handheld images you could ever hope for, earning him another nickname, the Human Tripod. The other guarantee is that you will, sooner or later, see him naked, basking in his full glory, the physical attributes revealed by this penchant also earning him the nickname the Human Tripod.

Jeff has a childlike sense of wonder, boundless enthusiasm and no shame. His nakedness is never intended to be cool or showy; more likely he just didn't bother to put on his clothes. I didn't quite know what to expect from this shoot, but I knew the hippie/cheerleader/pirate combination was sure to make things interesting.

We fired up the gear in Antananarivo and filmed a short scene-setting segment with Rey, then went to meet up with her Malagasy team of ten budding young field scientists. They'd arrived in the middle of the night, two days late, from their village fourteen hours away. But there was no time to rest. We had to catch a small plane for the next leg; it was a once-a-week flight and we couldn't be late.

At the tarmac we began to load our twin engine with gear, and that's when Rey made a startling discovery. For all our equipment, we were missing one very essential item: lemur traps. The traps are loaf-sized tin boxes with spring-loaded doors. Without them, mouse lemurs (scientific name Microcebus) would be very hard to catch.

Rey looked down in disbelief; she had expected twenty traps. "We have *no* lemur traps? None? Zero?" In their rush to meet up with us, Rey's regular field guys had let her down. The traps are hard to come by, and they weren't just back in the city - they were accidentally left *way* back in a village about two days drive away. Angelo, the most experienced of Rey's local team, sat flushed with embarrassment. We had no choice but to board our plane and leave without the traps. We'd have to work something out at our next location.

Our flight took us north along the eastern edge of the jungle to Sambava, and our three hours in the plane proved to be a great opportunity to inspect the landscape below. Madagascar is the fourth biggest island in the world and the diversity of terrain here is astounding, from barren desert in the south to thick jungle in the north. Madagascar is a rebel child that left its home, Africa, 165 million years ago, drifting away never to have contact again. Once out on its own, it developed unique species: palms that spout water like fountains, goblin-like tree dwellers with witchy fingers, frogs that hang their eggs from branches, large googly-eyed lizards that change color at a moment's notice. Unlike the rest of Africa, there are no lions or hyenas, no gorillas or zebras. The largest land predator on Madagascar is a mongoose-like creature called a fossa. The largest mammal is a type of lemur. The island's smallest primate is also a lemur, and both are wide-eyed members of a diverse primate family that lives nowhere else on the planet.

The human population within Madagascar is no less diverse. This is a place where it seems everyone has had some influence. My associate producer, Bill, would feel right at home in the north where pirates established the free colony of Libertatia, and before them Arab Muslims were here establishing trade routes. The Portuguese found the place by accident and tried to make it a colony, then the British stepped in and spread some Christianity. Local royalty took care of the Christians by killing some 150,000 of them, which they considered a good start, then the French came in.

The French took over the capital losing only twenty soldiers to fighting, but another 6,000 to malaria and similar diseases. They managed to introduce good pastries and held on until World War II when Germany invaded France and contemplated deporting all of Europe's Jews to the Malagasy colony. Then the British came back and successfully fought off the Japanese for the place. The Brits then let the French take it back to make sure the pastries were still of suitable quality, but that only lasted a few years before another revolt from the very beleaguered indigenous population. Finally, in 1960, Madagascar reclaimed its full independence. This entire time, the more isolated rural portions of Madagascar tried to keep it business as usual, but you can almost see a fearful confusion in their eyes. They try their best to welcome you with their intuitive friendliness, but suspicion is never far from the surface.

This tension is not helped by the one thing that two-thirds of them have in common: they all earn less than the international poverty line of $1.25 a day. Wherever we went we were regarded as wealthy celebrities, but no one ever seemed too sure that we weren't there to occupy the damn place. We always did our best to let everyone know that our sole interests were quality croissants, rum and lemurs very, very small lemurs.

The only place we knew to look for our quarry was where Rey and Ed had found their one and only sample, an area that was a speck in the middle of dense jungle. We were a lot closer after landing in Sambava, but still three days away from where we'd set up a base camp. No more planes - from here we'd go by vehicle until the road ran out, then by foot.

We took a day out to hit the markets and load up with supplies, mainly hundreds of pounds of beans and rice. This was not only the favorite local dish, it was really the only bulk calories available. We had a carefully laid out meal plan: rice with powdered milk for breakfast, cooked beans for lunch, then, joy of joys, rice *and* beans for dinner. What we could get from the trees would hopefully provide some relief.

Back in the capital, Rey had ordered a banana split and it was dutifully delivered short of one ingredient - a banana. They had run out. That wasn't going to happen here in the north. Fruit was plentiful, and at our lodging we picked mangoes straight from the trees, doused them in Malagasy vanilla-bean rum and made a meal of it. Buoyed by the rum, and no doubt influenced by the nature of our cameraman, we went for a late-night skinny dip in the ocean and generally tried to take it easy before the onslaught that was about to come.

While we were frolicking, Angelo had been hatching a plan to deal with his embarrassing trap problem. He purchased some large plastic soft drink and water bottles and cut holes in them. His hope was that a mouse lemur, entering the bottle to get some fruit bait, would be unable to get out. It was a fair effort. We also sent word to a photographer who was going to be joining us in about a week: "Bring traps."

We set off early toward Anjanaharibe-Sud, the area where Rey and Ed had been working about a year earlier. They hadn't set out to catch a mouse lemur; they were there to study larger primates, and putting out a few small traps had been more an afterthought. It rained hard overnight and the next day, huddled inside one of their spring-loaded tin boxes, they found something resembling a small wet mop.

They warmed up the tiny creature with an improvised zip-lock bag cum hot water bottle. As the animal dried out, they started to realize that this adorable little bundle of fur, with its large eyes and human-like hands, could be something quite special. They'd seen other species of mouse lemur before, but nothing quite like this one. Its features were a little different and its fur a little more golden.

If Rey could now find more and document them as a new species, it could be a much-needed boost for conservation. The attention generated by a rare and special primate like this could encourage the government to protect areas for wilderness. Loggers and slash-and-burn farmers had destroyed much of the formerly pristine wilderness like modern-day pirates, with the only pirate code being one dictated by the mighty dollar. Now these Long John lumberjacks were getting close to Anjanaharibe-Sud. The jungle was under siege and needed all the conservation help it could get.

After a long day of driving, the road eventually became a drain. We got a little farther by filling in holes and creating makeshift bridges, but soon enough it was time to call in porters. We sent messengers out to the nearest villages and spent our first night in the jungle, camped by our cars.

No problem with the jungle telegraph. By mid-morning the next day workers began showing up. We had thirty-three porters in the end - a record number for me - and with our mountain of gear, we'd need every one of them.

Our camp cook dished up oodles of beans and rice. Our porters squatted in circles, six to a dish - or rather bucket – and dug in with their hands to shovel in all they could. I watched in awe and wondered which of Madagascar's previous invaders had introduced the vacuum gene that allowed these Malagasys to suck up food like human hoovers.

They wisely ate first, *then* started to haggle over how much each porter would be paid. This was Rey's area. If you come to a place like this and unwittingly pay too much, you set a precedent. You can easily ruin a lot of budgets for conservation foundations trying to do good and fair long-term work.

After much huffing and puffing and walking away and walking back, they agreed on a price - the equivalent of about thirteen dollars per person, per day. With that, this scrawny-looking group of individuals transformed themselves into an army of supermen; in lifting our gear, some of them would have been carrying half their body weight or more. Up and down hills we went for most of the day. We forded a chest-high river, then left any semblance of a trail and turned into thick jungle.

In the distance we began to hear the distinctive whooping of large lemurs, a call that resembles a sound effect from a sci-fi video game. It was a welcoming chorus that briefly distracted us from our arduous hike.

A few porters in front carved our path with machetes. The terrain was muddy and slippery and the pace laborious. I grew tired of filming our slow going and was desperate to capture something less monotonous. When we turned to go down yet another long, steep, slippery section, I made a quick mental calculation and risk assessment, started the camera rolling, shouted, "Here I go," and slid down on my backside at a cracking pace. Like a scene from the movie *Romancing the Stone*, I didn't know where I was going to wind up - certainly not facedown in Kathleen Turner's lap, but hopefully not on anything too pointy either.

At the bottom of the slope, a hundred yards from the top, I came to a very muddy but fairly graceful halt. There was silence for a moment, then Rey shouted, "Me next," and down she came. As I'd hoped, others followed the short cut and just fifteen minutes farther on we reached the exact spot where Rey and Ed had found their mouse lemur. For the next two weeks, this was home.

It was a relatively open area between the mudslide mountain and a swamp, and just a minute's walk from a gushing stream. Not that water was a problem. The porters arrived behind us, deposited our gear in a heap and left, but before we could open a bag, the skies opened up for a torrential downpour. We all huddled under a tarp as an incredible amount of water dumped on us. I doubt it could have been thicker, and the sound resembled a jet engine at mach speed.

When the rain eventually eased, our tarp became the roof of a camp kitchen. With this sort of deluge, a mere tent would not be enough. We staked out our personal sites in a fairly tight circle, with at least one tarp as backup above every shelter. Rey, being the only woman, set up a little farther away, and Naked Man, being the only hippie, camped down by the river where he could be even more in touch with nature.

Angelo and his team immediately set up their makeshift lemur traps. They nestled the drink bottles in the forks of trees at precise angles so anything getting in could not (hopefully) get out, and they popped a bit of banana in each one. They laid about a dozen such traps, then it was back to camp to look at some more rain.

With this onslaught from the heavens it took a while to sort through our equipment, but soon enough Rey made another startling discovery. Her crew had also forgotten the small scales, those used specifically for mouse lemurs. It's impossible to prove you have the smallest primate in the world when you have no way of weighing your samples.

Angelo was again in the firing line as Rey flipped. "The mission here was to get *Microcebus*, why aren't there scales for the *Microcebus*? I mean, there's no reason. We pack scales for every trip; regardless of what we're getting, we pack the big one and the little one. This is a really big problem. There are just too many screw-ups this trip. This is unbelievable, Angelo."

Angelo stayed quiet; his sullen expression said it all, but his tactic did nothing to soothe Rey's temper. She continued: "We pack for every trip the same and then we come out specifically for mouse lemurs and we don't bring the scales? You guys can't wait until we are in the field to tell me this stuff - you knew it at the airport, we could have bought some on the way in."

Continuing rain over the next week seemed to reflect the overcast mood, and the twice-daily check of the bottle traps never produced anything more than soggy, ant-covered fruit. Rey and her team captured some larger lemurs for other research, and we filmed them, but the only other things moving were slimy, black, wriggling leeches.

The leeches seemed to come at us by the hundreds, somehow even entering our tents. No one escaped these little suckers, and each leech is capable of consuming three times its weight in human blood. Naked Man, not too surprisingly, found one attached to his backside, but the champion leech magnet was Pirate Bill. He began counting each one as he ripped it off and got to forty-seven before our expedition was done.

Instinctively, like Bill, most people just yank off a leech when they see it attached to a piece of body, but that's not the best move. A quick tug will detach the leech, but possibly leave its proboscis in your skin to fester. People talk about burning off leeches or dousing them in salt, but even if you manage to get a lighter or match lit in your damp swampy rainforest, you're just as likely to burn yourself. And if your salt hasn't congealed in the wet, you're better off saving it to add some much-needed flavor to your beans and rice. I discovered a superior approach many years ago while hiking in Tasmania, one of the leech capitals of the world. In leech territory I always carry a small pair of fold-out scissors, with which you simply cut the beasties in half. A little bloody perhaps, but in its dying moments the leech will withdraw its proboscis and fall to the ground in two pieces, never to suck again. The leeches in French Guiana that can grow more than three feet long may be a challenge, but for most of the 650 leech species, I'm sure a quick snip with the scissors works best.

I actually began to wonder if we shouldn't be doing a leech story instead of lemur story - they were so much easier to catch. But no, we came for a cute and cuddly new species of primate and we were stuck with that mission.

We soon realized our fate was in the hands of the Nat Geo photographer who was meant to be joining us. We could only hope that he'd gotten the message to bring in traps - that's if he could find us and if he was still coming at all. He was already a day late. Rey laid it out for me on camera: "Unless those traps come, I'm afraid this expedition is just going to be a complete failure. Our [homemade] traps are not proving to do the job, so I'm going to keep my fingers crossed because I cannot imagine having this expedition fail. Just can't. Before I was hoping for, you know, ten animals, now I'm hoping for one. Funny how perspective changes."

Rey is normally a light-hearted practical joker, and it was heartbreaking to see her so down. Naked Man thought he had just the way to cheer her up. He wanted to take her away from the group, upstream to a spectacular waterfall he'd found, and film her under it having a shower. Naked, of course. "Sorry," I said, "who's this meant to cheer up?" It wasn't an essential ingredient for the film, not as much as, say, a mouse lemur, but I also wasn't out to spoil anyone's fun. Naked Man talked Rey into the waterfall shower and off they went.

Upon return she did seem a little less gloomy - or was that Naked Man? But the shower bit proved unnecessary: just when I thought it couldn't rain any harder, sheets of water began to gush around us. It was by far the densest rainfall I've ever seen. It was so spectacular I had to film it. I retreated to my tent, where I kept a secondary camera, and filmed the water thundering down.

Pirate Bill, already sheltering in his tent, had the same idea and was filming with his camera as well. He turned it on me as I mockingly checked the laundry I'd hung out to dry "Still wet," I said. "After four days." Just then I heard a noise behind me and turned.

A voice said jokingly, "Dr. Livingstone, I presume?"

"Ahhhhhhh!" I yelled with joy. It was Mark Thiessen, Nat Geo's in-house photographer, very much out of house. A drowned rat never looked so good. He cut to the chase, no doubt quoting the famous Stanley's less-documented follow-up question to Dr. Livingstone.

"Do you know where a guy can get a beer around here?"

Mark had found us with the help of a local guide, a couple of porters and a VIP guest. He had hiked in with Dr. Russ Mittermeier, the president of Conservation International, a long-term sponsor of Rey's work. Russ had been a primatologist for thirty years and had boundless energy when it came to spotting new species. Think fanatic bird watcher, only with chimps instead of chickadees. Mireya and Ed planned to name their new primate after Russ - *Microcebus mittermeieri* - if we could find another sample to help properly document the species.

Russ and Mark were besieged upon arrival. First by leeches - Russ had one crawling into his eye - then by Rey. "First things first," she said. "How many traps did you bring?"

"I'm not sure," said Russ. "Check with the guides." They'd received the message to bring traps, but had no idea that we'd come with none at all and were desperate.

The guide looked at Rey, perplexed. "We didn't bring any traps."

"No!" said Rey in disbelief. "Someone has traps. Who brought the traps?"

"No, no," insisted the guide. "There are no traps." If Rey had any leeches on her at that moment, I'm sure they popped off from a sudden gush of inflated blood pressure.

She pleaded, "But Russ says there are traps."

"Oh," someone switched on a light globe, "oh yes." The guide immediately started looking through a bag. Rey watched with bated breath as he pulled out a shoebox-sized container marked "URGENT". It was filled with fold-up traps.

Rey counted, "One, two, three, four . . . five. That's it." Not the twenty she'd hoped for, but better than nothing. "It's disappointing," she said, "but at the same time it's a relief to have any traps at this point. Cross our fingers that a Microcebus will take one of these five traps."

Russ's presence added to the pressure of finding some animals. He'd just met with the Malagasy president and was convinced an important discovery, like a new tiny primate, would further conservation. That night, by candlelight, he told Rey, "I think with a new government like this, with a president who is really excited about conservation, there are real opportunities to turn the tide here and to develop a whole new approach to conservation in this country."

After dinner, the rain broke and we headed out into the swamp with our headlamps on. On the few dry nights we'd had, this was how we searched for mouse lemurs. These little creatures are nocturnal and we may have been able to spot the shine of their eyes, high up in the trees, reflecting back our flashlights. So far we'd had no success, but our run of bad luck was about to end when one of our guides spotted a reflection, then saw some movement.

We all focused on the same tree and, sure enough, a tiny little bundle of ginger fur looked down at our group with giant eyes. Finally, a mouse lemur, and it seemed to hold the same wonder for us as we had for it. The primate scampered around the canopy about fifty feet up and we followed it for as long as we could through another leech-infested swamp, but there was never any hope of catching it by hand. At least we knew mouse lemurs were around. It was a thrilling find and we set our traps in its area and left them overnight.

Rey was full of hope as we raced back in the morning, but each trap held nothing for us but disappointment. Russ left us no more than twenty-four hours after arriving. He'd made a huge effort to reach us, and in his brief stay he managed to tick three species on his list of new primates to see. With a few words of comfort and encouragement, he was off to more official duties. It wouldn't be long before we'd have to follow him. After two weeks in the field, we had just forty-eight hours before we needed to be gone. Our permits, our budgets and our crews were all exhausted - nearly expired.

That night, Rey sat around the campfire with her team and together they chanted a traditional Malagasy song used to summon good luck. It is a folk song about a good man who's strong without being rude, and singers then change the words to create their wishes. In this instance they were essentially saying, "We are going to be strong. We are going to get a mouse lemur in the morning."

There was a light shower as they sang, but very late that night, after we all went to bed, the rain stopped and the guides quietly headed out without us knowing. The next thing I heard was a great commotion. "Quickly, quick, come quick!"

I bolted out barely dressed, started rolling the camera, and followed Angelo around to Rey's tent as he woke her. "Quickly, Mireya. We saw a mouse lemur and the team wants to catch it so they are keeping light shining on it."

Rey slipped on her shoes - "I can't get out of my tent quick enough!" she cried and away we went.

On the way, I shouted for Bill to go get Naked Man. The river where he camped may have had a nice aesthetic, but it was too loud for him to hear any of what was going on.

About two hundred yards from our camp, there it was. One of our guides had spotted this mouse lemur atop a tree, about twenty feet in the air. It was a thin tree, its trunk no more than a few inches wide. All the guides had eyes on the lemur and they'd spent ten minutes or so knocking down other similar trees and plants around it. The lemur was now isolated and had no place to go but down and because it was so close to where Ed and Rey had found their first sample, it was almost certainly the same new species.

I filmed it for a moment, high on its perch, and Naked Man showed up with the big camera for an alternate and higher-quality angle. With two cameras we were sure to nail whatever happened next. One of the guides started to bend the tree directly towards me, to my surprise; it was the easiest way for the tree to bend. Slowly, slowly the top branch came down with its tiny little primate attached. I was ringed by guides ready to pounce should the little fellow make a dash for it, but no need. Sure but steady, they arched the branch over, and our new little friend went straight into the secure hands of our tallest guide.

Even before the pitch, I'd withheld a secret fear. Not that we wouldn't capture one, but what if we went to all this trouble to capture one and it turned out to resemble some nasty, mangy, big-eyed rodent? In this moment of capture, my fears were allayed. You're meant to be quiet behind the camera, but I couldn't help myself. In the finished film you can hear my relief on tape. "Oh my," I gasped uncontrollably, with awe and surprise, "it's beautiful."

We jumped for joy - especially Rey. "Oh my God. Thank you, thank you, thank you," she gushed. "Oh it's so cute. Huge eyes. They are incredibly wide and alert right now." It was late and there was not much to do with our discovery but keep it secure and as calm as possible until daylight. Rey popped it into a mesh sack and would not let it out of her sight. This lucky little primate spent its first night in a tent with a former cheerleader.

In the morning we got a closer look at our tiny pocket primate. Rey sedated it for a while to take measurements and collect samples of DNA and blood to verify that this was a new species. It had all the familiar primate traits, only in miniature: five fingers and five toes (with microscopic nails), opposable thumbs, forward-facing eyes, a large brain relative to body size. Only one surprise: Rey's little King Kong was female. Queen Kong. Without the small scales and more samples there was no way to tell if this was the smallest primate species on the planet, but it was definitely close.

Our photographer clicked away and Naked Man rolled the camera on the science. There was not much time left to get everything we needed when another problem emerged. Because of the equipment lost by Air France, Naked Man had been running the camera on disposable expedition batteries - and his last battery was close to running out.

While we pondered the power problem, Bill and I set about converting our largest tent into a mobile set. We needed shots of the mouse lemur scampering around its natural environment, but we didn't want it to get away. We made the tent look as jungle-like as possible, brought in our star, and zipped us all inside. Naked Man had barely rolled a frame of this crucial footage when the inevitable happened - dead battery, with no more left.

One luxury we'd brought was a cordless drill; we knew it'd be handy in securing our small jungle set to a folding table inside the tent. It also turns out that Bill, previous to his pirate days at Club Med, had been an electrician. He re-rigged the drill batteries so it would either run the camera for a few precious minutes or, quite possibly, blow it up.

There was hot debate between Pirate Bill and Naked Man on whether it'd actually work. The pirate, more preppie than hippie, had gotten on Naked Man's nerves this trip. He seemed to challenge much of what Naked Man did, and that eroded the Naked Man's usual carefree demeanor. At one stage, for reasons no one can really remember, Naked Man threw a glass of water straight in Pirate Bill's face. Now it was getting just as ugly, but with a $60,000 camera at stake if we made a misstep.

We knew the voltage was correct, but there was no way of telling if the make-shift battery would provide the right milliamperes. Making everyone even more nervous was a glaring fact: Naked Man had tried something like this on a previous shoot and totally fried the motherboard of a similar camera. It was a tough decision, but with all the humidity our other cameras were only working intermittently - and in any case, they didn't have the quality or the zoom abilities that we needed. Called in to adjudicate, I sized up the risks and gave my most advanced technical advice: "Fortune favors the brave. Let's try it."

With a deep breath, Naked Man turned on the camera and it worked. No "pop whoosh frizzle", just some glorious milliamperes surging through and rolling tape, and just enough to finish the job and record Queen Kong's movements in her tent jungle.

Rey grabbed our queen, now adequately documented and described, and released her on a low branch near the spot where she was captured. We rolled on secondary cameras as she shot up the tree and returned to the wild.

KING KONG IN MY POCKET: Malagasy Vanilla-Bean Rum

We'd gotten through by the skin of our homo sapien teeth. It had been stressful and traumatic, but we could now head home with heads high. Less than a week after our lemur capture, and still in Madagascar, our large group sat in a restaurant celebrating our success. I was grateful when Rey offered me some moisturizer for my beacon of a nose. On our trip out from the jungle I'd copped a good dose of sun; I can't stand the feel and smell of sunscreen, and my stubbornness on this point has exposed me to too many of the sun's rays on far too many occasions.

Rey passed me her lotion and I took a quick glance at the brand. It looked like a cheap factory second with the label on crooked and bending around the tube, very Malagasys. In the dark, I could see the letter P and the rest was too hard to make out. I applied it liberally to my nose and forehead and slowly realized that everything had gone quiet. I paused for a Wile E. Coyote moment.

Ever see the old Road Runner cartoons where Wile E. Coyote is tricked into running off the edge of a cliff? Then there's that moment where he looks at the camera just before plummeting into the vast void below. That looking-at-camera moment was what I was experiencing. I turned to see our entire crew gazing at me in silence. Grins appeared, then chuckles, then spontaneous bursts of splutter. I looked at Rey, who could no longer contain herself. Some of the side-splitting eruptions of uncontrollable laughter spilled onto the floor. It was clear that Rey's usual light-hearted sense of humor had emerged from the jungle unscathed. I knew I'd been gotten good - but how good?

I checked my fingers to see if I'd unwittingly painted myself a strange color - but no, it was clear. I lifted my tube of moisturizer into better light and paid closer attention. Reading around the label I saw the full extent of the joke. I cannot imagine where in Madagascar Rey had managed to purchase it, but I had just amply lathered my entire face with penis enlargement cream.

It was a good get and couldn't be topped, but one day, I'm certain, I'll have my revenge. Everyone back at the Club wanted to know if my nose grew any longer. I told them no, but strangely, I did wake up the next day with a stiff neck.

The vanilla-bean rum was a cut above our usual exotic alcohol. The conversation revolved around our Malagasy adventures and the Club's recent brush with HR. Then I was struck with an idea that linked the two. It was clearer than ever that presidents, with a meeting or a stroke of a pen, had the power to save endangered institutions - and indeed species.

The Exotic Booze Club

I called Rey as soon as we ran out of rum. "We need to go back to Madagascar," I said.

"Need more alcohol already?" She'd guessed correctly.

"Yes, but I think we can get more than that."

We were halfway through our edit of the film, but Earl Grey gave us permission to put it on hold while Rey and I raced back to Antananarivo. We were armed with a collection of images from our shoot, maps and scientific papers, and we asked to meet with the president.

One of Rey's good friends, Serge Rajaobelina, a behind-the-scenes mover and shaker in government circles, was pulling out all stops to get us in. After several days of waiting and cajoling, our meeting was granted, not with the president, but with Prime Minister Jacques Sylla. It was just as good. We both put on our best monkey suits and, with Serge as interpreter, we went in with me rolling the camera.

The prime minister had been briefed and knew what we wanted. Rey, with backing from Conservation International, did her best-ever cheerleading. In the area where we'd found the mouse lemur, she and Ed had previously documented two other large species new to science, all endangered. Our bold request was to upgrade the entire area, about 400 square miles, from a reserve to the status of national park. It needed to be done, and with the tree cutters not far away, it needed to be done now.

Prime Minister Sylla listened carefully, asked some questions and seemed to give our matter deep consideration. In his hands lay the power to safeguard this patch of jungle and all its occupants, or to politely brush us aside and send a clear signal to Madagascar's powerful logging interests that their clout was supreme. Finally, he turned to Serge and spoke quietly: "On va le faire."

Rey knew some French and couldn't believe what she was hearing. She asked him if he could confirm this in English.

"Yes," he said, doing his best to articulate his third language. "We will do it." He gave full and unconditional support for the plan. It was what we hoped, but never what we expected.

Our journey had taken us from the deepest jungle to the corridors of political power. Although there was much paperwork to be done, Madagascar was getting a new national park and our new lemurs would remain forever protected. Thanks, in no small part, to a humble alcohol-charged gathering of the Exotic Booze Club. Other even greater events were soon to challenge the Club, but for now we had plenty to celebrate.

Chapter 8

DANGEROUS ENCOUNTERS:
Chinese Godawfulgunk

We need to up the danger level. Time to raise the bar. This was the catchcry that launched me on a harrowing six-country tour through Africa and Asia with Geo's resident herpetologist. The bar they wanted to raise was the Brady Barr - and he wasn't happy about it.

After our Burma trip, Brady went from strength to strength as a host, but it was a lot for him to handle. He had his own series, *Croc Chronicles*, which had him capturing large reptiles all over the world; thirteen half-hour shows a year, every year, for three years. You wouldn't know it to see him on camera, but Brady was exhausted, cranky and missing his family. Now he was asked to do even more.

My mandate was to produce Brady's new series, bigger and better than anything he'd done before. I was just getting my head around this when we were assigned a series title that was going to make a tough job even tougher: *Dangerous Encounters*.

We knew this would be unpopular among the field scientists we needed to work with and rely upon. Most of them would rather be associated with a title suggesting loftier attributes, such as "Worthy Science in the Field of Herpetology" or even "Adventurous Endeavors Highlighting Credible Science". But no one targets an audience that narrow, so we were stuck with the far more commercial title. And, more importantly, we were charged with living up to all the expectations such a title creates. We needed danger.

Brady and I collaborated on an elaborate plan for four hour-long shows and got our green lights. Two shows would be world firsts; to pull them off would require every bit of gusto and ounce of luck we could muster.

The first of these, *Colossal Croc*, would have Brady capturing the largest known living Nile crocodile, a man-eating behemoth called Gustave. The other show, *Countdown Croc*, would make Brady the only person on the planet to capture, in the wild, every known species of crocodile. This last possibility, in particular, lifted his spirits.

There are twenty-three known species of crocodilian, and crazy is what I call someone who wants to catch one of them. Crazy to the power of twenty-three is Brady. This was his idea, but I confess I loved it and got everyone on board. Brady had already captured twenty of the species in the wild - how difficult could it be to get just a few more?

I discovered too late that it would be difficult to the power of twenty-three. It turned out that other producers had explored this idea for *Croc Chronicles*, doing a show on each capture. Every time, these last three crocs were deemed too tough, too expensive or too risky. Now I was stuck with having to deliver all three in one episode. Just the logistics of getting to where these animals live is complicated: northern Philippines, deepest Borneo and southern China. Regardless, we headed off knowing we had to make it work.

Somewhere through the thick haze of our first stop there was a city called Beijing. We timed our arrival in the smog-filled capital to coincide with a large international conference on crocodiles. A lot of people we needed to speak with would be in one room and it was an important opportunity for some crucial face time. Not only did we need to get Brady to the right location, he needed permission to capture wild animals. Ideally, he'd provide some hands-on help to already permitted scientists, but when it comes to some of the most endangered animals on the planet, hands on is a big ask. In the wild, each of Brady's final three species number not much more than a hundred animals.

I quickly found the scientists at the conference to be a jealous lot. Many wanted Brady's job, thought they could do it better, and/or just took exception to his having what appears to be the dream gig. But at the same time, I found most respected his talents and his dedication to science.

Brady had not been enjoying the same promotion or success as his Aussie counterpart, the late great showman Steve Irwin. Brady is every bit as much a croc man as Irwin was, perhaps even more so. But, unlike Irwin, Brady could also hold his own at a conference of leading herpetologists. It was one of the few benefits afforded Brady by his PhD status; though for the most part his doctorate just added substantial pressure - especially as a representative of National Geographic - to have a good scientific reason to capture animals.

Irwin never had this problem. Entertainment, in the name of education, was all the excuse he needed. Plus the Crocodile Hunter often worked with captive animals. Irwin could borrow some animals from a zoo, even his own zoo, do his shooting and be back at the bar sinking a cold one before dark. But captive animals are rarely any use on projects that involve legitimate behavior and science, so Brady had to trudge into the wild to find animals for his shows and success was never guaranteed.

We were doing well at the conference, espousing the history and merit of Brady's contribution to science, when one of the scientists critical to the success of our mission asked the question, "So what's your new series called?"

We fell silent for a brief moment, as if overcome by some strange group amnesia. Up until that point we'd just been calling it Brady's new series. I knew I had to pipe up. Stopping short of saying "Worthy Science in the Field of Herpetology", I instead said truthfully, We've been talking about a few titles, then quickly changed the subject.

Despite such close calls, we left the conference feeling confident that Brady would be permitted to help out with projects that could get his hands on animals in the Philippines and Borneo, but China was a harder nut to crack. That would take a lot more convincing.

We recruited David Shadrack Smith, aka Shady, from the camel and tornado shows. He'd worked as a freelancer in Beijing for seven years, spoke fluent Mandarin and understood Asian customs, so he would be useful as much more than just our cameraman. We flew out of Beijing and made our way to Anhui province in the southeast of the country, home of the last wild Chinese alligators.

There are only two alligator species in the world. One is the type you hear of in Florida's Everglades, which occasionally provides added levels of complexity to the water hazards on nearby golf courses. The other, much smaller, is the Chinese alligator. If there is a crocodilian that could be called "cute", this would be it, its short, rounded snout is almost doglike. This reptile is the basis of the famous Chinese dragons. These fictional dragons are not considered evil but spiritual symbols of benevolence and good fortune, both of which we could use in our search.

We had no trouble finding captive animals as the Forestry Bureau had an extremely active breeding program, with several thousand animals confined within a research centre of wire and concrete. They proudly gave us the royal tour, and in their sole natural-looking enclosure toward the back we saw one of the things that makes these animals so special: dens.

Chinese alligators are great diggers and build underground labyrinths where they can shelter through winter. Although it was a captive setting, it was good enough for a piece to camera for another Brady show called "*Dens of Notable Subterranean Species."* Actually it was called "*Dens of Danger,*" but we didn't want to get into that right then.

Mr. Wang Wen was in charge of this alligator city and the program that monitored the wild population. He knew what we really needed, and he knew he was in control. We had to woo Wang, but to woo Wang we first needed to woo Dr. Wu, the chief scientist. Would it actually work to woo Wang Wen by wooing Wu first? Who knew? We just had to try because it was such fun to say. Woohoo!

We offered Dr. Wu a supply of the latest high-tech tracking devices to help with his conservation program. He was excited by the idea, and of course Brady would help capture the wild animals and show Dr. Wu how to use the devices. But we were at the mercy of Mr. Wang's will - and he was clearly delaying giving us a definitive answer in order to check us out.

We took Mr. Wang and his twelve-strong entourage out on the town, treating them all to massages and dinner. Massage meetings are common in China: usually two businessmen take a room together, each with his own masseuse, sip green tea and try to relax while negotiating details of, say, how best to get your hands on a wild Chinese alligator. But it was at dinner that the real business got underway, and without a word of alligators spoken.

This meal was all about assessing the quality of our collective character. Mr. Wang ordered three ornate bottles of clear top-shelf Chinese alcohol and had our glasses filled. There are several things you should know about this particular kind of fermented-rice moonshine. One is that it is *extremely* alcoholic, around fifty-proof. Another is that it is the single most revolting liquid on earth - a mere whiff of its pungent odor is enough to put most westerners on puke alert.

One summer in my childhood, a large truck carrying oranges overturned at a crossroad near our country school in Marong, Victoria. The truck was taken away, but hundreds of the scattered oranges stayed. They were then mashed into the blacktop by passing cars and began to ferment in the hot Australian sun. After a few days, the rancid smell was thick enough to slice. When the wind blew our way, every teacher and child raced indoors from the playground and shut the windows tight.

That was nearly forty years ago, and the last time I smelt anything like the liquid tripe presented to me now.

There are two other things to know about this liquor. The Chinese themselves seem oblivious to its horrendous quality and, most importantly, when someone in China looks at you with a glass in hand and says "gan bei" (drink up, empty your cup) it is *extremely* rude for you not to down your entire glass. And now, in the midst of our intense negotiations, was not the time to be rude.

There was hardly any English spoken this night; gan bei seemed to be their new favorite phrase and was usually followed by a great deal of laughing. They had played this game before. Brady was the first victim. One of them pointed to him and shouted, "Gan bei," with a raised glass. Brady hesitated and pretended not to understand. "*Gan bei,*" his nemesis insisted, then a chorus of "dwink, dwink, dwink" followed.

There was no escaping his fate. Brady gulped down half a shot and could go no further. He winced his eyes closed, turned a shade of red, then an odd green color. He put the glass down and leaned over, seeming to struggle to keep his mouth shut. I thought for sure he was going to throw up. Our Chinese friends thought this the most hilarious thing they'd ever seen. They slapped each other on the back and watched Brady as he finally came back up to the table to suck in a deep breath.

"*Gan bei, gan bei,*" they urged him to finish his glass.

"Oh noooooooo. Brrrrrrryuckuckuckuck errrra ahhh."

Apparently unable to feel his tongue, Brady just threw his hands up in surrender. He was done.

The table erupted into a chorus of, "Ahhhh, girl. Girl. He girl." They didn't know much English, but they knew enough to hurt a guy. Their laughter was uproarious.

Next, one of them pointed to Shady. "Gan bei!" From his seven years in the country, Shady knew there was no way out. He and his Chinese counterpart both threw back a shot and everyone poised to see Shady's response. He bellowed a series of guttural noises, turned a similar green color and put his empty glass on the table.

"Ahhhhhhh! The crowd was impressed. One of them instantly went to fill Shady's glass.

"NO!" Shady screamed. Then, with the benefit of fluent Chinese, he told them that he humbly and politely declined any more.

This elicited a chorus of, "Ahhhh, woman. Woman." At least he wasn't a girl, but he wasn't doing much for our credibility. To detract the attention from himself, he pointed to me and said something in

Chinese that clearly threw down the gauntlet and got everyone very excited, something about me being Australian. I knew it was coming so I'm not sure the added encouragement was needed.

This time Mr. Wang himself looked me square in the eye. "Gan bei," he declared. At another time, in another land, he would be the one dressed in black with a big cowboy hat, spurs clinking as he walked down the dirt street, only stopping to say, "Draw." This was no time to flinch.

"*Gan bei!*" I yelled back, tossing the vile brew down my throat so quick that its wretched flavor barely touched my tongue. I threw my glass down on the table with a manly roar and beat my chest. They loved the theatrics. I immediately refilled my glass, pointed to the man beside Mr. Wang and said boldly, "Gan bei." No one saw that coming.

A bison being chased by wolves has a much better chance of survival if it stops running and faces its predators. I decided to play smart bison. Mr. Wang's wingman echoed my "gan bei" with some nervousness and together we shot another drink. The group was impressed, but it was not a strategy I'd thought through. I was outnumbered twelve to one, and now they all wanted a go.

After a few more, thank God the food came out and slowed the pace a little. I tried to numb my tongue with salt and several times, when no one was looking, I managed to refill my glass with water and merely pretended it was spirits. Somehow I got through the night. They were no less impressed when I bought a bottle for the road. It wasn't for me, of course; I just had to have some of this shite for the Exotic Booze Club. But it all helped with our credibility. Mr. Wang told me to come see him tomorrow about the alligators.

Not unexpectedly, the drinking game was only the beginning of much more serious negotiations. The next day he suggested we pay a location fee of $25,000 for further work that may or may not allow Dr. Barr to capture a Chinese alligator. That was out of the question – our budget was already too tight. But it is the Asian way to start very high with any bargaining. A location fee is not uncommon, and I said we'd be happy to pay the same as we had for the captive animals, which amounted to a couple of thousand, plus we could also donate the tracking devices to Dr. Wu's program. I threw in lots of stuff about the glory of a collaboration with National Geographic and the importance of establishing such relationships and blah blah blah.

He barely softened as we continued to haggle. This was going to be a big thing for him and he would be responsible if anything went wrong, a major factor to consider when living under Chinese rule.

He leaned in. "With the gan bei..." he started in his best English.

"Yes," I said, knowing he was referring to our drinks the previous night.

"How many water?"

"Three," I said, without hesitation, and cracked a smile.

We both knew I'd drunk more than my share of the real stuff, so I wasn't too worried about disclosing my few deceptive indiscretions. At one point in the night I thought he saw me sneak some H2O and I'd given him a wink, just in case, to let him in on the joke. He liked it.

"Ahhhhh, very good," he chuckled, "very good." Then he asked, "Would you be interested in seeing a nest in the wild?"

"A nest would be good," I told him, "very good." I didn't know what we'd do with a nest, but it was a start. He said he'd get back to me in a couple of weeks and our meeting was done. It was far from perfect, but it was the best we could do.

When I told Brady of the nest option he did some quick research. He learned that there was a nest on an island in the middle of a nearby lake and the eggs inside were due to hatch in a couple of weeks. If he was there at the right time, he may get to capture a baby alligator and help it to the water. Brady was not so proud to worry about size. This kind of capture would certainly count for the story - and his record. It was still a long shot, but it was all we had, and with that we left the country with hopes for a payoff on our return. It hurt to go empty-handed, but we had no time to waste. Our next croc awaited.

At the croc conference we'd laid some of the ground-work for our next expedition in Borneo, the world's third largest island, right on the equator between Australia and China. It's the only island divided between three countries, Malaysia, Brunei and Indonesia.

We landed in the southern Indonesian city of Banjarmasin, and although it's the closest city to croc country, we still had a fourteen-hour drive ahead of us. Shady had always blamed our endless vehicle-bound hours chasing tornados for his bad back and couldn't believe I'd talked him into a shoot where we'd be stuck in a car again for some very long bumpy hours. We knew the drill though, and in preparation we'd picked up some DVDs in China; at least this time I wouldn't be driving.

The good blacktop ended just a few hours out of Banjarmasin, and it got dark soon after that. We popped one of our movies into a laptop. It was a bootleg film (I'm not sure there was any other kind to buy in China) and you get what you pay for. This was a 99-cent copy of the disaster film *The Day After Tomorrow*. The voices were dubbed Chinese, and for the subtitles they'd translated back to a loose form of English. Key words were screwed up, but we persisted and worked it out like a kind of code.

"You just hail back from perilous journey," the female lead declared in subtitles, while conveying a great sense of pain and anguish. Then she asked, "You sink matter?" It was a recurring question, and soon enough we worked out that "sink matter" was most likely (and for some unknown reason) a translation for "okay". Once we knew that, it all made sense.

Our brains started doing these corrections automatically and we managed to black out the errors as if nothing was wrong and delve into the filmic experience. Then came the climactic nail-biting scene. A lieutenant rushed in to deliver the tragic news that one of our main stars was, and I quote, "in the soup". We burst out laughing at this somber moment and figured that either our hero was dead or his last name was Campbell.

Our other bootleg copies weren't as much fun and only seemed to make the trip longer. When we finally rocked into End-Of-Road Village, there were three choices of where to sleep: the car (an intolerable thought after all that driving), a local flea-bitten brothel (eek!), or on the powerboat we were taking on our next leg. Upon reflection there weren't any choices at all and we squeezed onto the boat for some precious shut-eye.

Rivers in Borneo operate like highways. In Banjarmasin, a city flanked by two frequently flooded rivers, boats are a way of life, and many houses are built on rafts. Our river highway soon became more of a country backroad. Over the next two days, the waterways narrowed and we jumped onto progressively smaller and smaller craft. This was why no one had done these trips before: in China it was near-insurmountable politics, and in Borneo the obstacles were near-insurmountable logistics.

Our objective, though, was an exciting one: an extremely rare crocodile known as Tomistoma, the false gharial. Not surprisingly, the false gharial resembles the gharial, another type of crocodilian. Both have thin, gnarly teeth that hang on the outside of their long and extremely slender snouts. They both use them to snag fish and it's a feature that makes them, by far, the strangest looking of the twenty-three species. The false gharial is the most mysterious and least studied of the crocodiles, but we know it inhabits the ever-declining peat swamp forests of Indonesia and Malaysia and is one of the largest species ever documented; reliable historical reports have it stretching to around twenty feet.

Such giants are no doubt long gone, victims of the habitat loss that continues to ravage this part of the world. We continued on our boats, and no matter how far we travelled into the country, we never escaped the sound of chainsaws illegally cutting down trees at night.

We eventually traded down to wooden canoes and moved along a muddy river in the province of West Kalimantan, once home to Borneo's famed and feared tribes of headhunters. But instead of wild ululating natives wielding poison-tipped spears we found a soft-spoken white guy with an Australian accent. Not even I realized that the tentacles of the Aussie mafia reached this far.

Mark Bezuijen is a leading international crocodile researcher fighting an uphill battle to save the last of the wild false gharials. He'd been doing field research on the species for ten years and had recently moved to Borneo to assess habitat and count animals. He was roughing it in a basic and isolated riverside shelter, at least three days from the nearest pub.

Mark had recently received a small grant from National Geographic's Expeditions Council and was keen to show us his work. We had little time to waste; commuting alone had sucked up more than a week of this trip and we had to get back to China fast. We had just a few days to work with Mark and capture a false gharial in the wild. It was a tall order and there was no room for failure. There was no way we could come back, so it was now or never. That's when Mark broke some disturbing news.

His count of animals had not been going well. Habitat loss wasn't the only problem for false gharials; locals had been poaching their eggs. Mark showed us some large fist-sized croc eggs he'd just acquired from a villager. They had expired and now represented three false gharials that would never be born. That may not sound like a lot, but by Mark's estimate there were only about a hundred animals left in the wild. In the last century or so, scientists had only managed to capture nineteen of them.

We had forty-eight hours to do the impossible. We decided to go to where the eggs had reportedly been collected - maybe mummy croc was still around. We jumped in our canoes and paddled up a narrow creek for five long hours. Downed trees, most likely left by the outlaw loggers, regularly blocked our channel. Our guides had saws and we often had to stop to cut and clear our waterway. Around dusk it opened into a swampy lake and the humid air filled with wild sounds - frogs, insects and some strange whooping I didn't recognize.

Once it was fully dark, we paddled quietly and said nothing above a whisper. Mark and Brady swept the water's surface with their headlamps looking for eye shine. After several laps of the lake we had nothing. We turned for camp knowing this bust had cost us half of our time here. The expedition rule of Last-Day Payoff usually gives you more than two days to think about it.

Brady thought the swamps looked a bit dry and he gambled that we should try our final night on the larger river - less hacking trees and more looking. Mark agreed it was as good a chance as any. We quietly floated along the river in our canoes until Brady saw a flash; he thought it was eye shine. We pulled over and waited for what seemed ages - five, ten, fifteen, twenty minutes. If it were up to me we would have kept going long ago, but I stayed quiet and tried not to slap the mosquitoes too loudly.

Without warning, Brady quietly got out of the canoe and into the water, leaving behind his snare pole. It was as if the pressure and the tropical heat had finally driven him mad. It does happen in this business. There's an infamous industry story of a cameraman who stared at a nest of eagle eggs, day and night, for more than three weeks, waiting to film them hatching. Sleep deprived and stir-crazy, he finally snapped and smashed them - only to discover they were all rotten.

Now I watched Brady wade deep under some low hanging branches by the shore - right where he'd seen the eye shine - as if on a suicide mission. Shady and I both stayed put in our separate canoes; I held an infrared camera that can see in the dark without white light, and Shady stood by with his big camera ready to go. If Brady tangled with a croc, all the lights could come on.

We couldn't see well and remained confounded as to why Brady had entered the water. What could he do without a snare pole? And if it was a baby croc, where was mum? You also have to understand that none of us ever enter the water lightly, and although these animals can grow longer than a minibus, that wasn't necessarily Brady's greatest fear.

Over a decade of croc hunting in filthy ditches and developing-world waterways, Brady, his producers and his cameramen have all endured a variety of waterborne illnesses, and we live in fear of a disease called schistosomiasis, otherwise known as snail fever. This disease starts as a parasite that burrows into the foot of a snail. Once inside said slug, it turns into an alien mother bee that produces thousands of new-and-improved larvae with an appetite for film crews. While the afflicted snail goes about its business, perhaps wondering about that strange gnawing feeling it's having on the inside, new larvae emerge from its skin daily, particularly when there's a disturbance in the water or the larvae sense chemicals found on human skin. This is where someone like Brady comes in handy.

As Brady wallows around looking for crocs, say in a stream in Borneo, the little nasties swim out of the snail and attach themselves to his skin and dig in. They move through the blood stream, hang out in the lungs for a while, then off for some R&R in the liver. They spend several weeks working out, feeding on red blood cells and growing to a worm about half an inch long. Then they start playing the dating game . . . and you know where that leads. They hook up, they marry, have some kids, and wonder what to name their young. It's hard not to get your children all mixed up when you're producing as many as 3000 a day. And there in your liver they can live, happily ever after, for up to twenty years.

I thank my lucky bourbon that my liver has never been so accommodating, but more than once Brady has found himself hosting more than a TV show. It starts with a bellyache, then a cough, then a fever, closely followed by fatigue and simultaneous bouts of vomiting and diarrhoea. Organ damage is quite possible, the chance of bladder cancer increases, and your friends no longer seem to love you in the same huggy kind of way. An estimated 200 million people in Asia, South America and Africa contract snail fever each year. It is the world's second most socioeconomically devastating parasite, beaten only by malaria.

Knowing all this, and knowing Brady's fear of parasites, I knew he hadn't just popped in for a cool down. But what? I watched him move slowly and softly under a maze of overhanging branches. Suddenly I heard the thrashing of water and a most incredible sound, like a deep-throated quacking duck. "Woooohoooo," Brady exuded. He spun to face us, revealing a grin from ear to ear and a three-foot-long croc. "Got my first Tomistoma, boys."

I maintain my assertion that Dr. Brady Barr is the luckiest man alive. He'd seen the croc just under the surface, but the overhanging branches had prevented a clear shot with his snare pole. In desperation, he went in and waited. When it popped up again he managed to blind the animal with his headlamp, creep up to its snout, and grab it barehanded.

Gushing with excitement, Brady told Shady's camera, "This is [a crocodile] I never thought I would get to see, let alone capture. This is a night I'm going to be telling my grandkids about."

Mark recorded some measurements, tagged the Tomistoma, and we released it back into the water. Finally, we had one in the can.

Boat, boat, boat, boat, car, car, car and several days later, we were back on a plane - or rather, two different planes. I got a message from

DANGEROUS ENCOUNTERS: Chinese Godawfulgunk

Mr. Wang Wen saying it was time to return to China to talk about the nest. But returning to Anhui province would jeopardize our plans for the third animal, the Philippine croc. I needed to head straight to the Philippines to get things rolling, so I sent Brady and Shady back to Anhui as a two-man team. All our hopes were with them and one single lousy alligator nest.

They moved fast and didn't waste time with protocol, instead going directly to the lake that held the wild Chinese alligators. The island with the nest was small and within sight from shore. Shady's language skills proved invaluable. He and Brady found four young assistants at a monitoring station across from the island, and Shady, from years of experience in China, knew what to do. He humbly pumped out his honorable chest, dropped names, flashed an official-looking document with who knows what on it, and spoke of already having permission to go out. He said they were in a hurry, and talked the assistants into a boat trip without getting a lot of people involved. It was a good strategy. But beyond that, they had nothing. They went to the nest with the greatest of hopes - and were devastated to find it empty.

The gators had all hatched and made their way to the water, maybe two or three days earlier. It was a crushing blow. In total despair, they stood looking at an empty hole surrounded by leaves and twigs. Brady began imitating the noise made by a baby croc, something of a closed-mouth swallowing sound. He hoped it would attract the mother, but nothing. As they were about to leave, one of the research assistants piped up, saying something in Mandarin.

"What's he want?" Brady asked bitterly.

Shady translated what at first seemed to be a confusing question. "He wants to know if we would like to see the other nest." Shady asked for clarification. "The other nest?"

"Yes, the other nest," the assistant confirmed. Who knew there were two?

"Hell, yeah," Brady said.

Just a short distance away they found a pile of foliage that Brady instantly recognized as a closed nest. Shady started rolling as they approached. Brady began making his baby-croc noise again, and this time he thought he got a reply - from underneath the foliage. Brady put his ear to the ground and listened hard. With everything quiet, he could hear tiny little peeping sounds coming from inside the nest. The crocs were hatching.

"These guys are ready to go," he said with bated breath. Mum was probably nearby, but they never saw her. Brady and the assistants gently opened up the nest and revealed the eggs. Brady picked up one that was cracking open. The shell was soft and he began to massage it. He continued to make a croc noise and the little being inside continued to answer back. Slowly it popped out its head and opened its eyes; the first thing it ever saw was Brady. If that were me I'd probably be shocked back into my shell, but this little guy continued to work its way out and right into Brady's big paternal hands.

"Look at that, look at that," Brady gushed over the eight-inch hatchling. "I'm a momma, I'm a momma."

Did I mention - the luckiest man alive? Brady and the assistants helped those that hatched get to the water. Birds and predators would normally make this the most perilous journey of these gators lives, but with a little help they made it to the lake safe and sound. Brady then covered the nest to give the other eggs more time. This one nest represented close to twenty per cent of the species entire wild population.

Within a few days, Brady and Shady joined me in the Philippines with the good news about the alligators. I was elated; two down, one to go. I had smoothed the final hurdles with the scientists in the Philippines, a team from Holland, and had managed to delay them from capturing and tagging a small group of animals at their site so Brady could help. This was the only known site where wild Philippine crocs had been regularly observed. It sat in a remote quarter on the large island of Luzon.

The Philippine croc population had it rough, thanks in no small part to the local practice of fishing with dynamite. One stick can get you a lot of fish, and the crocs become collateral damage. This particular freshwater species has a thick bony plate on its back, a kind of heavy armor, but even it doesn't do so well against TNT.

Our Dutch scientists understood what we were doing and that this was Brady's final species, but I don't think any of us realized what the capture of all twenty-three species, in the wild, meant to Brady. For me, up until now, it'd been all negotiations and logistics. But for Brady, this was something he'd dreamed about for much of his life, and there were plenty of times he thought it'd never happen.

He'd researched crocs on five continents, he was the first American ever to capture a wild gharial, was the first scientist to capture one of the legendary cave crocs of Madagascar, and was the first scientist in a hundred years to capture a wild Siamese croc. But now, beyond all that, his proudest moment was within reach. Just one more croc to go and he'd set a world record that may never be matched.

DANGEROUS ENCOUNTERS: Chinese Godawfulgunk

Lightning cracked through the night sky as we hiked to our known croc site, a dark murky pond. The small size of the waterhole should have made this last animal the easiest of the final three. The largest croc out there would be no more than a few feet long, and Brady wanted to try capturing it alone - no boat, just a snare, a headlamp, patience and nerves of steel. He slowly waded out. This one, more than any other, would be worth the risk of contracting snail fever.

Shady and I waited quietly on the shore with the Dutch scientists. Every now and then we'd feel a light sprinkle of rain. My camera was switched to infrared and I could see Brady, in black and white, as he wallowed around for a good twenty minutes. He imitated the baby croc distress call over and over, but nothing. After a few laps of the waterhole he started coming back.

Despite our anticipation, it was clearly a bust. There was no signature "woohoo", no relief-inducing "got 'em, boys". The supposedly easiest of the last three wasn't so easy after all. He walked back to us looking downcast. Shady and I were both still rolling but were just about to button off when Brady started to speak. Quietly he said, "I got a little teary-eyed out there." Indeed, he was choking back tears, but not from disappointment. I heard a little peep, looked down in his hand, and saw a tiny baby Philippine croc, about two weeks old and less than a foot long. Brady was overcome. Like a gift from the heavens, or perhaps the depths, it'd popped up right in front of him and he'd simply reached out and grabbed it. Did I mention lucky?

"I can't believe it," Brady whispered to himself. "I can't believe I pulled it off." His first-ever capture fifteen years earlier was a hatchling alligator, and this little find seemed to be a nice bookend. Brady composed himself as best he could but continued to gush, It's been a long time coming. He'd done it. We'd all done it.

The other scientists were thrilled by this capture too as it proved that the nests here had produced young this year. But as big as this moment may have been, it was still with the smallest of crocs. I was worried that *Dangerous Encounters* was looking more and more like *Kindergarten Croc*. We needed to dramatically up the scale of our quarry.

As much as Brady wanted to shout his record from the rooftops, we had no time to rest on laurels. We managed a quick celebratory drink, of course, but we now had our second story to get in the can - hopefully another world first. With a huge thank you to the team from Holland, we headed to East Africa. No more kissing babies; we needed one of the biggest, most terrifying man-eaters known to humankind.

Burundi is one of Africa's smallest and most troubled nations. It sits among the top ten of the world's poorest countries and, at last count, had the lowest per capita gross income in the world. Eighty percent of the population lives in poverty, and more than half its children are malnourished. While it sits to the north of the world's longest freshwater lake - Lake Tanganyika (420 miles from bottom to top) - with Tanzania to the east, Burundi is locked away from the ocean.

The ethnic situation in Burundi echoes that of the neighbor on its northern border, Rwanda. Under Belgian rule, these two were the same country, but the Belgians never did leave places better than they found them, and Burundi's eventual independence only sparked political assassinations, a continual slaughter of civilians, and a to-and-fro of ethnic refugees between the two African countries that continues today.

More recently, Rwanda has begun to heal, but Burundi still threatens to haemorrhage. At the time we arrived, insurgent groups representing the eighty-five per cent Hutu majority had been battling the Tutsi-dominated government for more than a decade. There's a third minority that no one ever hears about called the Twa, and about half of all three groups are Catholic. It seems strange to me that so many people can agree that the Pope is cool and not agree that killing each other is going to look bad at the pearly gates, but after 500 years of living together maybe they were starting to work it out. We heard that the ethnic rivalry had stabilized, peace agreements had been signed, and now might be the time to head in. The unrest was why Brady hadn't come here before, but now was our chance. All but one Hutu group seemed to have made peace with the country's elected leaders, and there was great hope for an election just a month away.

Despite research suggesting that our timing couldn't be better, the drive from the airport and into the capital, Bujumbura, was unsettling. The place felt like a shaken fizzy bottle with a loose lid. White UN trucks slowly drove down the main road amid random scuffles and general mayhem. Women scurried from our view, and men seemed to look at us with menacing eyes. It's one of those places where you don't stay in a hotel but a compound, one with high walls and armed guards. The relative stability we'd heard of was very relative. Just before we'd arrived, Hutu rebels raided a camp on the border and killed 160 innocent refugees. They were the poorest of the poor, who'd not long ago escaped the mayhem in war-torn Rwanda; all but four of the dead were women and children. And this was a "good" time to visit. It wasn't the kind of danger we were looking to insert into *Dangerous Encounters*, but Burundi did have one thing found nowhere else in the world: Gustave.

Gustave is a Nile crocodile of legendary proportions. Carefully analysing photographs taken from afar, Brady calculated him to be around twenty feet long. To put that in context, Brady's captured more than 3,000 crocodilians, and the largest was just over 15 feet. We guessed Gustave to be about sixty-five years of age with a weight of around a ton. Those are the facts of the matter, and then there's the *legend* of Gustave, certainly the most fabled croc in Africa. By some estimates he's killed 300 people, including the wife of an ambassador. Some locals say he hunts for sport and eats the bullets of those who try to shoot him.

A naturalist with binoculars counted three bullet-hole scars along Gustave's side, and this croc also has a large black scar on his head, which several eyewitnesses accurately described after seeing a loved one taken by the man-eater. There's also little doubt that Gustave would have fed on some of the civil war casualties that'd washed downstream from the conflict in Rwanda in 1994. In just three months, at least 500 000 people were butchered; according to some it was as many as twice that number. At one stage bodies reportedly clogged the mouth of the Ruzizi River where Gustave lived. But it's also certain that Gustave was blamed for every crocodile attack within a hundred-mile radius, and as crocodiles will happily go a month between a good meal - due to their slow metabolism - the serial-killing notion was farfetched.

Our ambitious plan was for Brady to capture Gustave and attach a tracking device. With that we would soon see if this croc was stalking human flesh, or if he was just a large version of every other opportunistic crocodile in the river. If he was truly a problem, we'd recapture him for a zoo.

At least one other would-be croc wrangler had tried to capture Gustave and that was the Frenchman who gave Gustave his name, self-taught naturalist Patrice Faye. Faye's obsession with Gustave, and his attempt to capture him in 2002, was the subject of a documentary where he built a giant metal cage by the river. The cage was five feet high, about six feet wide and nearly thirty feet long, and inside he tied a live goat. Thankfully for the goat, Gustave didn't bite. Faye went on to spice up the menu a bit, trying chickens and even a dog, but neither Gustave nor any other croc took the bait.

It was a harebrained idea. Crocs have been around since the time of the dinosaurs and a species doesn't get to do that by being stupid. As one croc song suggests, "don't be taken in by his foolish grin". These animals are acutely aware of their surrounds and rarely need to take unnecessary risks for lunch. If they have to, crocs can eat a fifth of their body weight in one sitting and make that feed last them for twelve months. That's it. Not three meals a day but one meal a year.

Brady told me his idea for capturing Gustave. It was simple and pure, and the most jaw-droppingly terrifying concept you can imagine. He wanted no big cages, no big boats, no large crews nor thick nets. For this twenty-foot-long man-eating legend, Brady gave me a short shopping list: one canoe, the smallest and narrowest we could find; one fearless volunteer to sit behind him and paddle; a head lamp; and a snare. I'd have to work on the volunteer, but everything else was ready to go, and clearly already in Brady's arsenal were balls of steel.

Once Brady crept up and snared Gustave, he'd race to shore and try to drag this toothy giant up the bank. Shady had commitments back in the States, so to film this whole wild affair I had a calm and collected cameraman from South Africa, Graeme Duane. And to help Brady with the croc we had ever-cheerful, easygoing scientist Hannes Botha, also from South Africa.

The political situation around town continued to make us nervous, but our plan to leave and head straight into the field hit a snag. Some scouts we'd hired told us that Gustave had moved upriver and was now closer to rebel fighting. Our local fixer went ahead as scheduled, but we held back to rethink our approach. Brady was going to be out there with a headlamp, the lone light in a dangerous country; he may as well tattoo a target on his forehead with the words "shoot here".

We mulled the situation over from the security of our compound and decided we would head out with some additional guards and turn around if it looked too hairy. Before we could act, journalist Michael McRae arrived with news. Michael was working on an article about Gustave for Nat Geo's *Adventure* magazine. "We've had three reports," he told us. "They've blown up a bus."

On the lone road to our destination, one of the rebel groups had chosen the day of our scheduled expedition to move south and make its first-ever daylight attack, swooping down on a checkpoint and throwing a grenade into a crowded minibus. One that looked a lot like ours. As if we needed further proof, a guide also came to warn us. He played a message on his phone that he'd just picked up, from our fixer at the scene of the explosion. "Turn around, turn around, you can't come," he yelled in the message. Behind his pleas rang the distinct sound of gunfire.

We all sat in stunned silence. That could have been us. It could even have been meant for us. What now? We all thought the same thing, but I think Brady said it first: "Let's get the hell out of here."

We were happy to deal with giant man-eating crocs, but gun-toting rebels were another matter. Our local team was upset that we were leaving so quickly; our expedition was good income for them. The government was also red-faced and offered us a hundred armed soldiers to form a perimeter around our croc hunt if only we would change our minds and stay. We thought about it for a nanosecond. A Tutsi-dominated military unit was just as likely to draw fire as repel it, and worse, people could be killed trying to protect us.

Producers will do a lot for a film. We miss birthdays, holidays, weekends and anniversaries. We risk marriages, lives and limbs and deprive ourselves and others of food, water, warmth, shade, sleep and more. The tools in our unpublished handbook include lying, cheating, seducing, gambling, rule breaking, law breaking, stealing, bribing, enticing, cajoling and other such things that our employers would never, and could never, encourage or condone. It's all for the holy grail of our profession - the film. We may not do so well in polite society, but all's well if we get to head out and do it all over again. Sometimes it's hard to decide where to draw the line, but this time it was clearly not worth the risk. It was time for the one thing we rarely have in our arsenal: a plan B.

Less than forty-eight hours after arriving in Burundi we were on a plane out. I didn't even have time to buy any rebel alcohol for the Club. What we most needed now was a new story, preferably one where we'd get to catch a nice big croc and where our cameraman would do the only shooting. We thought about Uganda; Brady had worked with big crocs there before, but permits for capture take more time than we had. The only solution was to head to Hannes's research area in South Africa where our accompanying scientist already had a permit to capture.

We landed in Johannesburg and drove three hours northeast to the lake formed by Flag Boshielo Dam. It was good to be in a safe country smelling the fresh South African air as we whizzed across the water in Hannes's fourteen-foot research boat. In the late afternoon we scanned the banks along a nature reserve that borders part of the dam and we found a cluster of very large crocs - not the reported size of Gustave, of course, but huge by any other standard. This was the spot.

Hannes was working on a long-term project here, looking at nesting ecology and the range size of large Nile crocs. Hannes had good scientific reasons to be catching crocs but wasn't necessarily after the largest he could find - until now. Gustave left a big gap to fill and we knew we wanted big, but that would only be part of it. Even if we got lucky, getting a big ol' croc is an event, not a story. Working out the actual plot was my problem and I'd have to deal with it sooner or later. I chose later. I didn't have any ideas, just a plan not to tell anyone back home what we were doing until I'd worked it out.

We returned to the croc hot spot after dark and set to work. After we'd drifted in and switched off all lights but for Brady's headlamp, Brady imitated the noise of a baby croc in distress and soon the eyes of crocs in the water shone back at us like reflectors on a bicycle. We played cat-and-mouse with some crocs for a while, then Brady spotted the one he wanted. The eyes were so far apart on this monster that Brady double-checked it was indeed one reptile and not two.

We all sat on the boat, quieter than mice. Brady was on the bow reaching out with his snare while I rolled on the infrared camera and, as usual, Graeme stood by with his big camera and lights ready to go. We waited for an age as Brady patiently lowered his snare, careful to aim his headlamp directly at his quarry, thus blinding it to our approach. Slowly the ring of rope went around the croc's neck and wham, Brady pulled it tight. In doing so he unleashed all the cold-blooded fury this monster could muster. As it thrashed about violently in the water, Brady quickly handed his pole to Hannes leaving Brady with just the rope. As he did so, the croc gave an especially violent jerk that knocked Brady off his feet and seemed to tangle him in the rope. Before he could recover, the croc pulled on the rope again, so fast and so hard that it yanked Brady clear over the bow of the boat and into the water. All I saw were his two legs flying up in the air and he was gone.

The audio from Hannes would have to be bleeped out. We all knew the danger Brady was now in, not only from the snared angry beast thrashing about with snapping jaws, and not only from getting tangled in the snare itself, but also from the other giant crocs that were undoubtedly racing to our area to check out the commotion. At this precise moment, I'd bet Brady would have been happy to be back in nice, safe Burundi. Crocs are highly attuned to any disturbance at the water's surface as this is where they get much of their food, and on tonight's menu, herpetologist al dente was looking good.

When Jesus walked on water, I imagine he did it with poise and grace. Brady's imitation was less serene but no less impressive. He stood up waist-deep in water and, just as the croc rolled towards him, he turned and hoisted himself back into the boat in one smooth adrenaline-pumped move. He was soaked, wide-eyed, and that gan bei shade of green, but in one piece. What's more, he still held the rope.

The thrashing croc rolled close enough to the bow that Brady could hoist part of it out of the water. The animal protested with a deep, disturbing growl. Hannes revved the engine and we headed to the nearest bank. We all jumped out and started pulling on the rope to get the croc up on the shore. It was hard work with four of us pitching in, and we began to realize that the animal we had was longer than our boat.

Eventually our giant came right to the water's edge. Brady threw another rope around its jaws to clamp them shut and gave me the job of keeping it secure. I appreciated his trust, but this was more responsibility than I cared for. Before I could protest, Brady jumped on the croc's back like a rodeo cowboy and put a strip of duct tape over its eyes; in the dark it would be calmer and less stressed. With another strip of tape he made good use of a fascinating bit of croc biology. Crocs have incredible power to bite down, but not much power at all for opening up, so Brady wrapped the second piece of tape around the croc's snout. That would be plenty enough to seal its jaws shut and I could relax my grip on the rope.

We all got behind the croc and tried to push it farther up the bank. With a "one, two, three" I heaved till I thought I'd have a hernia, but with no result. It was like trying to budge a car-sized sack of wet wheat. We'd have to get Hannes's measurements with it sitting where it was, at the crocodilian lunch counter, half in and half out of the water. I went on high alert to look for other approaching reptiles.

We didn't have much time. A big animal like this builds up a lot of lactic acid thrashing about, enough to kill it if it's then made to sit still for too long. Brady ran his tape down the croc. It was even bigger than he'd thought – just a hair short of 16 feet - and therefore the largest croc he'd ever captured. A great headline, but still not a mission-driven, hour-long story.

At Nat Geo headquarters I'd had our engineers make up a tripod adapter so I could run Brady's snare pole up in the air with a camera attached. There's never enough time or space on Brady shoots for a proper jib, but this make-shift contraption gave us an elusive aerial view that put 16 foot length in perspective; from above, Brady was a speck at the end of the tail. Before we released it, Brady had an idea. In his bag of tricks he had a bite-force gauge. Doesn't everyone?

The engineering wizards at Geographic had made the pressure gauge for another show where Brady tested the bite force of alligator snapping turtles. These turtles sit on the bottom of lakes and rivers with their mouths open and wiggle their worm-like tongues. When a fish comes in for a look, snap! The turtle slams its mouth shut with incredible bone-crushing power - around 1,000 pounds of force. Now Brady wanted to test the power of the largest croc he'd ever captured. Trick was, he'd have to undo the duct tape.

Hannes sat on the back of the croc to help contain any thrashing; I was back on rope duty. Brady again sat behind its head and carefully cut the tape from around the giant jaws, then reached down and put a hand on the end of the animal's snout to pull on its upper jaw. The croc was happy to open wide - maybe it could finally do something more than growl. Brady untaped its eyes and carefully moved his bite-force gauge into its mouth. *Whammo!* Its jaws clamped down hard on the gauge, as if it was venting rage. It then bit down even harder, bending the gauge with such power it looked as though it'd snap. Brady's eyes lit up as he read the meter: "Two thousand five hundred! - that's over one ton of bite force," he yelled, "and the animal's exhausted!"

Once it decided to release our gauge, we carefully removed its bindings, and Brady leapt off its back and let it slide back into the water. It darted a short distance away and kept a disturbing eye on us. We packed up, ever so careful not to fall from the boat on the return trip. After months of planning and replanning, darting between countries and throwing caution to the waters, we had twenty minutes of precious tape with a very large croc, and an incredible measure of 2,500 pounds of bite. We headed back for a well-earned drink. I knew we had just shot a great end to a film; we had a payoff, but to what?

We slept on it and by morning an idea was clear. I suggested to Brady we replace the Gustave pitch with a film called *Bite Force* and measure a range of different animals to see how they compare. We'd try to find the biggest bite on the planet, knowing that we probably already had it in the can. He loved it.

I'd worked on a pitch a few years earlier called *Animal Mechanics* where we planned to test the bite of a great white shark. That series never got off the ground, but this was different. From my previous research I knew testing a great white had never been done, but I also knew it was feasible. Brady threw in a bunch of big biters he thought would be worth testing. "Let's compare domestic dogs to wild dogs." He'd always been curious about that. Lions and hyenas were obvious. And why not start with people as a base reference? Who needed Gustave? We had *Dangerous Encounters: Bite Force*.

DANGEROUS ENCOUNTERS: Chinese Godawfulgunk

The new plan was well received back at headquarters, and in Africa we had most of the animals we wanted to test. Within a month we had the following top measures for pounds of bite force:

Human - 127
African wild dog - 317
Large domestic dog - 328
Lion - 691
Hyena - 1,000
Alligator snapping turtle - 1,004
Crocodile - 2,500

It seemed our croc bite was the strongest of any animal on record. We thought a large great white shark would be the only possible rival. It was time again to go fishing.

Shark activity in South Africa's Gansbaai area, just around the coast from Cape Town, is well documented. It's where twenty-foot-long great whites leap into the air as they torpedo up from the depths to grab hapless seals near the surface. You can induce this spectacular leaping behavior by dragging a seal carcass behind a boat. If you can't find a dead seal, a piece of foam that looks like a seal will do just as well. Not a recommended place to go waterskiing. Some of the largest sharks on the planet congregate here, weighing around two tons each, and they've earned this area the name Shark Alley. It's another good place to keep yourself *in* the boat, and I mean *all* of yourself.

Andre Hartman was *mostly* in the boat when he was recently bitten, proving mostly to be not quite good enough. Andre is a curmudgeonly character, a curly-haired boat captain who guides film crews, scientists and tourists through the waters of Shark Alley. He's a salt-of-the-sea, shark-watching veteran. With a bit of bait, he can get large sharks to surround his boat and bob their heads above the surface, just an arm's reach from his stern. It's only an arm's reach, of course, if at the end of this experience you still have both arms. If your timing is right you can reach out and touch the sharks on the nose as they pop up looking for food.

Andre was sitting on the back of his boat a few weeks earlier, embarking on such a perilous activity, when a shark came to the surface and charged his bait. For some reason Andre jerked the bait out of the water, but the captain forgot that his bare foot was still hanging. It was then the only thing left for the shark to sample. With a stroke of luck, or perhaps it was foot odor, the great white did little more than drag its razor-sharp teeth across the middle of Andre's right foot. Had it closed its mouth at that moment, Andre would have been reduced from a size ten to a size five. As it was, the slicing action split open the top of his foot and it took a bunch of stitches to pull it back together. A nasty wound, but by great white standards barely a scratch.

Andre was back in bare feet chumming the water for us while Graeme and I filmed Brady preparing a newly designed bite-force gauge - a sturdy metal construction that was about the size of a shoebox and entirely water-proof. The weak link was the cable that followed a rope back to the boat and connected to a meter. All going well, Brady would hold the meter and call out readings of bite force as the shark chomped on the gauge, but we could only hope that a wayward bite wouldn't cut the line in two.

Andre shoved the gauge into a large tuna and secured it with cable ties. "That oughta do it," he said. "One good chomp on this fish should get you a good reading."

It was a perfect day with barely a ripple on the water, and soon enough the chum attracted a couple of extremely large sharks. As they circled the boat, we estimated them both to be just over 15 feet. I had a waterproof camera on the end of a pole and leant over the side to film underwater. It's a hair-raising way to shoot. The images are fed into a pair of goggles and recorded on a video deck by your feet. With the goggles on, it feels like you're in the water with the camera - in this case, a few inches from some of those two-inch-long shark teeth. But the really scary part is not being able to see anything else, like what's coming up beside you as you hang over the boat. One can only hope it isn't more of those pearly whites.

Brady lowered the baited bite-force gauge into the ocean beside me. From the shoebox he had about three feet of attached pipe, then the rope and cable. A few buoys on the pipe helped it float on the surface. The sharks were instantly curious and quickly moved in to inspect their free lunch. Then there was a most curious and unexpected turn of events.

We think of sharks as indiscriminate eaters that feast mechanically on whatever floats before them. Not so. With my pole-cam I watched a giant shark approach the bait, bare its teeth and, with amazing dexterity, carefully strip the fish away without touching the gauge at all. I was in awe. But this impressive ability wasn't going to help us get a bite-force reading.

Brady pulled the line back in for a rethink. We needed to create more of a feeding frenzy. Andre switched tactics and put the gauge into a mesh bag and jammed it with bait. This time the sharks would have to rip into the bag, and hopefully bite hard on the gauge.

DANGEROUS ENCOUNTERS: Chinese Godawfulgunk

A new shark showed up, even bigger, and feverishly ripped into the bag. He violently thrashed it around, but before Brady could get a decent reading, the shark exerted such force that it snapped the rope and, with it, the attached cable. The shark swam off still munching free fish with its very own newly acquired bite-force gauge for dessert. Brady was left with nothing but ripped cables and a piece of frayed rope.

Geo's Wizards were prepared. Most of the stuff these engineers make seems to get destroyed in the field at least once, so they learned long ago always to send a backup. We had one more chance, and this time we used thicker rope. The bag was just a short reach from the back of the boat when the same shark returned for another go. Its eyes rolled to the back of its head giving the impression it was possessed as it bit down harder and harder on the bite-force gauge. This time it was unable to break away. Brady began excitedly shouting out reading after reading: "180, 382, 279, 530 - that's a bite there, boys."

We repeated the experiment several times and got more: 387, 669, 529. The top reading was 669 pounds of force. It seems that with such sharp teeth, great whites don't require any more bite force than a lion to secure their meals. Our croc, with 2,500 pounds of force, was the clear winner. It was a fun show to shoot, fun to put together, and fun to watch. All that helped to make it a huge hit and, later, other producers would work with Brady on sequels.

Before leaving Africa I picked up some flavored moonshine for the Club - curiously sold in test tubes - and back home I spun stories of our adventures from both shows. A visiting executive from the Nat Geo channel harped on about the first episode and the marvel of Brady capturing his last three species in the wild. "What were you going to do," he asked me, "if you didn't get one of those crocs?"

"Well," I said, "we knew that wasn't an option, so we got 'em."

"Wow," he commented, "you *do* like to live dangerously."

"Here," I said, "try a shot of this fine alcohol from China."

Chapter 9

ROLLING STONES ON THE BEACH:
Brazilian Caipirinha

In a push for better local ratings, Geographic's US Channel began to focus more and more on American stories, so documentaries requiring international travel became hard to find. As I searched for my next gig, only one good option stood out, a series struggling for money but promising nonetheless. Called "Inside," it would be a fly-on-the-wall look at what goes on behind the scenes at big international events. I signed on.

Needing to pitch six hour-long shows for the series, we immediately roughed them out: soccer's FIFA Club World Championship in Tokyo; the launch of a space tourist in Russia; Bonneville SpeedWeek on the salt flats of Utah; the Chinese New Year celebrations in Hong Kong; and the International Winemaker of the Year Awards in England (guaranteed supplies for the Club).

My colleagues soon replaced the name *Inside* with a new working title: "Where in the World Does Brian Want to Go Next?" All these shows were green lit, as well as the sixth show - one that would become the envy of producers everywhere - a Rolling Stones concert in Rio de Janeiro, potentially the band's largest show ever. No mountains to climb, no venomous snakes to dodge, no diseased mosquitoes to slap, just jumping Jack Flash and some beasts of burden.

We flew into Rio ten days before the concert and settled into a splendid beachside hotel with a bar by its rooftop pool. I know it's difficult to plead hardship, but we had earned our cocktails. Just getting to that point was a major accomplishment that involved months of hard work, planning and negotiations. And you have not really haggled until you've done it with Rolling Stones management. The experience makes some of their songs sound like warnings: "you can't always get what you want," and you're likely to "get no satisfaction."

From the time of our first brainstorming session, we knew we wanted to cover a big concert. Dana Kemp, my most delectable and tenacious coordinating producer, was on the case, and needed every ounce of her delectability and tenacity to get the job done. U2 had said "no" off the bat. The Dave Matthews Band was totally on board (Dana is a huge fan), but I knew they weren't big enough outside of the US. She tried the Rolling Stones and didn't get a "no", which was a good start.

After many, many delays, phone calls and emails, she finally bounced into my office, overjoyed. "Mick Jagger says he'll do it." Then the catch. "But only if he can also be in the magazine."

"Mick Jagger wants to be in *National Geographic* magazine?" I asked.

"He says that'd make his mum proud."

"Anything else?" I wondered out loud.

"That's it for now," Dana said. We both knew more would eventually come. "What do you think?"

I'm not sure what struck me most about this news: that I could be doing a story for Geographic that involved Sir Mick Jagger (how does that happen?), that Mick had a mother (who was alive and kicking enough to be made proud), or that we'd somehow have to get the magazine involved. I wondered which department Mick would fit into. Science? No. Nature? Not really. Maybe nocturnal wildlife, but it'd be a stretch.

If the Rolling Stones are the most difficult group to negotiate with, second on the list is National Geographic's yellow-border magazine. Both are notoriously selfrighteous and uncompromising, but we had to give it a go. It was too good an opportunity to pass up.

Initially we looked at getting the band packing up a Boston concert and setting up for a show in New York (a relatively cheaper domestic shoot), but something much better was afoot. South American sponsors had recruited the Stones to perform a free concert on Copacabana Beach in Rio. It had been nine months in the planning and had the potential to be the Stones' biggest audience ever. We'd film the stagehands packing up the previous concert in San Juan, Puerto Rico, and roll behind the scenes for a week or so before the big gig in Brazil. "Stones on the Beach" just had a nice ring to it.

The Exotic Booze Club

We thought Geographic's magazine would at least give such a story idea a decent hearing, but our initial pitch to the magazine's editors did not go well. "What sort of article would *Geographic* do on the Stones?" they asked, probably rightly. I suggested an ethnographic piece about the age of rock 'n' roll, because nothing would show the age of rock 'n' roll like a close-up picture of Mick, Keith, Charlie and Ronnie.

That didn't fly, and some of them thought the whole suggestion ludicrous and unworthy of further discussion. The real problem was the lofty air that circulates around the prestigious institution that is the *National Geographic Magazine.* No one told them what to print, especially not someone from (add spitting sound) *television.*

We needed an insider from the magazine to help, and we got him. Michael Nick Nichols is probably the magazine's most famous and highly regarded nature photographer and, more importantly, he's a rabid Rolling Stones fan. Nick, a wild and passionate artist, could see it clearly: "the Stones as a series of landscapes". I wasn't sure what that meant, but by using such language he managed to pitch his idea and get enough editors on board that it could happen.

The Stones wanted a written guarantee that an article would be printed. The magazine *never* gives such guarantees. They wouldn't do it for the President of the United States nor the Queen of England. And not even to make Mick Jagger's mum proud. We left the magazine to work it out and for endless weeks the chest thumping went on.

"Well, we're the Rolling Stones, and we want a guarantee."
"Well, we're *National Geographic*, and we don't give guarantees."
"Yes, but we are *the* Rolling Stones."
"Great, but *we* are National Geographic."
"Stones!"
"Gee-oh-graph-ic!"
"Rolling friggin' Sto . . ."
"Children, STOP."

We jumped back in and I spoke to the Stones manager, a savvy, sharp-as-a-tack Canadian with a take-no-prisoners philosophy of business. Michael Cohl began his career in the entertainment industry running a strip club when he was just eighteen. More recently he produced *Spider-Man* for Broadway, and in between he became what Fortune Magazine called the "Howard Hughes of rock 'n' roll." After a couple of lucky breaks that had him promoting Michael Jackson's *Thriller* tour in 1987, Cohl's client list began to read like a who's who of tour bands: U2, Pink Floyd and, since 1989, the gift that keeps giving, the Rolling Stones.

I pleaded with Mr. Cohl and explained that Nick Nichols was one of the magazine's best photographers and they wouldn't be sending him if they weren't serious. Finally he agreed to go ahead without a written guarantee from the magazine, trusting that they had the best intentions, and therefore we could proceed with our behind-the-scenes documentary.

"Great," I said. Then it came.

"But," added Mr. Cohl, as my stomach began to churn, "there are some conditions."

I knew "conditions" was potentially a very bad word. You have to understand that Michael Cohl is the king of merchandising. He practically invented it. He understands the value of *everything* and nothing avoids his gaze. If he could, he'd copyright the moon and charge you to look at it - and sue you if you didn't pay up. After Mr. Cohl took over the Stones, a rival promoter described the onslaught of Stones merchandise "like watching my favorite lover become a whore".

So what did Ol King Cohl have in store for us? He laid out his demands like an elaborately conceived business plan. It seemed to be coming off the top of his head but he didn't miss a thing: the magazine could only print a certain number of photographs, the copyright of all other photos would revert to the Stones, the Stones would have free use of all footage, there would be no home video sales, there were guidelines for the songs that we could use in the show, access to the band would be limited, we had to use Cohl's son as one of our cameramen, and Mick Jagger could claim shagging rights to all our wives, girlfriends and post-pubescent daughters. I'll confess I made up the bit about shagging rights, but I honestly sat on the phone waiting for it.

With considerable coercing and compromise, and a trip to a Stones concert in San Francisco to meet King Cohl himself, we worked his list of demands into an agreement that everyone could live with, including the possibility of home-video distribution. Our lawyers were left to put it in writing, with one final word of warning from Mr. Cohl: it had to be signed and delivered before the concert started in Rio or there'd be no further filming.

Dana and I were finally on our way to shooting the concert set-up in Rio. We sent another team to shoot the end of the concert in Puerto Rico, and it was these first scenes of roadies pulling down and loading up twenty-four large semitrailer loads of gear that began to illustrate the astounding magnitude of a Stones world tour. It was nothing less than a small city on the move. The full size of this travelling extravaganza included 370 tons of equipment that flew from venue to venue on four 747 cargo aircraft, and no fewer than thirty-seven shipping containers, each forty feet long, that would travel by sea.

According to what had to be where, and when, mountains of this gear would often leapfrog over each other to meet different concert deadlines around the world. The shipping and airfreight alone for this tour was a multimillion-dollar logistical Rubik's cube. Our twenty-six bags of equipment suddenly felt like carry-on.

With eight days to show time, Dana and I hit the beach in Rio where the Stones advance team had already spent a fortnight erecting the skeleton of a stage. Ian Kinnersley was charged with constructing six-storey-high scaffolding on the beach, directly across from the famous Copacabana Palace Hotel. Ian had no fewer than 160 crew to help him, most of them local contractors. He'd been frustrated by the pace; it was the wet season and they'd had to stop several times for rain. It also seemed to Ian that his crew needed to focus more on the job at hand and a lot less on the women strolling the beach. That was a tall order.

Brazil is famous for its beaches, its women, and probably the world's briefest bikinis. The local word for these bathing costumes is "fio dental," which literally means dental floss. It's a confusing array for the uninitiated. The triangular patch at the back looks as though it should cover the crack of the bum, but instead it's designed to cover the small of the back. In fact, nothing covers the bum and hence the constant distraction for Ian's workers.

We got to know Ian and moved freely around the stage filming both the work and the lack of it, and of course the offending floss. Rich Scholtz, from the tornado show, was happy to cover this job for us, but soon, as the big event drew closer, it would get too busy for just one camera operator. Naked-Man-Up-A-Tree Jeff was on the way to help us out, and we flew in Jeremy Ashton from Australia to manage all our audio needs. After what I put him through with the camels and mustangs, he'd earned it.

Another storm rolled over the stage, so we wrapped up filming for the day and retreated to our hotel. We had a couple of experienced local fixers helping us out and they figured what we needed most was an introduction to some sweet icy green cocktails. Who am I to resist such accommodation? They ordered us rounds of caipirinhas, a drink made from cachaça, the local rum. There are thousands of small cachaça distillers throughout Brazil. Instead of molasses, the traditional base of most rums, the Brazilians distil sugar cane in copper pots and age it in barrels made from a range of exotic woods: balsam, almond, brazilwood, cherry and oak, to name but a few. An alternative, known locally as a caipivodka, adds vodka to the mix, so these are less sweet and more potent, on both counts making it a preferred option for the end of every day.

Our rooms were positioned well. I could see the stage scaffolding on the beach from my window, so from there we set up a time-lapse camera to watch the concert façade evolve. From Jeremy's window we could see the famous 130-foot tall *Christ the Redeemer* statue, his arms outstretched atop Corcovado Mountain. This giant art deco sculpture overlooks Rio's twelve million Catholic-dominated inhabitants. It's also the feature that animators graphically crumbled and destroyed in the big-budget disaster film *2012*. We didn't need digital mastery to make our shots any more dramatic as we started filming the statue from Jeremy's room, a dark green and black sky rolling in and bolts of lightning flashing down Christ's back, equal parts breathtaking and ominous. One bolt seemed to be a direct strike, but this Christ is made of insulating soapstone so no harm done.

When the weather cleared we filmed more of the stage work. Over several days we got to know and like the advance team, and they liked us. We were feeling good about our relationships and that this crew would look after us come concert time. That's precisely when they were replaced.

Four days before show time, Brazilian police escorted two coaches from the airport to Copacabana Palace, a road crew of a hundred people. A week earlier, Brazilian gangsters had hijacked a bus coming from the airport and robbed the bewildered British tourists aboard. Now the red-faced government was taking no chances. Even the Stones equipment received an armed escort.

Heading up the newly arrived roadies was Dale Sherseff, a man known to everyone as Opie. He'd been on the tour circuit for about thirty years and was away from home nine months out of twelve. His job was to keep things moving and he did it well. He knew how to hustle and he constantly encouraged others to do the same with no-nonsense discipline and good-humored banter.

Their commute from Puerto Rico had been close to a day long, but Opie had no time for jet lag. From the bus he headed straight to Ian's construction site. For all of Ian's work on various productions, he rarely gets to see a concert. He handed over to Opie and left to start setting up a new stage in Argentina. Opie was our new commander in chief.

The Exotic Booze Club

We started again, getting to know Opie and his crew, filming as his experienced team took over and considerably upped the pace. Over two days they added more than 500 lights and positioned thirty-two tons of speakers and sound equipment. They had a jigsaw puzzle of a set to hang, one they'd never before seen. The new London-designed backdrop consisted of six giant arrangements up to eighty-feet wide and 200-feet long. Each of those was made up of some twenty-five car-sized colored kites. The roadies decoded it with some grumbling and began to transform the scaffolding into a work of art.

The lighting team had just two days to work out the light show that'd match the new look, a process that would normally take them two or three weeks. Opie's men positioned a shelter onstage that would protect Charlie Watts thirty-year-old drum kit from any rain. When they did, there was an enormous crunching sound as parts of the stage collapsed from the weight. The culprits were several panels of chipboard not accustomed to such strain. But nothing was going to slow these guys down. The full number of crew travelling with the Stones was 264, and fourteen of them were full-time carpenters.

Two other dramas unfolded at the same time, and we kept our cameras on both of them. Pyro Pete, their fireworks guy, was having trouble getting permission to finish the concert with a top-of-the-stage fireworks display. With the stage so close to the historic Copacabana Palace, and potentially in front of more than a million people, Rio's fire department was serious about safety. In contrast, Pete was a part-time stand-up comedian with a severe facial twitch, both unnerving traits to have around explosives. A clash was imminent.

Pete chose to wear a safari outfit as he met with town officials, complete with safari hat, crop and monocle. The administrators came carrying automatic rifles. Pete fought hard, and even lobbied the mayor, but there was no way. This time there would be no fireworks. He jokingly put his failure down to having a less impressive uniform than what the fire guys wore. In part, he was probably right.

The other drama unfolding was inside the Palace. When you hear that Beth Springer is on "wardrobe", don't think little old lady handstitching ornate fabrics. Think little bull terrier dynamo in charge of *constructing* dressing rooms out of portable partitions, and fitting them out with band essentials. As we filmed, one of the local promoters had unwisely decided to combat Beth for space, in particular toilets. He needed more for his sponsors and VIPs, and Beth needed a bathroom for the band. In her mind there was never any chance of sharing. Just think of it: some bloke, after a few drinks in the Rattlesnake Lounge, walks up to a urinal to spring a leak and cheerfully finds himself standing next to Sir Mick Jagger. "Hey Mick. Put it there." The possibility may have pleased the promoter but it was not happening, not with Beth on the case.

"This is Mick Jagger," she said firmly. "I need a toilet for them." The translator was working overtime as the Brazilian promoter refused to budge. In the course of an exhausting meeting, Beth realized she would have to go over this guy's head.

"Okay then, let's get the big boss." Within a day, Beth had her toilet, and VIP dreams of sharing a twinkle spot with Mick were shattered.

While a private privy may make sense for the world's most enduring rock band, there was plenty on their list of pre-concert requirements that seemed a tad excessive. All big travelling stars have lists called "riders", and some of them read like demands on a psychotic extortion note: Aretha Franklin has asked for part of her appearance money, "$25,000 in cash", to be delivered on the night of her performance; Britney Spears is paid $5,000 if someone calls her dressing-room by mistake; and rapper Lil Wayne has asked for half his six-figure fee in cash before the show, a presidential suite of at least 1,000 square feet in a five-star hotel, a chartered Learjet at his disposal and a two-vehicle police escort from the airport.

It's possible that many of these outrageous requests are invented and demanded by aides and agents rather than by stars, but they still carry weight. In Keith Richards room: a life-sized cut-out of Elvis; Italian silk draped over the furniture, statues and ornaments; and a snooker table racked and ready to go - all for pre-concert space he may use for no more than an hour. Not so much spoiling in Mick's room; his space is more about preparing himself physically. Humidifiers moisten the air so his voice doesn't dry out, there are music-playing devices, and he needs 150 to 300 feet of private hall space to do sprints before the show, that way he enters the stage already pumped. And, of course, that most vital of British necessities: hot tea.

We got on well with the worker bees preparing all this, and I think we earned their respect by rising at three am to film them unloading 220 tons of equipment. After a day or two we felt we had established an entirely new set of good relationships that would allow us to move around uninhibited. Wrong again.

With forty hours to show time, the band arrived with Michael Cohl and the "entourage", consisting of another forty-two people. Our schmoozing had to start from scratch, and it didn't start well. We were called to meet with King Cohl first thing the next day. He was blunt: "No more filming." He didn't have his signed contract.

Cohl had been clear on this point, but I was certain it had all been taken care of. This was the most crucial time for shooting and I didn't want to stop for a second but, based on my previous experience with Nat Geo lawyers, it could take days to sort out where the problem lay, maybe even months. King Cohl stood firm about the filming and it seemed I had no place to go. Out of desperation, I resorted to a diatribe of brown nosing. "This concert is a once-in-a-lifetime opportunity to document the world's greatest rock band on what's likely to be the most incredible event in rock 'n' roll history." That was a good start. I added in a few more ego boosters about how people will talk about this for generations to come, and without our documentary no one will ever know the tireless work of the unsung heroes behind the scenes, like him, that made it all possible.

Despite my efforts, I could feel our story slip, slip, slipping away, but in the course of my "blah blah blah" I was suddenly struck with an idea.

"So how about this," I quickly added. "We'll bring you every tape we've shot so far. We'll continue to shoot so we know everything is documented, and each tape we'll deposit in your care. When this contract is worked out, in good faith, we collect our tapes and continue as normal."

I didn't really know what "in good faith" meant, but I know it's a term lawyers use, so I threw it in there. Then I added, "And if it doesn't get worked out, you walk away with all the material, a good $80,000 of production for free, and you can make your own documentary."

He thought about it for a moment and agreed. "Phew."

"But," he said (damn this man and his buts), "any filming of the entourage has to go through our PR person, and all the filming of the band has to be done by my son, Jake."

Of course I had to agree. "And we are operating in good faith, right?"

"Right," he agreed.

I will never be totally sure if this wasn't actually Ol' King Cohl's idea all along, but it was getting me through the day, so I didn't mind.

Jake Cohl was about eighteen, but he was keen on camera work and had done a fair amount of shooting for his age. Plus he seemed like a nice kid. We had to upgrade his camera to something that would give us better quality, and that made us a little nervous. Ideally he'd be familiar with the camera he'd be using, but the basic functions would be the same and there really wasn't much choice. He had a friend to wave around a boom microphone and collect sound, and Rich, Jeremy and I jammed into their brains as much information about style and simple shooting techniques as we could without overloading them. I felt this situation was actually going to be a good thing. Jake grew up around the band; they all knew and trusted him, and they would be more relaxed and candid with a familiar face. Plus, Jake was very keen to do a good job.

The public relations woman we had to go through was Cheryl Ceretti. She pulled out a smile as sweet as brown sugar, but those pearly whites had a serrated edge. She was no honky-tonk woman, more of a Lady Jane dominatrix. I detected the faint smell of quality perfume and, like all good PR people, she was a control freak. We met and got along fine, so I thought it'd be better to embrace her role rather than try to work around it. It was her job to let everyone know that the Rolling Stones still had "it" after what was, even then, an incredible forty-three years in the biz. We enrolled her in our mission with the message that she'd be helping us help her. She was nobody's fool though, and another take-no-prisoners shark. We'd have to watch our step.

In relatively short order, schmoozing the new guys had gone as well as could be expected. At least we were still rolling. I went to contact the Geo lawyers to see what had gone wrong with the contract and left the crew to film more set-up. Rich and Dana shot the roadies playing instruments on a moving section of stage for the sound check. They also filmed the completion of the sixteen giant towers that were to carry sound and video to the masses, positioned at intervals down the beach totalling a distance of about two miles.

Naked Man showed up and had no context for the strain under which we'd been operating. On his flight from Hippiville he'd dreamed up scenarios where he'd engage in a kind of on-stage filming dance with Mick Jagger during the concert. He was gushing with such ideas and eager to tell me all of them. I reined him in as best I could.

"It's not like that," I said. "Imagine your balls are in a vice that gets a crank every time you glance the wrong way. Only no one is going to tell you which way that is. Keep your head down and your clothes on and we *might* get this done."

I sent him down the beach, charged with filming some of the 500-strong security detail and any passing dental floss. I knew he'd be good at that.

The hold-up with the paperwork related to a buried note from Cohl asking how many times the show would be broadcast. When it was noticed, the Geo lawyers were unsure how to respond. It was an unusual request and the show was yet to be programmed. No one knew.

Programming is not something done by we who make the films but by the broadcasters. Who knew what PBS would do? And internationally, different Nat Geo regions would run it at different times. The lawyers were waiting on some answers but no one they were consulting understood the urgency.

I was sure Cohl didn't understand what he was asking. I did some calculations on the maximum possibility of broadcasts, doubled it for good measure and had this ridiculous number written in, something like "no more than 74 in one year". I had the contract faxed to my hotel where I signed it, then I raced the decree over to the Copacabana Palace for Ol' King Cohl's approval. He noticed the number, raised an eyebrow, then laid it down and said in an unhappy tone, "That's a lot."

I explained that it was impossible to be accurate; PBS may just run it once in the US, but probably several times, then cable TV in Europe may run it four times in the first week to accommodate different time zones, then possibly again later in the year, then Asia will do its own programming, and Australia and etcetera, etcetera. I quickly put his question in context of our great revolving planet, gave him the impression that the show wouldn't be over- nor under-exposed, and waited for his response.

"Okay," he finally said, "looks like we're good to go." I sat there waiting for the "but", but it never came. At last.

I retrieved our tapes, but before I could exit, Cheryl came charging. "What the hell was your guy doing filming security on the bridge?" This production was like walking an invisible tightrope above a pool of circling sharks: you couldn't tell where your feet were treading, but below you could see razor-sharp teeth and detect the faint odor of Chanel No. 5.

The bridge Cheryl was yelling about was enclosed scaffolding built over the road between the Palace and the stage. It was the band's entrance and exit. The security she mentioned was their A-team.

Beyond the army of security protecting the stage there was, and always is, highly trained security agents that travel with the band at all times while on tour. There is one personal bodyguard for each band member and four floaters. In Rio, these were ex-military and the elite of their profession. They planned for every contingency, and even had a helicopter standing by for show time, just in case the crowd got out of control. If that happens, the bodyguards are prepared, and strong enough, to physically carry the band members to a chopper in a hasty but well-planned escape.

We'd met some of this team upon our first backstage experience in San Francisco. It was easy to meet them; they sat down at our table, introduced themselves, and started chatting. This was not just to be polite, although they were - it was a tactic. They saw our strange new faces backstage and it was their job to know who we were and if we presented a threat.

Eric Hausch was the unassuming young leader in charge of this detail, and Naked Man had filmed him and his A-team inspecting the bridge. Naked Man had then followed Eric up to their room for a security briefing. Neither Naked Man nor I had thought of these guys as part of the "entourage" so hadn't realized we needed Cheryl's permission to film them. It was just a mistake. Eric and his crew hadn't given it much thought either, until Cheryl crackling over Eric's two-way radio interrupted their briefing. She had spied Naked Man and Eric on the bridge a few minutes earlier. "Cheryl to Eric, you read?"

"Eric here."

"Get that Nat Geo crew out of there now."

They politely asked Naked Man to leave, which he did. The footage he managed to get while there was incredibly valuable, and just enough to cut together a sequence for the final film, but now I had to face Cheryl's wrath. I've been chewed out before, but rarely with such eloquent gnawing. It was like being run over by an icecream van: it smelled good and the music was annoyingly familiar, but it still hurt.

At the end of my Mrs. Whippy whipping, and my apology and my grovelling, Cheryl calmed down. Deep down, she may even have felt sorry for me. She asked if I'd met Arnold. It was not a name I'd heard. "Well," she explained, "if you want any access at all to the stage during the concert, it all has to be cleared by Arnold. I thought you knew that."

This was a detail meeting my eardrums for the first time. It echoed in my head and pounded my brain - yet another level of permission to go through.

I went to Opie, whom I *thought* was the stage master, and he confirmed. "Oh yeah," he said, like it was old news, "Arnold Dunn is the road manager, keeps the band on time. You need to meet him. Nothing happens back here during concert time without his say-so."

Our behind-the-scenes story would not be much of a story if we weren't permitted behind the scenes. I arranged a meeting and pulled our entire crew together for inspection, both our team and the local production hands you must hire as a condition of working in Brazil. One of these hires was Evandro, an assistant we assigned to work exclusively with Naked Man. We waited in the wings of the stage with just three hours to show time, and when Arnold was ready for our meeting he sent an aide to summon us forward.

The Exotic Booze Club

We walked onto the stage as a group, where Arnold Dunn sat like a guru in one of those elevated director's chairs. It felt so regal that I humbly introduced myself and wondered if I should kneel down and kiss his ring. Lord Dunn was clearly in command of this domain and his word was law. He was the ultimate authority for everything that would happen during the concert and a force to be reckoned with. His eminence sat quietly as I explained all that we wanted during the concert, the most crucial thing being a cameraman, with Jeremy on sound, operating out of sight but immediately behind the band. Our life was in this man's hands and we awaited his judgment with bated breath.

At this precise and crucial moment, Evandro, Naked Man's Brazilian assistant, decided to turn to scratch himself. Why, why, why would he do that? As he turned, the sound mixer hanging from his shoulder knocked the item standing right beside him. It wasn't much, just the priceless guitar Keith Richards had selected to play that night. It was one of those slow-motion moments in life when time seems to move at a snail's pace, yet you can't move quick enough to do anything about it. Keith's guitar hit the stage with an almighty crash. The crown jewels had been violated.

Lord Dunn's reaction was as instant as it was ruthless. "Right," he said "that's it! This meeting is over and done. Everyone leave NOW."

There was only one thing to do. There was no room here for "but" or "sorry" or "what about", we had to agree with him entirely. I turned to my team.

"Everyone go now. Go quietly, go carefully, just go, and make it quick." My dumbstruck crew was solemn and obedient. I turned to his worship as we left and added, "Those two," pointing to Naked Man and his Brazilian attachment, "you will *never* see them again." It was an honest promise I knew I had to make. My hope was that my unquestioning response would reassure him that we understood he was the ultimate authority. Then I would cross my fingers for some much-needed mercy in the next few hours.

Evandro understood the gravity of what he'd done and was mortified; if there was a guillotine around, he would have stuck in his own head. But I had no time to console him. I went to Cheryl and asked if she'd stick by Rich and Jeremy during the concert if we got permission to film backstage. She readily agreed and it was probably her intention all along. I let an hour go so things could cool down a little and sent the crews to film the ever-growing crowd that was now being sprayed by fire hoses in the sweltering 36-degree heat. I asked Opie to let Lord Dunn know of our arrangement with Cheryl, and arranged for Cheryl to speak to Lord Dunn on our behalf. It was a strategy that worked. Just an hour or so before show time we were in the clear. Another bullet dodged but, of course, yet another on the way.

We only had rights to use music the Stones owned, and much of their early work is actually owned by a former manager. They can still perform these tunes on stage, but we couldn't use them in our documentary. We desperately needed the first song to be one we could use. We'd asked, but we knew the Stones would only create their final list immediately before the show, and they certainly weren't going to choose their songs based on our needs. All we had was hope.

The more we filmed, the more I became convinced that the band members had no idea we were even on the scene. Less than an hour before show time we assumed our positions. Rich and Jeremy had been instructed to wear all black and not to look any band member in the eye. Cheryl kept them a good distance away, but not so far that they couldn't get what we needed.

We hired a local cameraman to get shots in the crowd and sent him out with our guitar anti-hero. We positioned Naked Man at the audio mixing booth, about a hundred yards in front of the stage, and I chose for myself the hairiest but ultimately most rewarding location, strapped in with the spotlight guys six stories up on the scaffolding. I knew it'd be a little risky because of the height, but the bird's-eye view would be extraordinary. The only problem was the big clouds that were beginning to roll in, and they looked electric. If so, the scaffolding would act like a lightning magnet. I'd already seen lighting strike Christ that week, and I thought myself slightly less lightning tolerant.

With thirty minutes before show time, Opie reported drops of rain hitting the stage. I donned a borrowed harness and looked up at the scaffolding in dread; it appeared to be constructed from hundreds of well-connected lightning rods. Jeremy saw my hesitation and came over.

"Don't worry, mate," he said in my ear. "Just remember, fear attracts lightning." Touché. He'd been waiting to say that since the camel shoot. And of course, now that my Aussie manhood was in question, I had no choice. I put on my bravest face and scurried up the top, camera in hand.

Somewhere out there, Nick Nichols was snapping stills for National Geographic magazine. I'd only seen him briefly as he was on his own mission. As a solo artist, he moved fast and with more ease than we ever could. I only hoped that he'd had a better time than us and that he was getting great landscapes.

Up top, I was astounded by what I saw. Chills ran up my spine. Spotlights from the towers swept over an enormous crowd that now stretched well over a mile down the beach, an estimated 1.2 million people. The energy from such a mass of humanity took my breath away. This was probably the largest beach party in history and I had the best viewing platform possible. To the side I could see some spectators being squeezed into the surf, and on the water a flotilla of boats had anchored to watch. Even a cruise ship came past.

Some people are afraid of flying, they hop on a plane fearful it will crash and they'll be killed and there is nothing they can do about it. This is exactly why I like flying. When you hop on the plane and strap yourself in, your fate is out of your hands. What you do on that plane is unlikely to have any bearing on whether you live or die - so you may as well relax and enjoy the ride. Lightning or not, standing directly above one of the world's greatest rock bands, in front of Rio's masses, I was finally able to relax. Of course I did stand on one leg now and then, but beyond that it was up to fate. Let the show begin.

From my privileged position I got a topside shot of the Stones walking over the bridge to backstage. The fifty-foot-high video screen came alive. A few minutes later, with Keith's distinctive guitar intro and an almighty crowd roar, the Stones launched into "Jumpin Jack Flash", a song they owned and we could use. It never sounded so good.

The rain and lightning stayed away, but there were a few nice little behind-the-scenes dramas. Six stories up with me, where *Christ the Redeemer* would have been happy to stand, a spotlight went out. The operator frantically tried to repair it but couldn't. With so many other lights, I'm certain no one in the crowd noticed, but it was a nice filmic addition.

Jeremy, ever watchful, turned to Rich at another point and said, "Hey mate, better film that guy there." Despite more than 500 security officers and the tightest of controls, it was Jeremy who noticed an intruder climbing the scaffolding. Apparently this man had crept in the night before and buried himself in the sand, where he apparently lay waiting all day for the concert. Once Rich was filming, Jeremy told Cheryl and got the attention of security. They had the interloper down as fast as fury and dragged him away like wild horses. I have no idea what methods they used, but when they took him out he was horizontal and motionless. Word to the wise: don't mess with Stones security.

When the crowd surged forward, ten people were crushed on a fence near the VIP area and were also carried out. All recovered. Farther out, it was much like a normal night in Rio. There were 688 people taken to the four medical tents, the majority for excessive alcohol intake, drug abuse and/or dehydration, forty-four had broken bones, three had stab wounds, and one woman went into labor. Another twenty-four people were rescued from drowning. There were 200 reports of theft, twenty-two reports of lost children and, the next day, 196 tons of litter to pick up.

The Stones rocked Rio, took a final bow, and returned safely to the Palace. Jake worked through a few tricky camera-filter switches and did a good job with the band. None of us ever met Mick or the boys, and Nick Nichols had similar problems getting access for photography. Without it, he never could shoot the landscapes he needed to make an article work. For all the haggling, the magazine article was forgotten about and never mentioned again. Mick's mum would have to make do with her current level of maternal pride.

The behind-the-scenes crew that had made the concert possible started packing up. They had to get it all down and moved to Argentina. After that they'd do it all again, and again, right around the world. Stage lights out, we let Opie have the last word in our finished film, deliberately alcohol related. "See you in Argentina," he says to a colleague. "Maybe we can have a cocktail together."

I liked this reference to *maybe* sharing a cocktail. It was how things were shaping up at the Club. With less and less overseas travel on offer, and therefore less exotic booze, maybe we'd be sharing more cocktails, and maybe not. As it turned out, not.

Chapter 10

ONE LAST DRINK?

Two factors, above all else, stymied the flow of exotic alcohol to my office. Firstly, the quest for "Generation Text", which is what I call the latest generation of TV viewers. The old saying was that "television turned the family circle into a semi-circle". Now members of the Text Generation, with their personal electronic devices, have turned that semi-circle into a bubble. It's a hard bubble to burst, and TV execs continue to try many things to command the attention of the Texters.

One of the general philosophies is that Americans prefer content based in America, that to them it's more relevant. In an early push to capture Generation Text, Club members were more and more confined to doing stories Stateside.

Secondly, the management at Geo's US channel began to think most expeditions too risky for film. An understandable position, really: why gamble a lot of money on a payoff? The new thought was to let explorers and scientists do their thing, and if it was a really good story it could be shown more affordably as a reenactment.

These shifts in strategy had serious consequences for the Exotic Booze Club. Fewer expeditions and overseas travel meant less alcohol for our gatherings; we all but dried up in the lull. Some of the regular non-travellers lent a hand. Catherine Yelloz, a beautiful French woman in charge of clearing film rights, brought in her homemade limoncello. Another regular brought some Chevy Chase Vodka; Chevy Chase, basically a suburb of Washington, DC, was about as far abroad as she ever travelled (it's the thought that counts). But ultimately it didn't prove to be enough.

ONE LAST DRINK?

The *Inside* series was helpful for a time in supplying the Club with good exotic booze, but when that series ended there was not much else for me to do other than jump onto some US-based shows. To accommodate the channel's growing needs, we did a restructure and I was ordered to move offices, up a floor and away from my beloved top shelf. I had kept one spent bottle of every kind of liquor we sampled, and the shelf of shame was now crammed with 109 empties. I took a photo of each and put the lot out for recycling.

The new shows I started doing were fun topics, but not serious expeditions. A few were based on engineering feats, but most were good, worthy programs on US national parks: Yellowstone, Yosemite, the Everglades and the Grand Canyon. I also produced the first ever made-for-broadcast film on the Appalachian Trail. I've been spoilt with pristine lakes, glacier-capped mountains, newly discovered waterfalls and abundant wildlife, but one thing I couldn't find in these places was exotic alcohol.

Once the Exotic Booze Club was gone, my superiors realized what they had lost. Five or six times they pressed me hard to restart "for the sake of morale", but the momentum was lost. The good news is that trends swing and the comparative lull in overseas travel may soon end; my creative documentarian friends are again finding excuses to shoot far afield. The EBC may have had its day, but the adventures continue.

Carsten Peter drinks less Coke now but is still photographing volcanoes and tornados and, more recently, incredible bus-sized crystals in a cave in Mexico. Dr. Brady Barr, even after capturing every species of crocodilian on the planet, still finds excuses to travel the world in search of dangerous creatures. Fabien Cousteau is a roving ambassador for his new Plant A Fish foundation. Naked Man splits his time between Hawaii and Bali, still travelling, shooting and falling in love on a regular basis. And wherever non-human primates hang out, you'll find Dr. Rey watching on and taking notes.

Ashley from the camel round-up and shark show was crazy enough to marry me. Our worldly adventures continue as a joint effort, kids now in tow. I run my own company now, Red Rock Films, which allows me to pitch a range of shows to a range of networks. My heart is still in the field and I am no longer confined by the wishes of just one network. As I write this, I'm on an aircraft returning from Guadalupe, Mexico, where we played with some supersized sharks. Next the Bahamas, and then down to New Zealand. More adventures for sure and most certainly more exotic alcohol. For better or worse, my personal mission remains unchanged: to create great programs that draw viewers and open eyes to the beauty, splendor, drama and humor of our incredible world - and sometimes the alcohol within it.

THE INVITATIONS

27 October, 2000

G'day drinkers,

Another question for you: What do Australians call the consumption of a million gallons of beer?

The answer: Monday.

Every day in my glorious homeland, a glass of beer is consumed for every man, woman and child. Of course some of the infants don't drink as much, but then some of the women make up for it.

Now I know you've all been brainwashed by marketing to think "Fosters is Australian for Beer". Poppycock. Fosters is Australian for "let's give the cat piss to the Yanks and save the good stuff for ourselves". But now the good stuff is finally here.

Drink of the night: Victoria Bitter.

VB, as it's better known, is a full-flavored brew that was created in the 1890s. Working-class Aussies quickly adopted it as a drink that rewards hard work with hard play and it is currently the number-one selling beer in Australia. It's not for sale in America, but Down Under it sells twice as much as any other full-strength brand, with the equivalent of one carton (twenty-four cans) sold every second.

By the time you've read this email, that's another 1608 cans gone. And we only have six cans to share tonight - so be quick for your tasting, before it all runs out. *(If you're too late, you'll be left to reward your hard work with our supplementary supply of cat piss.)*

Bar opens at five pm. All welcome.

Cheers,

Brian

5 October, 2001

Greetings divine ones,

Tonight's alcohol proves you can always get a good drink when you need one. Fear not the anti-alcohol dogma that seems ever-present in the eastern countries you may visit. You can always find plenty of Buddhist, Hindu and Muslim brothers who like to worship as we do - with a drink in hand.

In Burma (Myanmar), the beverage of choice is today's offering.

Drink of the night: **Htanyei, the Burmese toddy.**

Twice a day, Burmese farmers climb their palm trees to collect sugar-sweet palm juice. When the priests are watching, they use it to make lollies; otherwise they ferment it to make their personalized version of the toddy. It seems no two are alike, but in general the toddy has the strength of a beer and all the sweetness and light of a laughing Buddha.

Come join our global brotherhood for a brew. Bar opens at five.

Please be here, if you can, for a special toast at six.

Cheers,

The high priest of the EBC

7 December, 2001

Howdy partners,

It's just as well nothing goes together quite like drinkin and shootin'. We can thank this natural coupling for the name of tonight's brew. In 1940, distillery executive Thomas McCarthy brought some new warehouse samples on an annual wild-turkey hunt. I'm guessing that something about the potentially catastrophic consequences of mixing his firewater with firearms whetted the appetite.

After they returned, some of the drinkin'-shootin' survivors pleaded, "Hey Tom, got any more of that wild-turkey whisky?" He did. They took it hunting again, everyone but the birds had a great time, and the name stuck.

Drink of the night: Wild Turkey bourbon.

Bourbon, by law, can only be made in one country. It is the spirit of the United States. This special whisky is aged in charred American-oak barrels from which it gets its color and flavor. No food coloring is allowed; what you see is what you get.

The distillery that makes Wild Turkey bourbon started in 1905, and (apart from America's fourteen years of shame - prohibition) it's been brewing bird feed into beautiful bourbon ever since.

So come on over and shoot some gobble gobble - in shot glasses, of course - and see if this corn/rye/barley mix invigorates your senses in the same potentially catastrophic way.

Bar opens at five.

Cheers,

Brian

9 February, 2002

Buenos dias gringos,

Here's a free Exotic Booze Club speed tutorial in tequila, a lesson you should've taken pre-college.

For many Americans, licking salt, shooting tequila and sucking on a lime is standard university fare. Alas, this technique was devised to hide inferior quality and does not hide the hangover it causes. And if your bottle has a worm in it, you've been taken in by a gimmick introduced in the 1940s, specifically to help sell bad alcohol to gullible college freshmen.

There are basically three types of tequila:

1. Mixtos is partly made from the agave plant, but as much as forty-nine per cent of it comes from other sugars. I shudder to think. Use your salt and lime, and maybe an aspirin. (This group includes Jose Cuervo Gold, the world's most popular tequila.)

2. If you survive your freshman hangovers you may graduate to one hundred per cent agave tequila. Still not the best taste, but more pure and you will be able to roll out of your dorm in the morning with a clear head. And . . .

3. Añejo is one hundred per cent agave tequila aged for at least a year in oak barrels, usually longer. It's what you want to drink to celebrate your diploma when you complete Tequila College.

And if you can afford it, you would do well to get your hands on tonight's offering:

Drink of the night: Don Julio tequila.

Don Julio Gonz lez-Frausto Estrada began distilling in 1942. At first he just made his special brew for his friends. With his eye for quality, he soon had a LOT of friends. Now it is consistently rated in the top three of Mexico's most loved tequilas. That's out of more than 900 brands. This is one you savour, not shoot.

So come toast your misspent lick-sip-and-suck youth, and the sacrificed worms that fooled you, and acquaint yourself with Don, the old freshman-year roommate you wish you'd had.

Bar opens at five pm.

Adios,

Brian

6 September, 2002

Hail all,

Even if you haven't been to India, you've probably at least seen alcohol displayed in the exquisite artwork and tapestries that depict the country's rich culture and heritage. In these images, Indian maharajahs, surrounded by buxom and veiled dancing women, sip from long-necked ornate vessels of silver and gold. Beside them, men of great importance also sample good heady liquor. The rums they lugged over the mountains and across the seas were of the highest possible quality, worthy of exchange and trade. Tonight's alcohol is not one of those.

Drink of the night: Archer XXX rum.

It's likely this rum has never touched the lips of anyone in upperclass India. It is mainly brewed for the masses, and particularly the poorer paid troops in the

Indian army. It is only sold in West Bengal and is manufactured by the notable establishment Eastern Distilleries & Chemicals Ltd. It's true the distillery is part of a group better known for its caustic soda and bleaching powder, but they've also been brewing grog now for more than fifty years.

So come drink like the masses do. But be quick: there are some things floating in the bottom of this bottle that'll be saved for the latecomers.

For the more tender of palate, I also have some beer and wine.

Bar opens at five-thirty.

Cheers,

Brian

18 April, 2003

Bonjour drinkers,

For tonight's special brew we must thank a tropical island, a love-struck goddess and a twelve-year-old slave boy.

Drink of the night: Dzama Rhum.

Rum is usually made from molasses, but when you see it spelled "rhum" it's likely from a former French island colony, and made with more readily available sugar cane. That's the case with this aged rhum, named for the Malagasy city where it's produced, Dzamandzar.

You'll notice a hint of vanilla, and inside the bottle you'll see a whole vanilla bean. Vanilla beans are originally from an orchid native to South America. Legend has it that Princess Xanat fled into the forest with her lover after her father refused to let her marry a mortal. Dad had very high standards and wasn't one to be crossed.

He caught them both and lopped off their heads. Where their blood fell, orchids sprang with vanilla beans inside. European slave drivers lopped off many more heads in frustration, trying for 300 years to grow vanilla bean outside of South America. They didn't realize that the plant requires a very particular native bee for pollination. Or, as it turns out, a twelve-year-old French-owned slave named Edmond Albius, who worked out how to quickly do the bee's work by hand.

THE INVITATIONS

Ed got to keep his head and the beans spread to Madagascar, which now grows half the world's supply. And currently trading at around forty dollars a pound, the vanilla bean in this bottle may be the most expensive part of tonight's drink.

Come by for some heady rhum.

Bar opens at five pm.

Cheers,

Brian

26 September, 2004

Greetings fellow drinkers,

Some historians credit the Chinese as makers of the world's first fermented drinks. This early grog was first poured into gourds about 5,000 years ago, and the Chinese immediately declared their brews sacred. You have to love them for that - because you won't love them for tonight's concoction.

~~Drink~~ Smell of the night: Baijiu.

Baijiu is the Chinese word for "white alcohol". Our version comes from southern China where they make it from glutinous rice. It's a clear liquid, sometimes called Chinese vodka - but that's really unfair to vodka. Baijiu is more alcoholic, it is distilled merely once rather than four to five times, and is less thoroughly filtered - all of which gives this brew its own unique and, shall we say, penetrating flavor.

Fragrance is actually how the Chinese class different kinds of baijiu. As I translate the smell categories, you have: "stinky tofu", "barnyard doo doo", "noxious", "vomitous" and, tonight's special, "paint thinner".

So come for a smell, a sip if you dare, and I have some good beer and wine to aid your recovery. Hey, at least it's a pretty bottle.

Bar opens at five pm.

Cheers,

Brian

21 April, 2006

Hello drinkers,

Tonight we're pulling out the blender - and it could get messy. This is a potent and infinitely drinkable tropical cocktail from a country famous for scantily clad beach babes and fun.

Drink of the night: Brazilian caipirinha.

The name comes from the word "caipira", which is Portuguese for "hillbilly" - but this ain't a backyard brew, more like a beachside national treasure.

Caipirinha is Brazil's official national cocktail (you have to love a country that has one of those). And it's not just for the tourists. The ingredients are ice, lime, sugar and cachaça, the latter being the most popular distilled alcohol in all Brazil. They make more than 285 million gallons of cachaça each year and only send one percent of that out of the country.

So make like a Brazilian hillbilly and come on over for a taste of the tropics. Thong bikini compulsory.

Bar opens at four-thirty.

Cheers,

Brian

11 August, 2006

Loyal patrons,

I feel a poem coming on . . .

One Last Drink

At National Geographic we've travelled the world, though the flavor wasn't always first class,

From far East Russia to the Kalahari, we've studied the globe with our guide - a tiny shot glass.

Venezuelan rum, Scots whisky, exotic liqueurs, mystery mixtures and good Aussie beers,

French wine, Bavarian schnapps and homemade brews - every odd Friday for more than five years.

THE INVITATIONS

The illegal absinthe, the Georgia moon, and the aphrodisiac that helped Pirate Bill get hitched,

Catherine's limoncello, that Chinese blah, oh the brain cells and tastebuds we've ditched.

We survived the mess, the spills and the scrutiny of HR (thanks largely to one TK),

But I'm sad to report it's time for our beloved EBC to finally call it a day.

It's been a pleasure to have you bravest of souls drop by my office for a drink or four,

But change is afoot and it's kicking me up the ass-emblage, and up to the sixth floor.

Alas there's no room for a fridge and a couch, nor one-oh-nine bottles from the world's top shelf,

So please bring a friend and come for one last drink, God knows I can't drink it all myself.

Bar opens at four-thirty.

Cheers,

Brian

ACKNOWLEDGEMENTS

Television is a collaborative medium, best enjoyed with the support of a great team - just like life. I not only need to thank a range of people for their help with this book, but also for supporting my expeditions with National Geographic and the Club itself. Without these people, the stories in this book would not be as rich or maybe even possible.

First and foremost, thank you to Ashley Hoppin, my number-one partner, editor and dream sharer. Your support, faith, love and encouragement make me strong.

Dearest Oliver, Henry and especially Jessie, sorry Dad's always away so much. But wherever I am, know you are on my mind and always in my heart.

Thank you, Lotte Lent: I truly appreciate you holding down your end of the fort. Kevin Krug, Gregg Solomon and John Ford, your contributions to this book have been invaluable. You're great mates. Likewise Clif Wiens - this project began with your support for a crazy idea. At the other end, Brian Cook and Foong Ling Kong came along with wonderful energy, expertise and support. I hope we get to do it again in the near future.

Nancy, Shady, Grenda, Colette, Bill, Patty and Dana: associate producers ensure my world keeps spinning. I'm sorry most of you are now producers, only because we don't get to work with each other as much.

A big thank you for the most silent of the major contributors to the films in this book. My stories from the field omit the editors, who sit back at the office, in small dark rooms, for months on end and turn all these adventures into watchable programs. I hope you at least liked some of the booze.

Thank you, Davie Royle: you have my greatest gratitude for your leap of faith in hiring me. Let's have a cup of tea sometime - or maybe an Irish coffee?

ACKNOWLEDGEMENTS

Maryanne Culpepper, Maggie Stogner, Jon Goodman and David Hamlin, thank you for getting me through the rocky ones with tender care. Tim Kelly, thanks for sticking up for the Club.

There is no better place in the world to write a book than Halemano on Maui. Thank you to my friends there, and to Naked Man for that introduction.

And finally, thank you to the many who brought alcohol to the Club from far-off lands. Let's get together again for a toast sometime. I still have some leftovers – and some fresh stuff I'm always willing to exchange for a few good stories from the field.